TWA IN RWANDA

This book is a contribution to the growing field of global legal ethnography. Through engagement with the global discourses of indigeneity, conservation, and development, this empirical study shows how power and legal normativity are enacted and experienced in the everyday life of the Batwa in Rwanda. By exploring how Twa negotiate their position within society, the regulatory power of these global jurisdictional encounters to construct (subjects, communities, normative frameworks), to reframe, and to discipline comes into sharper focus. Focusing on agency instead of resistance, on a desire for inclusion rather than difference, this book provides a critical contribution to the scholarship on counter-hegemonic narratives of globalisation. Rwandan Twa are positioning themselves within national and global narratives to demand progress and belonging – not as part of a political movement based on their ethnic distinctness or indigeneity but as Rwandans.

MORAG GOODWIN is a professor at Tilburg University, the Netherlands, and holds the chair in Global Law and Development. She was principal investigator of a Dutch Research Council (NWO)-funded project researching barriers to inclusion in Rwanda.

GLOBAL LAW SERIES

The series provides unique perspectives on the way globalization is radically altering the study, discipline, and practice of law. Featuring innovative books in this growing field, the series explores those bodies of law which are becoming global in their application, and the newly emerging interdependency and interaction of different legal systems. It covers all major branches of the law and includes work on legal theory, history, and the methodology of legal practice and jurisprudence under conditions of globalization. Offering a major platform on global law, these books provide essential reading for students and scholars of comparative, international, and transnational law.

Books in the Series

Intimations of Global Law
Neil Walker

Legalized Families in the Era of Bordered Globalization
Daphna Hacker

Transnational Sustainability Laws
Phillip Paiement

The Sociology of Law and the Global Transformation of Democracy
Chris Thornhill

Authority and the Globalisation of Inclusion and Exclusion
Hans Lindahl

Property Law in a Globalizing World
Amnon Lehavi

The Law of the List: UN Counterterrorism Sanctions and the Politics of Global Security Law
Gavin Sullivan

Democratic Crisis and Global Constitutional Law
Christopher Thornhill

The Redress of Law: Globalisation, Constitutionalism and Market Capture
Emilios Christodoulidis

9/11 and the Rise of Global Anti-terrorism Law
Arianna Vedaschi and
Kim L. Scheppele

On Tyranny and the Global Legal Order
Aoife O'Donoghue

Entangled Legalities beyond the State
Nico Krisch

Designing Indicators for a Plural Legal World
Siddharth Peter de Souza

Lawyering Imperial Encounters
Sara Dezalay

Cultural Property: Law, Policy, and Markets
Amnon Lehavi

Global Governance by Data: Infrastructures of Algorithmic Rule
Fleur Johns,
Gavin Sullivan and
Dimitri Van Den Meerssche

Twa in Rwanda: Situating Global Discourses of Indigeneity, Conservationism and Development in Daily Life
Morag Goodwin

The African Renaissance in the Age of Globalization: What Role for International Investment Law?
Edited by
Valentina Vadi,
Saudin Mwakaje and
Tarcisio Gazzini

Digital Justice: Technology, Impartiality and the Law
Antoine Garapon and
Jean Lassègue

TWA IN RWANDA

Situating Global Discourses of Indigeneity, Conservationism, and Development in Daily Life

MORAG GOODWIN
Tilburg University

CAMBRIDGE
UNIVERSITY PRESS

CAMBRIDGE
UNIVERSITY PRESS

Shaftesbury Road, Cambridge CB2 8EA, United Kingdom

One Liberty Plaza, 20th Floor, New York, NY 10006, USA

477 Williamstown Road, Port Melbourne, VIC 3207, Australia

314–321, 3rd Floor, Plot 3, Splendor Forum, Jasola District Centre,
New Delhi – 110025, India

Cambridge University Press is part of Cambridge University Press & Assessment,
a department of the University of Cambridge.

We share the University's mission to contribute to society through the pursuit of
education, learning and research at the highest international levels of excellence.

www.cambridge.org
Information on this title: www.cambridge.org/9781009768542

DOI: 10.1017/9781009768528

When citing this work, please include a reference to the DOI 10.1017/9781009768528

First published 2026

Cover image: 'The good life'. Photo by Morag Goodwin.

A catalogue record for this publication is available from the British Library

A Cataloging-in-Publication data record for this book is available from the Library of Congress

ISBN 978-1-009-76854-2 Hardback
ISBN 978-1-009-76853-5 Paperback

CONTENTS

PREFACE

The project upon which this book is based began slightly over ten years ago. It came about as a collaboration with my colleague, Dr Felix Mukwiza Ndahinda. Felix had written an excellent analysis of the concept of indigeneity in Africa in his 2009 doctoral thesis (later published with Springer). This work included several case studies, one of which was the Twa in Rwanda. My interest in a potential new project was methodological, more particularly in testing the potential of a cross-cultural methodology for examining social exclusion that drew on Wolff and De-Shalit's 2007 study. While I had been researching the relationship between social exclusion and law for almost a decade at that point, I was a total beginner to the Rwandan context. Being able to be part of this project – to learn from my colleague, partners, and our interviewees – has been an incredible experience, from the initial discussions with Felix in Tilburg, through our regular partner meetings and interviewer trainings in Kigali, to observing interviews in the field, to transcription, analysis, and re-analysis, and, finally, writing.

In my visits to Rwanda across the decade of 2014–2024, I have witnessed the physical transformations of the phenomenon that I describe in this book. As a result of pro-poor programming, roofs have transformed from vegetation to metal, and brick houses, pigs, chickens, and goats, along with cows, have proliferated in villages throughout the country. Almost every child, even in the remote villages, now wears shoes and the telltale swollen stomachs of Kwashiorkor are a thing of the past. Land reform is visible as swamps have been drained and cultivated, and as tea plantations have appeared where previously smallholdings had been. My photographic record across the decade shows roads in the Nyamirambo area of Kigali changing from dirt tracks to paved streets, and then to pedestrianised zones decorated with beautiful street murals and encouraging slogans.

The decade has also seen a dramatic rise in conservation tourism, observable in arrivals at the airport and in Kigali's ever-increasing range of luxury hotels for would-be gorilla watchers stopping off on their way north to equally luxurious mountain lodges. The success of Rwanda's positioning as a regional and African-wide hub has similarly been made tangible in the completion of the Kigali Convention Centre and in the surrounding conference infrastructure, capable of hosting thousands of delegates, that has sprung up over those years. And where, in my first visit, I needed to carry several thousands of Euros in cash into the country to pay for project expenses and then carry around a rucksack stuffed with Rwandan Francs, doling out cash like a mafia boss, now nearly all payments are done by apps, like MoMo – even with the ubiquitous motorbike taxi drivers, for whom helmets are now compulsory. Equally visible are the scars that the country bears from decades of violence: in the prisons and in the pink boiler-suited prisoners that can be seen working the land, and in the genocide memorials in every settlement.

These developments are evidence of a country undergoing rapid change. Many lives have improved across Rwanda in this decade in innumerably small and sometimes big ways. Yet, many of these same lives remain incredibly difficult, whether as a result of the physical and psychological scarring of violence or of poverty, of landlessness, or of discrimination and exclusion. The changes that my observations detail are distant from the daily existence of large parts of the Rwandan population, who will never see the murals in Nyamirambo or the new arrivals hall in the airport, or witness the luxury lodges. As such, while the naked eye (or photographic record) can witness 'development', it cannot tell us about the experience of being a Rwandan in this period. What our project wanted to do was focus in on a group within Rwanda that are understood to be the most distant from the visible markers of development: the Batwa. Our data reflects the impacts of change against the background structure of economic, social and ecological patterns: our interviewees lamented the poverty and suffering of their daily lives, but mixed with despair was also the desire for a better life and hope focused on the future.

I am an outsider to Rwanda and this book would not have been possible without my project colleagues. At the project's core was the partnership between Tilburg University, Communauté des Potiers du Rwanda (COPORWA), and the Kigali-based Institute of Research and Dialogue for Peace (IRDP). The project was designed and implemented by a team drawn from these institutions: Felix Mukwiza Ndahinda and me from Tilburg University; Jean-Leonard Karuranga and Athanase Kayijamahe from IRDP, and Omar Rugwiro from COPORWA. It was a wonderful team – not so good on the paperwork demanded by European academic funders but excellent on ideas, collaboration, and results. In addition, we were lucky to have as interviewers Alex Ingabire, Selemani Muhoza, Faustin Munyanziza, Beline Niyotwagira, Elizabeth Twizeyimana, and Florence Yankurijec. They travelled the length and breadth of the country in rain and heat, persevering in locating interviewees who were frequently not at home at the agreed time and persuading often-hungry interviewees to continue reflecting on their lives when what they wanted to be doing was something useful, such as collecting firewood or preparing a meal. Their tenacity, as well as their ability to connect to interviewees and to implement the project methodology at the ground level, was essential to the project's success. Jean-Leonard Karuranga created a visual record of the project through film and photographs, a limited number of which are reproduced here. This book is a result of all these people's work, and I am incredibly grateful for it.

Our methodology involved the attempt to form a dynamic public reflective equilibrium about Twa exclusion, which is a pompous way of saying that we extensively brainstormed our methodology, pilot-stage results, and later findings with a dedicated group of stakeholders. We benefited greatly from their input, with special thanks to the late Senator Zephyrin Kalimba and to Dr Ezechiel Sentama. This book is based on the willingness of our interviewees to give up their time and to share both the physical and emotional reality of their lives with us. The interview transcripts are packed with raw emotion, and it has been both distressing and a privilege to engage with them. Thanks are due, too, to the sector and district leaders who gave up their time to be interviewed; and to the (I)NGO workers and the non-Twa community members who all helped provide us with context in which to understand what our Twa interviewees were telling us.

The research funding that enabled this project was awarded by NWO-WOTRO, the now-disbanded development section of the Dutch Research Council, under their Strategic Actors research programme. In addition to the financial support – for which I am very grateful – the specialist expertise and experience of WOTRO colleagues were invaluable in seeing the project through to completion. The disbanding of this section is a real loss to Dutch academia and beyond. My particular thanks to Dr Martijn Wienia.

I have chosen here to frame the story of our data through the lens of global jurisdictional encounters in daily life. This is because my scholarly interest is in the role of law in structuring exclusion and inclusion in relation to questions of participation, agency, and resistance. I am particularly interested in how these dynamics shape and are shaped by global discourses. I go into more detail about the reasons for this choice in Chapter 1. One of the regrettable consequences of this choice was that my colleagues in the project did not collaborate on this book. I hope that there will be future opportunities to reflect afresh on our data and to write something together.

As the manuscript has taken shape, I have benefited from the opportunity to present chapters at various fora, including at a research session of the Belgian Royal Academy of Overseas Sciences (KAOW), the weekly fika of the Constitutionalising the Anthropocene research group at Tilburg Law School, and the Law and Development Research Network's 2019 conference at Humboldt University in Berlin. Thank you to all who were willing to engage with my work and offer feedback. An early version of Chapter 5 was published as 'Becoming Rwandan? The impact of two decades of unity policies on the Batwa' in (2021) 63(2) *KAOW Bulletin des Séances/Mededelingen der Zittingen* 187–208. Thanks to Ambreena Manji for her willingness to read and comment on several chapters; I very much value her support and critical engagement; and to Deval Desai, who gave great feedback at an early stage of my thinking about the book.

As well as thanks to those who have given up their precious time to engage with my work, I wish to express my gratitude to the institution that has given me the space to work on this book project. I am very fortunate to work in a scholarly community at Tilburg Law School that has moved away from the 'publish or perish' doctrine and that understands that original scholarship or new directions in an individual's scholarly development take time. I wish also to express my thanks to the team at Cambridge University Press, who have shepherded the book through the process with professionalism; and, in particular, to thank the copy-editor, Sally Evans-Darby, who has done a wonderful job.

As anyone in academia knows, getting to the end of a writing project implies that sacrifices have been made, and not only by the author. Weekends have been ring-fenced for writing, which means invitations have been declined, birthday parties skipped, and promised trips postponed. Those closest to me have had to live with this project for a decade and I am more grateful than I can say that they have put up with it and me. Thomas Mertens has read and commented on the whole manuscript, showing remarkable forbearance as the deadline was repeatedly postponed and providing moral support when my confidence deserted me.

This book has been written – although not published – using the Candara typeface, invented by Gary Munch (according to Wikipedia), which has made a world of difference to my struggling lupus-brain. I am including this acknowledgement here for other brains out there that are easily overwhelmed by visual input and who might not yet have discovered that a different font can be a simple game-changer. I wish that I had known about this earlier.

It feels necessary at this stage of human–AI interaction to state that every word of the book has been written by me and without the assistance of AI – although it is quite possible that any reader who makes it through to the end of the book may have preferred it otherwise. Where I have used AI to assist with translations, it is clearly flagged in a footnote. Lastly, I am solely responsible for the analysis and opinions expressed: the generous engagement with my work by those thanked above does not entail that they share any of the thoughts or conclusions given expression here.

This book is dedicated to the memory of my father, George Frederick William Goodwin (1941–2019), who cared deeply about social injustice; and to Beata Mukakazine, and to all the female survivors of the genocide, who work every day to lay the foundations of a Rwanda at peace with itself.

GLOSSARY

Abasangwabutaka	'those found on the earth or on the land', a term for 'indigenous'
abunzi (pl.)	local community mediators who help resolve disputes
agaciro	dignity
amoko (pl.)	clans
Batwa	the Twa people
gacaca	literally 'short grass', a traditional dispute resolution or community-based justice mechanism used to try genocide suspects
Girinka	'one cow, one family', a development programme
imidugudu (pl.)	villages
imihigo	a Rwandan tradition, now understood as performance contracts
imiryango (pl.)	lineages
Impunyu	forest-dwelling Twa
ingando	solidarity camps
intore	an individual who has completed the Itorero programme
inzu (pl.)	families
iterambere	literally 'the stuff of the future', development
itorero	civil leadership
kuneena batwa	a purity code excluding the Twa that covers all forms of social interaction
Mutwa	singular of Batwa, an individual Twa
Ndi Umunyarwanda	'I am Rwandan', a unity programme launched in 2013
ubudehe	government socio-economic categories, 1–4 (after 2020, A–E)
ubuhake	a cattle-based client–patron relationship
ubumwe	unity
ubureetwa	unremunerated manual labour
ubwenge	a traditional language practice referring to intelligence and prudence in public speech
ubwoko bw'abantu	ethnic groups
umuganda	communal work carried out at the village or community level
urugerero	national service or community duty
Urugwiro	presidential compound, the site of the Urugwiro Process – a series of weekly meetings between May 1998 and March 1999

ABBREVIATIONS

ACHPR	African Commission on Human and Peoples' Rights
ADBR	Association pour le Développement Global des Batwa du Rwanda (Association for the Global Development of the Batwa of Rwanda)
APB	Association pour la Promotion Batwa (Association for the Promotion of Batwa)
AREDETWA	Association pour le Relèvement Démocratique des Twa (Association for the Democratic Recovery of the Twa)
CAADP	Comprehensive Africa Agriculture Development Programme
CAURWA	Communauté des Autochtones Rwandais (loosely, Community of Indigenous Rwandans)
CBD	Convention on Biological Diversity
CBHI	community-based health insurance, also known as Mutuelle de santé
CIP	crop intensification programme
COPORWA	Communauté des Potiers du Rwanda (Community of Potters of Rwanda)
EDPRS	Economic Development and Poverty Reduction Strategy
ELD	Economics of Land Degradation
FAO	Food and Agriculture Organization
FPP	Forest Protection Plan
GGCRS	Green Growth and Climate Resilience Strategy
HMP	historically marginalised people
HRBA	human rights-based approach to development
IMF	International Monetary Fund
INGO	international non-governmental organisation
IRDP	Institute of Research and Dialogue for Peace
IUCN	International Union for the Conservation of Nature
IWGIA	International Working Group for Indigenous Affairs
LDC	least-developed country
LODA	Local Administrative Entities Development Agency
MINALOC	Ministry of Local Affairs
MINECOFIN	Ministry of Finance and Economic Planning
MRG	minority rights group

NAFA	National Forest Authority
NDC	National Dialogue Councils
NFP	National Forestry Plan
NGO	non-governmental organisation
NLP	national land policy
NST	National Strategy for Transformation
NURC	National Unity and Reconciliation Commission
OECD	Organisation for Economic Co-operation and Development
ORTPN	Office Rwandais du Tourisme et des Parcs Nationaux (Rwanda Office of Tourism and National Parks)
PRSP	Poverty Reduction Strategy Paper
RDB	Rwanda Development Board
REMA	Rwanda Environment Management Authority
RIB	Rwanda Investigations Bureau
RPF	Rwandan Patriotic Front
UN	United Nations
UNDP	United Nations Development Programme
UNDRIP	United Nations Declaration on the Rights of Indigenous Peoples
UNEP	United Nations Environment Programme
UNESCO-MAB	United Nations Educational, Scientific and Cultural Organisation's Man and the Biosphere programme
UNPO	Unrepresented Nations and Peoples Organisation
VUP	Vision 2020 Umurenge Programme
WB	World Bank
WEF	World Economic Forum
YCD	Youth Connect Dialogue

1

Setting the Scene

This book is about the Batwa of Rwanda.[1] It is an attempt to understand how this group are situated by, and situate themselves in, various forms of global jurisdictional ordering. Based on four years of fieldwork data, collected between 2014 and 2018, it relates how Twa navigate their present and their future – their place in the world – in the context of global and national discourses of indigeneity, belonging, progress, vulnerability, unity, faith, and environmental preservation. In short, it is a book about intersecting global discourses that, refracted through the policies of a post-colonial state, together form the context in which Twa negotiate their lives. It is a story of ordinary Twa: of their struggles, frustrations, hopes, and aspirations. It is also necessarily therefore a book about Rwanda,[2] about government policies on national unity, conservation, and development.

Few countries divide opinion like Rwanda. It is either celebrated as a pro-poor, development success story that has overcome the ravages of civil war and genocide through strong, non-corrupt leadership or it is denounced as an autocratic state, ruled by a military strongman, who murders opponents, stifles political opposition, and imposes a false narrative of reconciliation and national unity (inter alia Reyntjens 2011; Thomson 2013; Makhunga 2019; Wrong 2021).[3] I will not engage here with this debate. Instead, my goal is a different one.[4] I am interested here

[1] Batwa is the plural form of Twa, where Mutwa is the singular. I shall, however, largely use the term Twa to refer to both individual members of the community and the community as a whole, despite the sensitivities surrounding the naming of this community within Rwanda (see Chapter 2).

[2] I do not attempt in this book to situate Rwanda within a wider African, or East African, context. This is perhaps a next step, but it was beyond the scope of this project.

[3] Clark has characterised this dichotomy as a disagreement between the 'developmentalists' and the 'human rights activists' (2014b).

[4] To be clear, I am not claiming to write a 'balanced' or 'better' account, as if those who stake out one of the positions sketched above are in some way unbalanced or their work not well grounded. I am simply doing something else.

in studying situated forms of global jurisdictional ordering – the claims, imaginaries, identities, and power that emerge in transnational encounters between the local, the national, and the global, or what has variously been labelled as inter-legality or, more recently, translocalism or inter-polity law (de Sousa Santos 1987; Canfield, Dehm, and Fassi 2021; also Benton and Cluclow 2023). Such studies are an attempt to shift scholarly focus from the top-down framing of global law to how power and global legal normativity are enacted in everyday practices and jurisdictional claims. The three global jurisdictional claims considered here – the discourses of indigeneity, development, and conservationism – constitute Twa variously as indigenous peoples, as development actors, or as poachers, thereby transforming them and their daily lives into a matter of global concern. These globalising claims to regulate everyday life in a particular domain intersect – are negated or magnified – not only with each other but also with the national legal framing of Twa as only Rwandans. In this study, these global jurisdictional claims, refracted and reframed through the encounter with the state and with local forces, are brought together into focus as jurisdictional encounters.

I am therefore concerned within Rwanda with how policies and laws frame the space in which Twa are able to make choices for themselves and not with how they may also legitimise the Rwandan government. One story does not cancel out the importance of the other; that is, a policy can be a form of narrative control (Doughty 2016) and yet still be mostly welcomed by a portion of society. Instead, what is important, as the writer Chimamanda Ngozi Adichie reminds us, is not to reduce a society to a single story.[5] In our data, the Twa are critical of state authorities – of, as they perceive it, their inactions, of the unfairness of the implementation of government policies, and of attempts to rename them – but these criticisms reflect different concerns to those whose focus is, for example, the rule of law or media freedom. The Twa are concerned above all with the daily lived reality of their own lives and, as such, of improving their socio-economic position. This includes concern with their place as Twa within Rwandan society and hence is of course political; however, for ordinary Twa, the focus of their concerns is not on an overly powerful government but on being left behind.

[5] Chimamanda Ngozi Adichie, 'The Danger of a Single Story', TEDGlobal, July 2009: www.ted.com/talks/chimamanda_ngozi_adichie_the_danger_of_a_single_story.

1.1 Global Discourses and Global Subjects

Throughout this work, I make use of the term 'global discourses' to refer to discourses that are intended to have global effect (Walker 2015). Following Foucault, discourses are understood here as cultural phenomena made up of interconnected vocabularies and shared systems of meaning within social ecosystems; for example, the way in which the rule of law is understood by development practitioners regardless of their individual background or the location of their development intervention (Leach 2021). They are a systemic or shared means of talking about actions and people, of understanding their relationship to others, to nature, and to the notion of how a human life should be lived (Foucault 1980); that is, discourses represent authoritative stories or narratives. Actors function within the available discourses, internalising their vocabulary and rules, which provide both the tools to motivate and understand their own actions and those of others. Discourses, then, frame our actions, determining what can be said and done (i.e. the scope of our imagination), and, in this way, they materially constitute and shape the context in which individuals and communities live; for example, the production of the Third World through the discourses and practices of development (Escobar 1995). Studying discourses means to focus on the mechanisms and relationships that enable the formation of permissible modes of being and thinking while at the same time disenabling others (e.g. Mudimbe 1988). For Foucault, the key to studying power is to focus on forms of resistance against specific forms of power (Foucault 1982: 780).

A discourse constitutes a system of rules or an implicit language of control embedded in ordinary life. Seen as a disciplinary force or technology of governmentality, discourses are thus not merely a description of the world but contain a disciplinary imperative. As such, they combine definitional, interpretative, and normative power, going beyond the explicit power of formal legal enforcement. This entails that, following Charles Taylor, modern systems of power come dressed not only in the conventional forms of physical compulsion but as science or liberation, or, we might add, rights or ideas about progress and nature (Taylor 1986). Within the global conservation discourse, for example, a nature reserve is defined by reference to global scientific standards, with limited inclusion of local understandings of nature or the human–nature relationship (Igoe 2010). Global discourses draw on and feed into global legal regimes: the combination of hard and soft law instruments, located and applied in a wide variety of legal and non-legal sites (Twining 2012), and involving a range of different actors. Whereas international legal regimes tend to focus on explicit rules and on institutions of enforcement, global discourses work to regulate the behaviour of actors – states, communities, organisations, and individuals – through a combination of persuasion and coercion, while asserting their legitimacy to do so based on the global standards or norms that the discourse itself asserts. It is this combination of explicit and implicit, of a body of authoritative norms and discursive practice, that constitutes the basis of what I mean by global law (Goodwin 2012; Zumbansen 2021).[6] As Manji, following Cutler, has put it, 'what links the local order of the nation-state with . . . [the] global order is law' (2006: 67; Cutler 2002).[7] The focus here is thus on the regulatory power of global discourses to construct narratives, to function as imaginaries, and to discipline. Moreover, by examining the narratives that underpin the hard and soft norms of global discourses, I am attempting to highlight the values that these norms encode.

Global discourses are not top-down, cooked up in Washington or Geneva. They go beyond the dualism of the national–international relationship, whereby international law seeks to regulate the behaviour of states. Instead, the sites of power within a discourse are multiple, with many different actors with different agendas and differing powers to act, all engaging with and remaking discourses in everyday practice (e.g. Allen 2009; Perry-Kessaris 2021). Global discourses address a wide variety of actors directly, as well as in mediated forms and at different scales. The global indigenous narrative speaks to and is spoken by international organisations, corporations, states, communities, individuals, courts, and more, making claims about what indigeneity is, what it means for those that are formed as indigenous subjects, and how it should shape the behaviour of other actors in response. These discourses transform local struggles and the actors involved in them into global struggles. In appealing to the language of indigeneity, for example, a group draws on the resources of a global discourse, introducing it into a local conflict, whether for recognition or for access to resources (Hodgson 2011). Indeed, 'the global' can only appear when manifested in particular places at particular moments; that is, it is necessarily localised (Anders 2009). The classic image of a rigid hierarchy of normative ordering, from the

[6] This understanding draws on Benton's ideas of global institutional ordering (2002) and the work of Zumbansen on transnational legal pluralism (2020).

[7] While Cutler's work is focused on the role of law in the globalisation of capital, the understanding of global law here is broader.

global to the local, with legal norms nested by reference to location or levels (Twining 2012), is thus reimagined as entangled legalities (Krisch 2021), inter-polity law (Benton and Clulow 2023), or translocal legalities (Canfield et al. 2021); or, in the words of Nyamnjoh, 'a world of hegemonies of all kinds' (Nyamnjoh 2002: 111).

Yet, within this plurality, a global discourse aims to standardise by subjecting individuals and communities to a single narrative framing; for example, as an indigenous people or as peasants subject to development imperatives. The discourse of indigeneity, for example, seeks to view a community – their relations with each other, the natural world, with other groups within the same society or place, and with institutions such as the state – through the lens of indigeneity. To do so necessitates structuring that community and their relations in this way – and not, of course, in any one of a myriad of other ways, such as class, gender, or local-based identities. To view a village through a development lens requires us to view the relations between individuals and groups as co-participants in the development enterprise, in which the shared goal is an agreed understanding of a better life. However, global discourses do not cohere into a single frame, subjecting individuals and communities instead to often contradictory normative systems; for example, between indigenous rights that seek to preserve groups in their original habitat and conservation ideals that demand pristine wilderness shorn of people. Similarly, the global development discourse that promises progress and inclusion can, in practice, conflict with notions of indigeneity, which seek to preserve distinctness. Twa live within and across these jurisdictional encounters between a range of global discourses: indigeneity, environmental protection, evangelism, and development.

The plurality of narratives provides that actors can attempt to move between them, framing and reframing what matters to them in different forms and via alternative positioning within daily struggles.[8] Determining which vocabulary to use to explain one's life – the naming of a problem – is itself an act of power, although this individual power is of course limited by the discourses available and to the force of any particular discourse in a given context. As an exercise of power, a discourse makes a jurisdictional claim to be *the* frame of reference or

[8] For example, see Escobar's study of the emergence of Black ethnicity in the Colombian Pacific (2008). Reframing oneself will not, though, always be possible and it is likely to require a great deal of effort over several years.

way of talking about a particular actor or aspect of life (Walker 2015).[9] The social power of a discourse is determined by the ability of the institutional structures behind a discourse to make good on this claim. Viewing global law in this way entails that instead of searching only for order and compliance, we are concerned with what Tsing calls 'contaminated diversity' (2015), or the friction that occurs in the encounter of one jurisdictional ordering claim with another, and between those who are subject to those claims (Tsing 2005). As Canfield et al. note, 'encounters between different legal orderings, like chemicals, produce different reactions' (2021: 337). As framing or jurisdictional claims, discourses are engaged with, negotiated, and resisted (Scott 1985; Escobar 2008); they allow creative space for individual and community manoeuvre within and between jurisdictional orderings. Against Foucault, then, subjecthood can also be creative and playful, as well as being concerned with discipline and domination (Werbner 2002).[10]

Subjectivisation through global discourses is an attempt to standardise in order to make legible at a distance. How one is subjectivised matters because the power of global imaginaries and their disciplining force are able to invest that imagination with a reality that becomes material – not because it is objectively real but because people and institutions act in accordance with the described reality in such a way that they produce it. Yet discourses, while potentially dominant as framings of the world, are not totalising. In Foucault's words, power 'incites, it induces, it seduces, it makes easier or more difficult; in the extreme it constrains or forbids absolutely; it is nevertheless always a way of acting upon an acting subject or acting subjects by virtue of their acting or being capable of action' (1982: 789). I understand this as meaning that power allows for a range of responses; that discourses structure the field of action of others but do not determine it totally. As Foucault wrote, power can only be exercised in situations in which individuals are free (1982: 790).

The contingency of these encounters and the room for manoeuvre in how we engage with and between jurisdictional orderings entail that we are subjects of these discourses and not objects. While the concept of the subject is deeply debated within both philosophy and sociology (and much less so in law),[11] subjecthood here is understood in

[9] This follows the understanding of a legal order as an exclusive claim to ultimate ordering authority (Walker 2003; Lindahl 2013).

[10] Mbembe has articulated the post-colonial African subject as 'homo ludens par excellence', suggesting the subject's 'talent for play and a sense of fun' (1992: 5).

[11] Although see Boyd White (1985) and Balkin (1993).

a Foucauldian sense that follows from his definition of power. Where power is understood as a force producing new relations, forms of desire, objects, and discourses, the subject is produced through these power relations and does not precede it (Foucault 1978; Butler 1993). This leads, famously, to the paradox of 'subjectivation', whereby the processes that create an individual's subordination are the very means by which they emerge as a self-conscious agent (Foucault 1982). A subject is therefore always and necessarily embedded in relations of particular operations of power and/or discourse and cannot be separated from them; that is, the individual is not prior to the social. This does not, *pace* Butler, result in an individual being trapped in domination, but agency is instead to be found in the performativity of power. That is, in the repetition or constant performance of social norms comes the possibility of reappropriating or destabilising these norms, and this allows for 'the possibility of [a discourse's] undoing' (cited in Mahmood 2006: 46; see Butler 1997). This locates the possibility of agency within a discourse rather than outside it.

Building on Butler's work and feminist theory more broadly, Mahmood – in her work on female piety within Islam – articulates a concept of agency that moves beyond an agonistic framework; that is, one that views agency beyond the dichotomy of resistance or subordination (Mahmood 2006: 36). For Mahmood, too much of our thinking about agency universalises the desire to be free from relations of subordination, whereby agency is posited as resistance to relations of domination. However, this view of agency as necessarily liberatory in nature, she writes, 'elides dimensions of human action whose ethical or political status does not map onto the logic of repressions and resistance' (42). Instead, she suggests that 'we think of agency not as a synonym for resistance to the relations of domination but as capacity for action that historically specific relations of subordination enable and create' (33–34). Agency, and the practice of exercising agency, exists therefore in the multiple ways in which an individual 'inhabits norms' (42). In this way, it is possible to include motivations, desires, and goals that are not captured by the resistance/subordination dichotomy.

This understanding of agency necessarily eschews the idea that it is something that one has or does not; instead it becomes part of everyday living (e.g. Haraway 1988). As Mbembe writes:

> In Africa today, the subject who *accomplishes the age* and validates it, who lives and espouses his/her contemporaneousness – that is, what is

> 'distinctive' or 'particular' to his/her present real world – is first a subject who has an *experience* of 'living in the concrete world'. She/he is a subject of experience and a validating subject, not only in the sense that she/he is a conscious existence or has a perceptive consciousness of things, but to the extent that his/her 'living in the concrete world' involves, and is evaluated by, his/her eyes, ears, mouth – in short, his/her flesh, his/her body.
>
> (2001: 17; emphasis his)

If we accept that subjectivities are, in part, performed rather than simply imposed, then subjectification, or the process of becoming a subject, is an interactive process that is also determined by the engagement, refusal, acceptance, witnessing, and participation of the subject themselves, through which they render themselves subject to a discursive regime. Or, in the words of Lambek, 'people are agents insofar as they choose to subject themselves, to perform and conform accordingly, to accept responsibility, and to acknowledge their commitments' (2002: 38). Where engagement is always intersubjective, subjecthood is an exercise of strategic imagination, in which individuals and communities imagine the future they desire in relation to other beings and in the context of social structuring forces, such as discourses. Following Mahmood, a key argument of this book is that we need to move away from a singular focus on agency as resistance and instead investigate agency as situated and multifaceted (also Ampumuza et al. 2020; Menzel 2020; Wainaina 2022: 88–89 for a situated understanding of female agency). Agency practised as the inhabitation of norms requires no less strategic imagination than what we look for as resistance. This means that, to understand global discourses, we need to study not only how individuals' and communities' worlds are shaped by these discourses but also how they are received, reworked, and inhabited in what Whyte (2002) has called, following Rorty, 'the practical wisdom of everyday life'.[12]

The exercise of strategic agency, of positioning oneself within society, relates in the contemporary world, in which questions of differentiation predominate, to questions of identity. I attempt here to heed Brubaker and Cooper's warning of the 'flattening rubric of identity' (2000: 9). Following Hall (1996), I understand identity as something that one does or performs rather than has or is. This moves away from an

[12] I note, however, Nyenyezi Bisoka et al.'s warning that an actor-orientated approach can overplay the possibility of individuals and communities acting as strategic actors (2020). Mahmood also comments that a situated, contingent approach to agency risks orientalising non-Western Others (2006).

essentialist approach and positions identity as a claim.[13] Baynham suggests that, connecting performance to narrative, we need to pay attention to the idea of 'speaking position' (2006: 380) in order to analyse how identities are constructed moment by moment in different contexts. The advantage of focusing on speaking position over voice is that the former draws attention to how speakers are placed in certain positions, as well as how they take up certain roles within a discourse (Baynham 2006: 381). In this way, an individual's identity is an outcome of complex positioning based on the socially available resources. These resources are determined locally – that is, they are situated – but can have their origins far away, such as in the global concept of indigeneity (Hodgson 2011). The idea that groups or communities position themselves in a dynamic and complex landscape clearly draws on earlier work by anthropologists in the field, particularly those focusing on indigenous peoples, as well as post-colonial cultural theorists (e.g. Hall 1996; Li 2000; Povinelli 2002; Hodgson 2011).

Positioning is a response to our recognition needs as human beings. However, it is about more than simply how we feel or wish to be seen. How we position ourselves can determine access to resources, such as funding and access to services and goods, whether at the local, national, or global level; as Mbembe has cautioned, we should be wary of viewing all struggles as struggles purely of representation (2001: 6). Yet, how one is able to position oneself depends upon the available resources or capital, whether social capital, in terms of access to networks and media; education and the skills to capitalise on opportunities; or financial capital, to be able to fund campaigns or finance media access (Bourdieu 1990). It also depends on the discursive resources available. But these resources are not necessarily directly available; that is, these resources are refracted and reformed by other actors. In Rwanda, this work of mediation is done almost entirely by the state. In order to examine identity and agency within Rwanda, it is necessary to consider not only how state policies shape the many aspects of identity – for example, how policies on land inheritance shape how gender is experienced – but also how those identities, and crucially the interaction between them, determine how individuals interact with the state and with each other, and what space they have to make choices about how they frame their lives.

Hodgson writes that the concept of 'positionings therefore encompasses and signals the interlocking struggles over representation,

[13] It does not suggest, however, that identity is an exercise in cynicism.

recognition, resources and rights that are central to any form of political action, especially in the "postcolony"'. As such, they 'incorporate and index agency, structure, meaning and power; they demonstrate the articulation of political economy and cultural domains of meaning, signification, and representation' (2011: 8–9). Tsing calls upon us to use ethnographic stories or fragments to interrupt tales of a singular and successful globalisation (2005: 271). Igoe responds to this invitation by suggesting that special attention needs to be paid 'to the ways in which processes of alienation and fetishization effectively exclude some groups from global connections and the collective imaginings that they sometimes allow' (2010: 389). I take up these invitations not by examining exclusion from global connections but by considering the ways in which Rwandan Twa are embedded within the entanglement of global discourses.[14]

1.2 Genocide and Beyond

1.2.1 Arriving at Genocide

Rwanda has been the target of a great deal of international interest over the past thirty years, as scholars have sought to describe and understand the origins, processes, and aftermath of the Rwandan genocide (e.g. Newbury 1998; Mamdani 2001; Lemarchand 2009; McDoom 2020; Reyntjens 2024). Lawyers and genocide specialists have explored the international and national efforts to prosecute the perpetrators of the violence and to achieve justice for the dead and the survivors alike (P. Clark 2010; Ndahinda and Muleefu 2012; Doughty 2016). International development practitioners, sociologists, and anthropologists have equally sought to understand how Rwanda has rebuilt in the wake of the physical and social devastation left behind by genocide and civil war (Ansoms 2009, 2011; Ingelaere 2010b, 2011; Strauss and Waldorf 2011a; Purdeková 2015; Kimonyo 2019; Sentama 2022). In more recent scholarship, political scientists, governance specialists, and journalists have focused on the formation of an authoritarian state in Rwanda (Reyntjens 2011; Thomson 2013; Wrong 2021) and on the country's role in the wider region, particularly in the Democratic Republic of the Congo (DRC) (Van Hoyweghen 1996; Hintjens 2006;

[14] This draws on what Nader has called a 'vertical slice' approach, in which one attempts to link local sets of practices and knowledge production back to the global (see Meyerstein 2007).

Doughty 2016: 62). Nearly all these studies have engaged with Rwanda's national unity and reconciliation agenda and are deeply critical of it. Some of these critical accounts focus on the gains to the government, others on the likely ineffectiveness of achieving their goals, claiming that the current unity policies equate to, following Ricoeur, an 'enforced ethnic amnesia' (Lemarchand 2009: 106) that can only lead to a 'false unity' (J. N. Clark 2010: 138). This, they claim, works to prevent reconciliation. Others, notably Reyntjens (2024), have asserted that the regulation of ethnicity through law is a tool to control a population that the state distrusts.

While the past is always a contested ground and the creation of a historical narrative is a key part of all nation-building (Smith 1991), history – and the desire to control what C. Newbury has termed people's 'mental maps of history' (1988b: 7) – is central to understanding Rwanda's reconstruction. Rwanda's political elites have long used historical claims to legitimate their rule (Vansina 2004; D. Newbury 2009); and its contemporary rulers are charged with the creation of a 'cognitive glue' of historical narrative of both the distant past and the recent, post-1990, past (Reyntjens 2005; Lemarchand 2009; Phillips DeZalia 2014; Doughty 2016: 45). Despite Rwandan history being particularly contentious, there are nonetheless points of scholarly consensus on facts, if not necessarily on interpretation.

Pre-colonial Rwanda is most simply described as a monarchy or military kingdom, which gradually expanded its control over much of what is contemporary Rwanda (C. Newbury 1988a). Social and political life was governed by lineage and client–patron relationships. However, the formation of identities as 'Bahutu' and 'Batutsi' and the extent to which it is possible to speak of pre-colonial harmony between them have long been contested; ideas about the formation of these categories and the relationship between them played a key mobilising role in the post-independence violence that culminated in the genocide. It was held that Tutsis arrived as pastoralists long after the area had been settled by Hutus, giving rise to claims that Hutus were autochthonous or indigenous to the land and the Tutsis mere foreigners (Mamdani 2001; Twagilimana 2003; Vansina 2004; Ndahinda 2011). However, rather than being the result of waves of migration of different people to the area, scholarly work suggests that the differentiation between 'Bahutu' and 'Batutsi' began to emerge with the formation of state structures in the north across the seventeenth and eighteenth centuries

(C. Newbury 1988a; Vansina 2004).[15] The formation of the kingdom among groups of pastoralists saw the emergence of a political identity and, according to Newbury, the emergence of a self-consciousness as Tutsi and as superior (C. Newbury 1988a: 207–209). In contrast, Hutu identity grew out of the attempt by Tutsi elites to distance themselves from everyone else. Both identities consciously distanced themselves from the forest-dwellers and hunters known as Batwa (Vansina 2004; Taylor 2011). These distinctions were then institutionalised via state structures, notably through the military (Vansina 2004).

The characterisation of these pre-colonial hierarchical distinctions – as entrenched and exploitative or as fluid and social – is another key part of the contested historical narrative. Under what Doughty has termed the current regime's 'master narrative of history' (2016: 55), these distinctions were flexible and harmonious; for the Hutu power movement that emerged around independence, relationships were feudal and unjust. Much of the dispute hinges on the characterisation of the practice of *ubuhake* – a cattle-based client–patron relationship (Newbury 1978; Vansina 2004). In this hereditary relationship, the patron would offer his protection and assign one or two head of cattle to the client for his use. However, the cattle remained under the ownership of the patron and the client was required to provide whatever service the patron required in return for protection. The practice ensured that Rwandans were woven together in tight social networks of obligation; yet, as Doughty observes, it entrenched socio-economic inequality by ensuring that Tutsis retained economic, social, and political power.[16]

However, historical scholarship has nuanced our understanding of the *ubuhake* practice, suggesting that, although deep inequality did exist in pre-colonial society, the relationship was not purely exploitative of subordinate Hutus (Vansina 2004; Newbury 2009).[17] Moreover, the

[15] D. Newbury cautions that ethnicity was an important part of the social process: 'ethnic identities were not primordial; they were contextually created, they altered over time, and they evolved differently in different places and contexts' (2009: 297).

[16] Again, caution is needed: historical research has questioned the centrality of *ubuhake* as the key form of clientship in early modern Rwanda, with Vidal highlighting a 'fetishism of the cow' in much historical anthropological work (Newbury 2009: 47). Land clientship appears to have been more politically significant (Newbury 1978). Moreover, the *ubuhake* contract was not necessarily ethnically based (see Vansina 2004 for an account of the development and waning of the practice).

[17] Alongside the *ubuhake* form of clientship, a particularly hated system was *ubureetwa* (unremunerated manual labour for the chiefs), which became synonymous with Hutu oppression under colonial rule, but which predates it (C. Newbury 1978).

categories of Tutsi and Hutu were primarily socio-economic in nature, with Tutsi being a term to describe the wealthy with control over cattle, and Hutu characterising the poor, including poor Tutsi. The labels were applied with some flexibility, so that, over time, a family could move back and forth across the categories as their fortunes waxed and waned (Vansina 2004; Newbury 2009). This form of identity also co-existed alongside alternative ways of identifying oneself and others and was not even the most important. Region, lineage, and clan were arguably more significant as forms of social organisation, and a clan was constituted by all three ethnic groups (Newbury 1978, 2009; Vansina 2004), changing over time as alliances were forged, broken, and remade. These deeply entwined social relations entailed that Rwandans shared the same language and were bound together in the same cultural and religious practices (C. Newbury 1988a).

Under colonial rule, however – first of the Germans and then the Belgians – these distinctions were further engrained and racialised, fixing socio-economic and ethnic identities into biological certainties. Racial theories became the basis of the administrative apparatus of Belgian rule in Rwanda, with Tutsi power entrenched in the colonial structures (J. N. Clark 2010).[18] This essentialisation of ethnicity as race was based upon European notions of racial superiority, with the Twa characterised as Pygmies and thus at the bottom of the hierarchy (Ndahinda 2011), whereas Tutsis were, in line with the so-called Hamitic Hypothesis[19] (Sanders 2009), viewed as Caucasian in origin – having allegedly migrated from northern Africa – and thus as racially superior. This superiority was not only determined by physical characteristics – height, facial features, and so on – but also determined moral characteristics. Tutsis were courageous, capable of leadership, and intelligent. By way of contrast, Hutus were hardworking and obedient but not clever (Maquet 1961). The indirect manner of colonial rule through Tutsi chiefs enabled them to accumulate further wealth and privilege, while farmers and rural dwellers, primarily but not only Hutus, bore the brunt of colonial exploitation (Newbury 1988a; Twagilimana 2003).

As momentum gathered for independence, so too did the animo for revolution. The revolution that then occurred – the Hutu Revolution

[18] Instead of Tutsis being co-opted into the colonial power structure, Des Forges has made a forceful argument that the relationship was a joint undertaking, welcomed by both (1999; also C. Newbury 1988a).

[19] As Chrétien notes, this thesis has been comprehensively debunked (2003: 69). See also Vansina (2004).

(1959–1962) – was directed, according to C. Newbury, not against the Belgian colonial authorities but against Tutsi rule and rural injustice (1988a). Widespread violence throughout the country broke out against Tutsis at the start of the revolution and occurred periodically throughout the post-independence period of Hutu-power governments. Tutsi were excluded from power and subject to regular pogroms and displacement, creating an extensive diaspora community across the wider Great Lakes region (Lemarchand 2009; Mayerson 2015; Doughty 2016). The Hutu-led post-independence governments created and entrenched ethnically based dynamics of fear in which moderates from all groups were marginalised (C. Newbury 1998a; Doughty 2016).

In 1990, the Rwandan Patriotic Front (RPF), a largely Tutsi-based group of armed Rwandan exiles, invaded the country from its base in Uganda and civil war ensued. Anti-Tutsi massacres proliferated after the invasion as the government labelled all Tutsis as RPF supporters, claiming that the invasion was an attempt to reinstate Tutsi domination. The violence across the country culminated in the 1994 genocide, which unleased grotesque levels of violence against Tutsis and moderate Hutus, and which ran from the downing of President Habyarimana's plane over Kigali on 6 April to the victory of the RPF three months later. During that period, some 800,000 Rwandans were slaughtered by their compatriots, their neighbours, their fellow parishioners, classmates, colleagues, and, occasionally, their relatives and friends – although the exact number of victims is also contested, as are the mass killings that took place in the months after the genocide had officially ended (Mamdani 2001; Lemarchand 2009; Doughty 2016).

However, we should not make the mistake of assuming that the genocide was solely the result of an ethnic hatred stoked over many decades. Musahara and Huggins' work suggests that poverty and landlessness were key factors in the violence that followed independence. They note, for example, that Tutsis were not the only target of violence during the genocide but that violence across the various communes was also targeted at those involved in land disputes (2005: 274). Indeed, poverty and inequality in relation to access to land grew during the post-independence period, partly as a result of population growth, creating social instability and social disconnection – particularly for those in rural areas and especially among young men (C. Newbury 1998; McDoom 2020; McNamee 2021). The global political economy also played a role in destabilising Rwanda, with coffee prices collapsing in 1989 and the International Monetary Fund's (IMF's) structural adjustment programmes requiring the devaluation of the currency a year later – both of which resulted in serious cutbacks in public services, limiting access for ordinary Rwandans to education, healthcare, and water (Newbury 1998; Mamdani 2001). Together, these factors saw a dramatic increase in poverty for the majority of Rwandans (Uvin 1988) – conditions that occurred at the same time that the Hutu-majority power structure was under pressure to open up political space to a multi-party structure; that is, those in power feared losing it, under pressure from both above and below. The genocide was thus not a spontaneous outburst of ethnic violence but was deeply seated in the country's political and organisational structure (Mamdani 2001; McDoom 2020) and in its socio-economic structures, all of which had been formed in the pre-colonial period (Newbury 1998), as well as in Rwanda's post-colonial position vis-à-vis global economic structures.

By the time the genocide had been stopped at the beginning of July 1994 by the RPF's victory, the country was utterly broken. The social, legal, and economic fabric of society had been torn apart. Vast numbers were dead or displaced; survivors were physically and mentally broken. And the background issues, such as population growth, regional instability, the colonial legacy of economic dependence, land shortage, and environmental degradation, were all still pressing. Moreover, although the genocide was over, violence continued between the RPF and Hutu insurgents until the 2002 Pretoria Accords (Lemarchand 2009). The destructiveness of the genocide and the total victory of the RPF created space for radical transformation. To the victors fell the task of rebuilding the country. They did so by putting unity and reconciliation at the heart of their efforts.

1.2.2 *Reconciliation through Unity*

Unity is at the core of Rwanda's national reconciliation and rebuilding efforts. The National Policy on Unity and Reconciliation, launched in 2007 by the National Unity and Reconciliation Commission (NURC), puts it succinctly: 'unity and reconciliation is the only option that Rwanda has chosen' (NURC 2007: 6). On first reading, this sentence appears to be ungrammatical. On further reflection, this sentence can be understood as capturing the essence of reconciliation in Rwanda, where reconciliation in Rwanda *is* unity and where the process of reconciliation is a process of creating a single Rwandan identity. The first guiding principle of the National Policy on Unity and Reconciliation is thus 'To promote the spirit of Rwandan identity and put national interests first instead of favours based on ethnicity, blood relations, gender, religions, region of origin etc.' (NURC 2015: 5). This vision of unity as the core of reconciliation is mainstreamed through all national institutions, sectoral policies, and local governance structures (NURC 2007: 134).

This focus on national unity was born out of the Urugwiro Process, a series of weekly meetings of Rwanda's elite at the presidential residence, Village Urugwiro, between May 1998 and March 1999 (NURC 2016: 49; Longman 2017: 151). The diagnosis of the RPF leadership was that ethnic discord had caused the genocide and hence the replacement of ethnic identity with an inclusive Rwandan citizenship as a 'monolithic identity' was the solution to decades of ethnic hatred and violence (Sentama 2022: 9). Moreover, that ethnic discord was, they concluded, in part a result of bad governance. Good governance therefore became central to overcoming ethnic strife and this required a change in the relationship between the governed and those in power, whereby a subculture of passive obedience that made the people vulnerable to sectarian manipulation was undone (NURC 2016: 69). The creation of a national unity as the core purpose of the post-genocidal regime in Rwanda thus places the genocidal violence at the heart of reconstruction (Turner 2014; Doughty 2016).

This 'single categorisation' vision of unity, whereby only one identity has salience (Moss 2014), is constructed in a number of distinct ways. The first pillar of national unity and reconciliation policies is legal. The use of the categories of 'Hutu', 'Twa', and 'Tutsi' is not merely taboo but was effectively criminalised in the 2001 law on discrimination and sectarianism, which makes discrimination a crime (Law N° 47/2001). In 2003, the new Constitution introduced the criminalisation of public reference to ethnic identities directly into the Constitution and created additional crimes of divisionism and 'trivializing the genocide'; indeed, the 2003 reforms made eradicating ethnic divisions one of the six fundamental principles of the Constitution (Article 9). This was followed up in a new law in 2008 to punish genocidal ideology (Law N° 18/2008). In addition to criminalising divisionism, the 2003 Constitution also institutionalised unity at the core of the post-genocidal state, for example in the new national motto: Unity, Work, Patriotism (NURC 2007: 71). The legal approach to the immediate aftermath of the genocide and the question of what to do with thousands of killers and accomplices was also an important element of the drive towards unity. The *gacaca* trials placed the emphasis on reconciliation rather than on justice for the victims and punishment of the perpetrators (Clark 2010, 2014b). Perpetrators were jailed only when reconciliation was not possible because they did not seek forgiveness. Doughty has suggested in her work that the emphasis on unity in legal forums in Rwanda has created a '"total environment" of reconciliation' (2016: 70).[20]

The second element of unity is an appeal to a pre-colonial past that was prior to the country's contamination by European racist ideology. The opening sentence of the 2016 Report on Unity and Reconciliation Process in Rwanda reads: 'Rwanda is a country, whose past was characterized by division, exclusion, and violence *since the arrival of colonial powers*' (NURC 2016: 1; emphasis added). More explicitly, the report's author goes on to note, 'nationhood and unity among Rwandans have been destroyed during colonization, through colonizers "divide and rule" policy' (NURC 2016: 5). The 'real Rwanda' posited in this reading of history is one in which the various groups had previously lived together harmoniously. The seeds of hatred and of divisionism are thus alien to Rwandan culture and must be rooted out. Reaching back into a shared past provides the unity narrative, and the authority that enforces it, with a strong sense of legitimacy. This attempt to use history to legitimise the unity narrative has been the subject of much academic disquiet (e.g. Pottier 2002; Ingelaere 2011; Doughty 2016; Thomson 2018).[21]

The third pillar of national unity is the rooting of reconciliation in home-grown solutions and values, an appeal to a specifically Rwandan way of living together (NURC 2016: 4). These home-grown mechanisms – emphasised throughout NURC documents – are intended to create a space in which Rwandans can come together to achieve unity and reconciliation. In addition to the legal element of reconciliation efforts, notably the *gacaca* trials, these mechanisms focus on civic education; community sensitisation and consultations (which includes sensitising Rwandans to respond positively to government programmes); and 'combating poverty and ignorance' (NURC 2007: 14). Educating citizens about pre-colonial traditions

[20] On the pressure on victims to reconcile and heal, see also Williamson Sinalo (2018).

[21] For example, Pottier reports that in 1995, Rwanda's then-home affairs minister, Anastase Gasana, said that rewriting history was one of the priorities of the new government (2002: 127). Pottier takes that to mean that the government is deliberately subverting scholarly accounts of Rwanda's history to suit their own goals. A more generous interpretation could be that the leadership understood the role that creating a shared national myth – one in which ethnic hatred is un-Rwandan – could play in rebuilding a society shattered by violence (cf. Anderson 1983).

and shared societal values is thus central to the vision of unity and takes place via programmes such as Itorero (Civic Education Academy), Ingando (Solidarity Camps) (Mgbako 2005), and Ndi Umunyarwanda (I Am Rwandan) (Purdeková 2015; Sundberg 2016). According to the NURC, 'these home-grown solutions had to be embedded within a solid groundwork characterized by a strong political will, a capable state, and good governance, which has always been at the core of all actions of RPF and the post 1994 Government of National Unity' (NURC 2016: 4).

Finally, the fourth pillar of the national unity and reconciliation policy is socio-economic development in the form of poverty reduction and self-reliance. Notable policies in this regard include the Girinka programme (one cow per poor family), under which the community decides which household should be honoured with a free cow; Ubudehe ('a homegrown solution rooted in Rwanda's culture of mutual support' (NURC 2007: 96)), in which households are classified into socio-economic categories for targeted support; and the best known of these programmes, Umuganda, which is a national collective action programme on the last Saturday of every month to do communal work, such as sweeping and tidying of public spaces, and involving all Rwandans. These communal socio-development programmes are underpinned by the Vision 2020 Umurenge Program (VUP), run by the Ministry of Local Affairs (MINALOC). VUP is a cash transfer and support programme that provides direct support to households to ensure that basic needs are met, including providing free health insurance to the poorest households. It also includes a public works programme to provide employment, credit packages of VUP-insured micro-loans to encourage entrepreneurship and investment, and savings co-operatives in the form of savings and credit co-operatives at the sector level. These programmes are concerned with social inclusion (understood as financial inclusion), fostering Rwandan values, creating self-reliance, and dignity. The National Dialogue Council (NDC), an annual event that brings together the country's elite to discuss government policies and the way forward, has made dignity – and the connection between development and dignity – one of its core topics. The topic, for example, of the ninth NDC in 2011 was 'Strive for our dignity, together we pitch for rapid development'; the topic of the tenth Council in 2012 was more straightforwardly '*Agaciro* (dignity): Aiming for self-reliance'; and the banner for the thirteenth NDC in 2015 was 'Rwandans' choices: Foundation of National Development and Dignity'. Dignity is strongly connected here to self-reliance and self-improvement and is a core part of Rwanda's reconstruction efforts (Rutazibwa 2014; Mwambari 2021).

1.3 Introducing the Twa

Although there are many accounts of post-genocide Rwanda, the Twa[22] are often absent as Twa from the analysis.[23] This has much to do with their numerical position in relation to the rest of society. While it is impossible to gain accurate population figures for communities because of the restrictions on identifying individuals as members of ethnic groups under Law N° 47/2001, Twa are generally understood to constitute around 0.3–0.4 per cent of Rwanda's population, so 26,000–50,000 individuals.[24] This small size means that population samples in empirical research are unlikely to include many, if any, Twa, unless the sample size is huge or the research specifically targets the Twa community – the difficulties of navigating Law N° 47/2001 notwithstanding.

Moreover, the outlawing of divisionism since 2001 has also entailed that the Twa are recognised neither as a minority group nor as an indigenous people, and thus they are not accorded the special status within society that such labels entail (Lewis 2000; Thomson 2009; Ndahinda 2011). Where Twa have been the focus of scholarly or global efforts, it is often to call attention to how official narratives in the post-genocide societal landscape have rendered them invisible (e.g. Thomson 2009). For example, in her account of Rwanda's grassroots legal forums, Doughty suggests that access to the benefits of citizenship is determined by one's position to the violence of the 1990s (2016: 59). Her work – and that of others – therefore focuses naturally on the two groups that have been assigned the key roles of victim and perpetrator in official narratives: Tutsi and Hutu. The Twa, however, have not been assigned a formal place in the official accounting of the genocide (Ndahinda 2011), along with other groups, such as Rwanda's Muslim population. The inability to identify Twa as Twa under Rwanda law has, further, made advocacy on behalf of this group to address their marginalisation

[22] Chapter 2 introduces the Twa in more detail, drawing out three important ways in which the Twa are positioned within different discursive structures.

[23] An early and notable exception is Ndahinda (2011), notably chapter 6 for his excellent introduction to Twa in Rwanda, including Twa activism.

[24] Numbers cited differ considerably, so much so that the International Committee on the Elimination of All Forms of Racial Discrimination passed a resolution in 2016 requesting that Rwanda collect data on the Batwa (cited in Ndikubwimana et al. 2024).

difficult and the relationship between advocacy or representative groups and the government has often been fraught (Ndahinda 2011). In a genocide citizenship story, the Twa are indeed invisible, and the government instead uses a catch-all term of 'Historically Marginalised Peoples' to capture the continuing socio-economic marginalisation of this group.

While Twa are relatively neglected in scholarly accounts, they are very much on the agenda of international non-governmental organisations (INGOs) and international organisations, particularly those focused on human rights and indigenous rights. The Twa of Rwanda are widely believed to form part of a larger Batwa population in the Great Lakes region, including Rwanda, Burundi, Uganda, the DRC, and, more broadly still, a population of forest-dwellers located across Equatorial Africa, once known as Pygmies (Ndahinda 2011: 216). Across the range of socio-economic indicators – in education, health, housing, labour, access to land, and property ownership – Batwa continue to lag behind other parts of the population (MINALOC 2011: 13; Ndahinda 2011: 216; COPORWA 2014). In Rwanda, members of this community live a settled life in small communities across the country, mostly on inhospitable and unproductive lands. Those who have taken up farming have no or limited lands to farm, and this limited access to land entails that they live a hand-to-mouth existence, surviving as day-labourers or by eking out a living in their traditional economic activity of clay pot-making (Dawson 2018). Policies of dispossession and displacement from forest land that pre-date the genocide led a 2011 United Nations Expert report on Batwa in Rwanda to conclude that the damage caused to Twa lifestyles, livelihoods, cultures, and traditional practices was irreversible (UN 2011: para. 93).

The refusal by the Rwandan state to recognise a special status for the Twa has met with widespread condemnation and is understood to reinforce their socio-economic marginalisation. This marginalisation was described in a joint 2005 report by the African Commission on Human and Peoples' Rights (ACHPR) and the International Working Group for Indigenous Affairs (IWGIA):

> In Rwanda . . . the Batwa suffer from marginalization, discrimination and extreme poverty, and they are neglected in all areas of development. Prejudice means they are considered undeveloped, intellectually backward, hideous, unsavoury characters of sub-human. The Batwa are allowed to share nothing with the Hutus or Tutsis, neither food nor drink. Even sitting down with a Batwa would be considered an insult or dishonour to the friends and family of any Hutu or Tutsi who agrees to do

> so. If an individual non-Batwa should sympathise with the Batwa and become their friend, his peers will treat him as ridiculous or mentally disturbed.
>
> (ACHPR/IWGIA 2005: 35)

The voices calling for recognition of Rwanda's Twa as indigenous include those of Twa from neighbouring Uganda and the DRC where Twa indigeneity is either recognised or at least not explicitly denied by governing forces, and where indigeneity is an important platform for claims to inclusion, development, and restitution (Ampumuza et al. 2020; Kokunda et al. 2023).

The concept of indigeneity has become a powerful global rallying cry for recognition and equality within states. Indigenous leaders and activists have successfully managed to push their claims at the global level so that respect for indigenous rights has become a fundamental strand of the human rights, rule of law, and good governance agendas.[25] At the same time, as Engle has so well detailed, indigenous development has largely proved to be 'elusive' (2010). The promise of respect for indigenous rights, anchored at the global level, remains a struggle for existence, respect, and inclusion at the national and local levels. Yet, the language of indigeneity has given communities a powerful means with which to articulate their claims, one which Twa leaders within Rwanda have made use of in the past and which Twa communities in neighbouring countries, such as Uganda, continue to claim. While claims to indigeneity are no longer possible within Rwanda, Twa remain subject to the discourse of indigeneity through the claims of external actors.

Although the Twa are not formally visible in Rwanda as a distinct ethnic group or indigenous people, they continue to be visible as Twa at the local level and in unguarded moments of officialdom. Moreover, they are visible to the state and are rendered legible through alternative subjectivities. For example, the Rwandan government has adopted strong pro-poor policies and Twa – because of their lowly economic status – are targeted for assistance, albeit not as Twa but for their socio-economic marginalisation. Twa are visible in this way as development subjects. Similarly, as Chapter 3 details, the Rwandan state's enthusiastic adoption of the principal tenets of the global conservation narrative sees Twa subjectivised – in contrast to their positioning within narratives of

[25] For example, the revised draft (May 2022) of the new convention on the right to development now includes a separate article on respect for the development rights of indigenous peoples (Article 17) (A/HRC/WG.2/23/2).

indigeneity – as potential encroachers on the sanctity of nature-only spaces; that is, as poachers.

Global subjecthood, refracted through state narratives, thus makes Twa legible in different ways: for example, as poor, development subjects rather than as ethnic, political subjects. The space in which the Twa are able to negotiate their existence is, as it is for all of us, delineated by normative ordering or law – whether that law is labelled global, international, national, local, hard, or soft. However, law is, as de Sousa Santos reminds us, not simply 'heavy normativity' but 'also imagination, representation, and description of reality' (1987: 281). As such, law can continue to exist after revocation by existing in the memory of things, practices, and people. In this way, practices of social ordering that place Twa at the bottom of the social hierarchy continue to reverberate despite attempts to write new laws into the social imagination via the stick of criminal law or the practice of civic re-education. For this reason, there is a tendency in accounts of Twa to see them as passive victims of societal discrimination and to focus on the government refusal to recognise the community as indigenous. There are, however, a growing number of ethnographic studies that seek to understand how Twa view government policies and actions from the bottom up and to understand how they navigate their position in society, despite continuing discrimination in daily life (e.g. Adamczyk 2011; Ndahinda 2011; Ntakirutimana and Collins 2017; also, in Uganda, Nyenyezi Bisoka et al. 2020; Kokunda et al. 2023). This book is a contribution to this work, adding another tale to the story of Twa in Rwanda.

There is good reason for trying to do so, beyond the simple idea of the more stories being told, the better we will understand and appreciate a place and its people. It has been suggested that the well-being of Twa is symbolically important in Rwanda and that their treatment by the rest of society is something of a bellwether for the health of Rwandan societal relations more generally. This is because, according to Taylor, the Twa were the first people in Rwanda to suffer ethnic stigmatisation and stereotyping. The adoption of negative ethnic stereotypes played an important role in the development of ethnic dichotomisation, whereby stereotypes coalesced around ideas of 'esteem' at one end and 'disgust' at the other. From here, it was only a small step to categorising people as 'human' versus 'less than human' (Taylor 2011: 205). It was the Twa who first suffered the categorisation of not being quite fully human or, in Taylor's phrasing, as the negative pole of alterity (2004: 354). Thus, while Twa have always been integrated economically, socially, and politically in

Rwandan society, this has often been via their social exclusion (Bahuchet 2012: 16–17; also Vansina 2004). Yet a place at the bottom of the social hierarchy is still a place within society, and an important one. Whether Twa now feel that Rwandan citizenship is fully open to them in their daily lives, and thus whether they feel that they are being treated as equally human, can tell us about how deeply the narratives of reconciliation and unity have penetrated into society. As will be developed throughout this book, our data suggests that the Twa are able to make use of the concept of Rwandanness[26] articulated in national reconciliation and unity policies to negotiate a new place in society; that is, despite their absence from the official genocide narrative, the Rwandan citizenship articulated in the post-genocide era is open to them.[27] Beyond Rwanda, how the Twa view their daily lives and their future possibilities also tells us something about the promise of global development or of the local salience of global indigeneity and the impact of conservation narratives.

1.4 Research in Post-colonial Times

1.4.1 The Data

This book draws upon data collected as part of a Dutch Research Council (NWO)-funded research project investigating Batwa socio-marginalisation in Rwanda, conducted together with the Batwa-representative organisation, the Communauté des Potiers du Rwanda (COPORWA), and the Kigali-based Institute of Research and Dialogue for Peace (IRDP). The data was collected by a team of specially trained researchers across 2014–2018 using semi-structured interviews and focus groups. Members of the Batwa community – selected using purposive sampling on the basis of location, age, gender, and level of education – were interviewed in two waves: twenty-four interviews within a pilot study that allowed us to test and refine the methodology; and an additional sixty-five interviews. Interviews took place in all districts of the country, including the capital. A third wave of interviews, focus groups, and other types of interaction were conducted with strategic actors at the

[26] While this translation is clunky, it best captures the concept of shared national identity that national unity and reconciliation policies promote (NURC 2016: 53).

[27] As Purdeková wisely notes, 'not all [political] space is equally disempowering and all groups equally disempowered' (2015: 97). This is an important reminder that the findings presented here of how Twa are navigating their place in society may not be true for other groups within society, ethnic or otherwise. It seems reasonable to suggest that the tiny size of Twa proportionate to Hutus and Tutsis will give them more political space to navigate.

local and national level, such as sector and district leaders, members of parliament, and other public bodies. The interviews ranged from two to four hours in duration and were audio-recorded; a representative number of interviews were also filmed where the participant gave additional consent to being filmed. The interviews were transcribed and translated by colleagues in the project. The data collection process was also visually documented by a project photographer – some of whose photos are included – and videographer. Data interpretation drew on this visual archive.

We chose in this project not to focus on contemporary socio-economic conditions – by, for example, attempting to detail the general living conditions of community members or their disadvantage in accessing public services. A wealth of (I)NGO, government, and United Nations (UN) reports have done just that and therefore we already know a lot about the external perspective of Twa marginality. Instead, we sought to collect information on how Twa individuals view their own position within society, their relationship to each other and other Rwandans, and how they experience their marginality. We chose to do this by focusing not on the past or even on the present, but on an imagined future. The overarching question, then, was what inclusion looks like for them. By using this lens, we hoped not only to develop a picture of how members of the Batwa community envisaged their own inclusion but – by comparing their vision with their reality – to also understand how they viewed their exclusion. Our interviews were not explicitly focused on identity, and we needed to be very careful about asking individuals such questions. Instead, we asked interviewees to tell us about their lives and, more importantly, to tell us about the good life as they saw it.

The methodological approach of the project drew on the work of Wolff and de-Shalit (2007) that sought to investigate socio-economic exclusion by means of a dynamic public reflective equilibrium methodology that itself draws heavily on the capabilities approach (Sen 1985). The advantage of Wolff and de-Shalit's methodology is that it takes the excluded person – their reflections on their own situation and on what matters to them – as the starting point and brings their thoughts together with a broader group of stakeholders in an iterative process of reflection and learning. We wanted to understand what constitutes the good life for members of Rwanda's Batwa communities, broken down as categories of functionings. As part of the methodological process, we started with Nussbaum's ten categories (2000: 11). Following discussion with our feedback group, this list of ten categories was extended to fourteen. Certain categories were also modified for a better cultural fit.[28]

1.4.2 Data Interpretation, Positionality, and the De-coloniality Imperative

In her account of her doctoral fieldwork in Rwanda 2008, Larissa Begley has described an atmosphere among ordinary Rwandans of debilitating fear and suspicion in everyday life (2013). She is not alone in highlighting the difficulty of conducting community-based empirical research under high levels of government control, or the silence and secrecy that it engenders. Thomson, in her 2011 article and follow-up book, details the resistance of Rwandan peasants to the government's reconciliation policies. In her evocative language, following Scott's notion of hidden transcripts, it was only possible to 'whisper truth' (Scott 1990; Thomson 2011; also Buckley-Zistel 2006). Williamson Sinalo has noted that Rwandans frequently harbour resentment and mistrust of outsiders and that, as such, their data may be affected (2018: 11). Purdeková writes of a public silence that is structural (2015: 98). How then should we make sense of our interview data that sees the majority of our interviewees apparently eschewing indigenous identity as Twa – confidently or indifferently assigning it to the past – and investing instead their hopes for the future in progress as Rwandan development subjects?

One way of doing so is to accept that we did not manage to build sufficient trust and that – simply put – our interviewees repeated back to us the government line on national unity. The government tells them that discrimination and Twa identity is a thing of the past, and hence this is what they told us, whether because of their assessment of the risks of possible repercussions or because they did not find the topic important enough to be bothered to deviate from the government's line. On the latter point, it is necessary to remain cognisant of the risk that our subjects are not as riveted by certain topics as we are as researchers, or that our framing of issues simply does not resonate. Thus, it is of course possible that our interviewees simply told us what was convenient for them – their 'truth' – and one would be foolish to discount this possibility entirely.

[28] Nussbaum's category of 'play', for example, was reframed as 'to enjoy life' in order to avoid interviewees interpreting it as something meant only for children.

However, Williamson Sinalo also noted in her study that it is not always the case that Rwandan interviewees dissemble when faced with interviewers. Indeed, the archival testimonies on which her work is based show that survivors are willing to speak openly about deeply intimate matters and be critical of the government. More recently, in his fieldwork among Kigali-based youth between 2022 and 2024, Beloff found no hesitations among interviewees in speaking openly about identity and ethnicity (2025). Similarly, interviewees in our project were frequently critical of government policies and some of their reflections on identity shocked our (mostly educated and Kigali-based) workshop participants. Our interviewees were also encouraged in the interview to push back against the framework of the questions by reflecting on elements of their lives that they had not been asked about; and a test question, designed by our local interlocutors, was used to establish the extent to which the participants were engaging in the reflective process. If the interviewee did not contest the framing of the test question, the interview was excluded from analysis.

One does not need, however, the difficulties of conducting research among wary subjects to reflect on one's positionality in relation to interpreting data in a culture that is not one's own. Africa, according to Mbembe, is one of the West's key imaginary significations, a way of understanding ourselves through our desire to assert our difference from Africa (Mbembe 2001; see also Wainaina 2022). Similarly, Grayson warns that there is a real danger in 'mislaying' Western notions and constructs on to African post-colonial subjects (2017). Karanja is harsher, noting the complicity of researchers in the perpetuation and continuation of African colonialisation (2018: 154). In the context of Rwanda specifically, Rutazibwa has noted that 'most of us seem incapable of transcending the Hutu/Tutsi, rural/urban, men/women, rich/poor, dictator-autocrat/democrat, pro/contra Rwandan Patriotic Front (RPF) regime categories' (2014: 292).[29] I have tried hard not to reduce the complexity of Twa lives into easy binaries and to understand rather than judge.

Instead, this book is an effort to contextualise Twa voices within the narratives that frame the space in which they live their lives. It is not a single story about the Twa: Twa as silent victims; Twa as indigenous people; Twa as development subjects. Rather, it draws upon different framings or subjectivisations in order to make sense of their stories as

[29] To this list, I would add the dichotomy of resistance/assimilation.

they told them, thereby purposively highlighting the plurality of interpretations. Put differently, I have started from the position that there are multiple versions of 'Batwa-ness' (Ampumuza et al. 2020), even within the same individual, just as there are different versions of Rwandanness.

I have taken a grounded theory approach to data interpretation (Bentzon et al. 1998), allowing the voices of our interviewees to frame the good life for themselves. For example, it was our interview subjects that determined that inclusion within Rwandan society and being valued as equal is core to their vision of a good life. This grounded approach drives the focus on agency, and I have attempted to take seriously decolonial critiques of Western notions of subjecthood and the relationship to agency by using situated notions of agency that draw on post-colonial studies of situated subjectivity (e.g. Werbner 2002; Menzel 2020). I remain aware, however, that a grounded approach does not change the fact that by analysing the data, I am producing knowledge about a community (Ballakrishnen 2024). Taking a self-critical approach also means being honest about the story that I chose to tell; for example, in the choice of the three global discourses explored here. They were not the only possible options, nor are they the only global discourses or institutions that play an important part in Twa lives. A European, secular, and disciplinary bias meant that we did not consider the role that religion might play in our subjects' lives in the design of the project and hence we do not have sufficient data on this question to explore it further.[30] However, our interviewees frequently raised the question of faith, religion, and spiritual belonging, and international Christian networks played and continue to play an important role within Rwanda (Lemarchand 1970; Van Hoyweghen 1996; Kubai 2016; Cantrell 2022).[31]

Moreover, one's responsibility as a researcher does not stop at being aware of the power dynamics inherent in the production of knowledge. I have struggled in the writing of this book with the relationship between scholarship and political responsibility, notably in how the findings presented here may affect political claims, now and in the future. It is therefore important for me to be clear that I understand political identity as collectively imagined and needing to be claimed – rather than an essentialised 'is' – and, thus, as something that can only ever be more or less made good on. Identity is dynamic and constantly changing. That

[30] As lawyers, we unthinkingly overlooked spiritual faith for faith in institutions, such as the rule of law and human rights.

[31] Another relevant global discourse is land reform, what Patrick McAuslan has called the 'global intellectual climate for land law'; see McAuslan (2013) and Manji (2006).

the findings as presented here suggest that Rwandan Twa do not view themselves at present through the lens of indigeneity does not mean that the work of developing just such a collective imagination may not succeed later; nor does it entail that other interpretations, other findings, might not conclude something different. Those that claim indigeneity for Rwanda's Twa are making a political claim and for me to suggest that there may be little resonance within Rwanda's Twa for such a claim during the period that our data was collected does not make those putting it forward dishonest. Hodgson poses the question of whether those engaging in an 'anthropology of the middle' are academics, advocates, or activists (2011: 13). However, while research is necessarily political, and research on questions of indigeneity feels very political, I am not seeking to advance a political claim here, either for or against Twa as indigenous or as Rwandan.[32] I hold myself instead accountable to those who participated in our research to represent their voices as best as I am able and not to any particular established viewpoint, including those held by partner organisations in the research project on which this book is based. Further, I do not view our findings normatively; that is, as either a good thing or a bad thing. This is not for me to judge.

Mudimbe astutely notes, 'the will to truth in Europe seems to espouse perfectly a will to power' (1994: 212). Our idea of Africa is a product of this. Yet the idea of Africa, as the idea of any one African country, is complex, many, and contradictory. The story that I offer here makes no claim to a truth about the Twa, or Rwanda, let alone Africa; it is partial and distorted, as all research encounters necessarily are.

1.4.3 Post-colonial and African

In the scholarly literature, Rwanda is most commonly viewed through a post-conflict lens (inter alia Pottier 2002; Lemarchand 2009; Strauss and Waldorf 2011a). To label Rwanda a post-conflict state is to see it as one of many states dealing with the aftermath of civil conflict, for example Colombia or Bosnia and Herzegovina. Yet, while this captures the extent of institutional and social destruction, it may overlook the special harm of genocide or the particularities of the African context.

[32] On this, see Wendy Brown's observation that 'It is the task of theory ... to "make meanings slide", while the lifeblood of politics is made up of bids for hegemonic representation that by nature seek to arrest this movement, to fix meaning at the point of a particular political truth – the nonfluid and nonnegotiable representation – that one wishes to prevail' (2001: 41; cited in Mahmood 2006: 59).

Alternatively, one can label Rwanda a post-genocidal state, which is, in important ways, to see it as a unique case because genocide is, thankfully, rare. However, to see Rwanda as unique runs the risk of missing the structural influences – including global discourses – that impact the state's ability to shape its future. Such accounts include the colonial perspective only in a narrow way: for example, on the role of the particular colonial power, or the Catholic Church, in solidifying societal differences into racial characterisations; or to analyse whether the colonial history endorsed within the Rwandan government's narrative is 'true' or not.

The approach that I take here is instead to see Rwanda as a post-colonial state that is at once unique (post-genocidal) and similar (the legacies of colonial rule, both specific and structural). The term 'post-colonial' is intended to contextualise both the historical legacies of colonialism (e.g. Mbembe 1992) and Rwanda's exposure to and place in the global economic, social, and political order. As Benton's work on law and colonial cultures elucidates, hegemony is both a social force and a map of the world (2002: 28). A post-colonial approach views colonial dynamics as extending beyond formal independence and instead is attuned to 'colonial encounters' in the present (Anghie 2005; Pahuja 2013; Kothari 2019a), or what Mertens et al. have framed as 'colonial durabilities' (2022).[33] As Hodgson notes, the key terms of political struggle in Africa are colonial in origin: the state, the nation, citizenship as the privileged form of belonging, ethnicity, property, development, and modernity, as well as, as we will see here, notions of mind-set (2011: 9). A post-colonial framing attunes us to the continuities and discontinuities of political forms as process and practice, and allows for a broader understanding of the space and dynamics in which the Rwandan state is rebuilding and shaping the country's future. It is also to lay bare the embeddedness of African states in global power structures; that is, to situate African states as post-colonial is to de-provincialise Africa (Chakrabarty 2000).

Moreover, Mamdani's influential study on the impact of late colonialism details how Africa's cultural history was instrumentalised and ethnic differences were politicised under policies of indirect rule. One of the legacies of indirect rule was thus the creation of hard categories based on

[33] A post-colonial framing is also an important corrective to the construction of development (and, arguably, globalisation more generally) as a forward-looking narrative of progress, which is thereby uninterested in accountability or the rectifying of past injustices.

racialised difference and the subjugation of rural subjects to the power of the local chief. In Mamdani's account, African states have until now taken one of two routes to overcome this legacy: ethnic clientelism – that is, continuing policies of tribal differentiation – and centralised administrative force, thus an attempt to unite a space divided politically and legally from the centre (1996: xiv). At the same time, in thinking about subjectivity in the African post-colony, Mbembe cautions that:

> the postcolony is made up not of one coherent 'public space', nor is it determined by any single organizing principle. It is rather a plurality of 'spheres' and arenas, each having its own separate logic yet nonetheless liable to be entangled with other logics when operating in certain specific contexts: hence the postcolonial 'subject' has had to learn to continuously bargain and improvise. Faced with this … the postcolonial 'subject' mobilizes not just a single 'identity', but several fluid identities which, by their very nature, must be constantly 'revised' in order to achieve maximum instrumentality and efficacy as and when required.
>
> (Mbembe 1992: 4–5)

In this seminal work, Mbembe puts forward the case that post-colonialism in Africa is different to that elsewhere.

To situate the form that the progress imperative takes in Rwanda in a post-colonial context allows us to view the government's choices in more structured and less personal ways; that is, less located in what is often reduced to the authoritarian drive of a single man. Of course, doing so is not to suggest that forms of governmentality were identical under the colonial regimes or that the response of African states to the governance challenges bequeathed to them by colonial rule are pre-determined; however, the post-colonial framing helps us in contextualising the Rwandan government's response to, for example, the global development imperative. That Rwanda should choose an approach that attempts to unite the social and political space is connected to Rwandan political history, which has a long thread of centralised power (Mamdani 2001; McDoom 2020), but is also a logical response to the ethnic violence that followed independence. In this light, development as a normative project in Rwanda is necessarily viewed as post-colonial (see also White 2002).

A post-colonial frame is, further, a helpful corrective to the tendency in Western development writing to see the African state as always already failing (Karanja 2018: 156), where a well-functioning, pro-poor state is either surprising or viewed as a symptom of some malign intent, such as attempting to legitimise its rule. Following Ferguson, it is important to situate this book in the context of development's engagement with Africa as a post-colonial phenomenon (Goldman 2005; Ferguson 2006), which Mbembe has characterised as networks of conservation, commerce, and state existing in the fragmented spaces of the post-colony and in which neo-liberalism is engaged with the remaking not only of nature but also of society and of notions of human well-being (Mbembe 2001). Situating African states as post-colonial challenges lazy assumptions that aspirations to modernity are 'failed copies, faint copies, mere shadows of the original' (Ferguson 2006: 16). My claim in the book is of more than a shadowing or haunting relationship between the West and African states, specifically Rwanda – even as these states participate in the global forums that perpetuate the civilising mission of global law.

1.5 The Argument of the Book

This book argues that Rwandan Twa are choosing the possibility of inclusion and material improvement to their lives, not as part of a political movement that makes demands based on their ethnic distinctness or indigeneity but as Rwandans. That is, they are drawing on the global development discourse and the national narrative of Rwandanness to position themselves as Rwandan development subjects. In the terms of Mahmood (2006), they are choosing to 'inhabit' the norms of global development as refracted through Rwanda's post-colonial legacy and the contemporary drive for unity. The Twa view these intersecting narratives – of development and unity – as together offering them the possibility of material progress and the security of belonging.

This positioning is understood here as an exercise of agency. While counter-hegemonic cosmopolitan studies have rightly highlighted the dangers of de-politicising resistance – of being deaf to alternative voices and the knowledge and legal forms that they draw upon (e.g. Kothari 2001; Rajagopal 2003; de Sousa Santos and Rodríguez-Garavito 2005) – there is a risk that by focusing heavily on resistance, we are primed to find a 'sociology of emergence' (de Sousa Santos 2014) rather than to understand agency as embedded in complex social and institutional structures. Moreover, by applying resistance as an analytical frame to whole populations or categories, we can miss the nuances caused by power differentials within communities (Palmer 2014). Taking counter-hegemony as a frame places conflict at the heart of the analysis and pushes us to find either resistance or oppression rather than other forms of agency that may be, variously, assertive or co-operative (Mahmood 2011). Where Rodríguez-Garavito and Arenas have asserted that 'global social movements are as much about difference as they are about equality' (2005: 242), the Twa are instead negotiating their place in society and a better life through everyday participation in the community, in church, and in government programmes. For example, by refusing to cede discursive authority over how they are named, Twa are asserting their own naming authority quietly but insistently. They have not adopted the government-approved language of historic marginalisation, choosing instead to embrace the language of self-improvement, progress, and Rwandanness. They are thus not passive adopters of government policy.

By accepting the framing of Twa interactions and positionings as resistance, or as the 'weapons of the weak' (Scott 1985, 1990), we can overlook gentle navigation over time and political claims that are rooted not in difference but in (aspirations to) commonality. A focus on resistance as an analytical frame can blind us to the enaction of agency that we do not understand or perhaps wish to see: where we, for example, are conditioned to view autonomy as a negative freedom from state interference, then we will see a strong state as interfering in the freedom of its citizens and their responses as resistance. But this is not how the Twa in our study view the Rwandan state. Yet, while agency is not an all-or-nothing force – one cannot possess it in the abstract – it is also important not to overstate it. One can have agency in the context of how one identifies oneself and still feel powerless in relation to accessing the basic necessities of life, such as sufficient food (Schlosser 2019; Menzel 2020). If one is to take seriously Blaser's notion of 'globalisation as pluriverse' (2010), my argument here is that we need to attempt to articulate an agency that exists within the regulatory power of global discourses, and not only in resistance to them.

Mbembe criticises studies on Africa for reducing the constitution of the African self to a struggle for representation. This, he claims, reduces engagement with materiality to irrelevance except insofar as it relates to struggles of representation and resistance (2001). As Mbembe writes, what is important is 'what African agents accept as *reasons for acting*, what their claim to *act in the light of reason* implies . . . what makes their action intelligible to themselves' (2001: 7 (emphasis his)). Alongside resistance, I wish to suggest the notion of membership as an additional framing for studies in the post-colonial – a membership that is fluid, yet material (Kalua 2009). This notion draws on the work of James Ferguson. Writing about documented imitation practices within the colonial order, Ferguson suggests that 'imitation was less about sympathetic magic and accommodating white power within indigenous cultural orders than about claims to membership within modern society and negotiations of the rights proper to such membership' (2006: 164). By decomposing modernity, Ferguson suggests that the promise of development has been abandoned, leaving the Third World not just with the notion of 'alternative modernities' that see African cultures as co-eval to the West (to be welcomed), but with a ranking of nations in which modernity is no longer a *telos* (2006: 189–190). Post-colonial (as opposed to post-development) is a way to hold on to the temporalisation of future progress, that living conditions for billions of people can and should improve. Viewed in this way, Twa are not resisting their inclusion in global discourses of modernity, notably development, but are claiming their membership in it through inclusion in Rwandan society.

2

Tales of Rwanda's Twa

Indigenous, (Self-)Marginalised, and Poor

Telling a story is always fraught with choices: what to include, what to leave out, where to lay the emphasis. One can tell the same story in any number of different keys (Cohen 1997).[1] This does not make one version more or less true, or more or less 'factual', than another. Yet, to be believable a story has, of course, to attend to certain realities as perceived by the intended audience. Tales are told in order to make sense of the world around us and thus need to reflect the normative frameworks in operation between the teller and the listener if they are to resonate with the audience (Boyd White 1985). As Trouillot cautions us, there is not a 'true' account of history, which is instead always produced (rather than merely told or recounted) in a specific context (1995: 13).[2] Just as historical accounts cannot make a claim to truth, they equally cannot be understood as neutral: telling a tale is an attempt to exercise control over the present. The ability to have one's version of a story adopted, or acquiesced to, is ultimately a question of power, whether of the power to create a convincing imaginary or to require acquiescence to one's version of events (Anderson 1983; Trouillot 1995; Sentama 2022). Either way, a successful narrative will necessarily suppress other versions of the tale or push them to the margins. Telling a story, therefore, although necessarily drawing on historical happenings, is an act of world creation in the present; that is, the production of knowledge that concerns claims to status, recognition, and material resources in the here and now. As such, stories or narratives can be understood as forms of social ordering, encoding our understanding of relations between societal actors that we then act upon in the present. Being able successfully to assert one's narrative is a continuous act of authority that manifests itself as the authenticity of a tale (Boyd White 1994). In Foucauldian terms, within a discursive market,

[1] Cohen's fascinating book concerns the different ways of telling the history of the Boxer Rebellion using three keys: as event, as experience, and as myth.

[2] Further, 'historical authenticity resides not in the fidelity to an alleged past but in an honesty vis-a-vis the present as it re-presents that past' (1995: 148).

some narratives are authorised and legitimated and others are not (Taylor 1986). The authority with which a tale is told and received is derived in part from the position of the teller but also by the resonance of the norms and symbols with the audience.

Narratives, and the labels or positionings that result from them, in allowing us to make sense of the world in our daily lives, also serve the function of making communities legible at a distance. They can transform the scale of subjectivity from a member of a village to a global subject. The subjectivities that are constructed influence not only the space for identity but also access to material resources: for example, whether the tale told is one of indigeneity or of a poor development subject determines the amount and type of resources available: ontologically, politically, and materially. This does not mean that one cannot attempt to create a new narrative about oneself, but it is harder, slow, and must necessarily resonate with an audience in order to gain credence. It cannot come out of nowhere (Anderson 1983; De Fina 2006).[3]

My aim here is not to tell a history of Rwanda's Twa, or to delve in great detail into the historical accounts that chart the socio-political development of Rwanda from the earliest records to the devastation of the genocide.[4] Instead, I will draw out three key stories that are told of the Twa.[5] These tales, or narrative productions, involve multiple actors over both space and time that interact to create the (more or less) authenticity of a tale. Knowledge about the Twa is thus being produced by a variety of actors. These include international organisations, such as the World Bank; international human rights actors, such as the United Nations (UN) Special Rapporteur on Minority Issues; INGOs, such as the Unrepresented Nations and Peoples Organization (UNPO) and Minority Rights Group (MRG); academics; and the Rwandan state, including local authorities. The post-colonial context in which these different actors are telling stories about the Twa entails that it is important to pay particular attention to the dynamics of knowledge production (Mamdani 1996; Mbembe 2001; de Sousa Santos 2014; Rutazibwa 2014). This chapter will attempt to draw attention to these dynamics as they

3 Anderson (1983) has shown convincingly how acts of imagination or of storytelling have societal force by affecting behaviour in the present. This, he insists, does not entail that individuals or communities cannot resist or attempt to reshape those narratives.

4 See, here, C. Newbury (1978); Vansina (1990, 2004); Chrétien (2003); D. Newbury (2009). I do, however, draw on these works of historical scholarship to highlight the articulation of the different narratives.

5 A tale of how some Twa think about themselves will be told in the remaining chapters.

manifest in the different tales told. Framing my tale as forms of jurisdictional encounter is, in part, an attempt to do just this: the tales constructed here are neither global nor national, but the form they take in this context is the product of the encounter between global discourses and the post-colonial Rwandan state. Understanding how these different tales are constructed and are made authoritative, and by whom, is important if we are to make sense of the space in which Twa in Rwanda negotiate their lives. Moreover, to understand the tales told of the Twa, we need to pay attention to how they account for their marginalised position within Rwandan society: their poverty and the continuing prejudices that exist against them. We also need to consider how these tales use or eschew history, what claims to authority they make, and the resources that they draw upon in their attempt to make good on those claims – for example, the assertion of national identity and culture as providing 'home-grown solutions' as opposed to 'foreign' intervention that brings division. The purpose of this chapter is thus to set the stage for a more detailed investigation of the space created by jurisdictional encounters in the chapters that follow.

2.1 The First Tale: Separate, Distinct, and Suffering

The most common tale told of the Twa – the dominant narrative outside Rwanda for activists, scholars, and international organisations – depicts a community or people distinct from the rest of the population.[6] That distinction is composed of multiple threads. These threads are woven from essentialist arguments, historical-factual assertions, narratives of dispossession, displacement, and discrimination, calls for equality, and demands for recognition. This tale of the Twa follows a globalised narrative of indigenous peoples' claims,[7] drawing heavily on historical arguments to assert an identity that is part ethnic, part cultural, and part

[6] The purpose of analysing the narrative that provides the title of this section is not to ridicule it or to suggest that it has no basis in historical sources. It is instead intended to highlight the constructed nature, over time and by many hands, of a particular way of seeing the Twa. For example, it is intended to highlight how meaning in the present is given to the likelihood that forest-dwellers were already present on the territory when communities of Bantu-speakers expanded into the area thousands of years ago.

[7] For a nuanced analysis of the global indigenous movement that suggests the right to culture, in its different guises, has displaced other approaches, such as those focused on dependency, discrimination, and lack of autonomy, see Engle (2010). There is, further, a vast and excellent literature on global indigeneity: see also Povinelli (2002); Blaser (2010); Hodgson (2011); Birrell (2016).

biological/physical.[8] As Ndahinda has persuasively argued, 'the claims [to indigenous identity for the Twa] are intrinsically linked to the rise of the global indigenous movement during the last three decades of the twentieth century' (2011: 56).[9] This is a tale that was clearly adopted by Rwandan Twa representatives in the immediate post-genocidal environment with the formation of Communauté des Autochtones Rwandais, or the Rwandese Community of Indigenous Peoples, known as CAURWA, in 1994 (Lewis and Knight 1995: 101; Ndahinda 2011). The organisation's name was changed in 2002, as a result of government pressure, to the Community of Rwandese Potters (COPORWA) (Ndahinda 2011: 239), and the claim to indigeneity has been quietly sidelined.[10]

The story of Twa as a separate (indigenous) people can be characterised as a tale of two halves: the first is a history of apartness. The second focuses on the more recent past and present, centring on dispossession, displacement, and discrimination. The best-known modern account of Rwanda's Twa, the 1995 report for MRG by Lewis and Knight, encapsulates the two poles of this indigenous narrative: difference based on historical fact and physical divergence, and on suffering. They write:

> The situation of the Rwandese Twa, as a 'Pygmy' people of Central Africa, is in many respects atypical. Most of them have long ago been forced off their lands and have abandoned life in the forests that were once their home. Yet, in other ways, their situation is similar to many other forest-based groups, especially in terms of the discrimination and prejudice which they face.
>
> (1995: 19)

This second part of the tale references the type and degree of suffering as grounds for a distinct identity, building to an existential crescendo in which failure to recognise Twa as indigenous will lead to their disappearance.

2.1.1 A People Apart

The tale of Twa as distinct typically begins with the claim of original presence on the land that is now Rwanda (e.g. UNPO 1994: 8). The

8 This chapter is not an attempt to interrogate the notion of indigeneity but focuses instead on how it is used or articulated, and on how it is substituted. For an excellent discussion on the concept of indigeneity, see Birrell (2016: chapter 6).

9 Ndahinda has suggested that there are two ways in which indigeneity is asserted in the African context: the first is as marking a difference in the types or sources of marginality and the second is as a claim for special protection. In Rwanda, both assertions are visible (2011).

10 This process is described in more detail in Chapter 5, Section 5.2.2.

earliest archaeological records, going back before the beginning of the Iron Age, suggest that there were human groups occupying the equatorial forests that covered much of the land. This account asserts that these first inhabitants of the Great Lakes region were subsequently invaded and conquered – first by agriculturalist Bantus, later by cattle herders, and finally by Europeans (Fordham 1968; Lewis 2000). In relation to these agriculturalists, the forest-dwellers became identified as Batwa and, with the arrival of the Europeans, as Pygmies (Bahuchet 2012: 11). The tale of Twa as original inhabitants receives support from the fact that they were frequently referred to, prior to the genocide, as *Abasangwabutaka*, the literal meaning of which is '(people/those) found on the earth or on the land' (Ndahinda 2011: 224), and by the role accorded to Twa in legitimising rituals in the enthronement of Rwanda's leaders (Lewis 2000).[11] The claim to firstcomer status is thus an important part of establishing a separate identity for Twa that requires recognition. As Lewis notes, 'as original inhabitants of the land the Twa deserve respect' (2000: 3).

This tale of first occupation also identifies a distinct way of life. In contrast to the agriculturalists and to the pastoralists, Batwa were forest-dwellers with a hunter-gatherer lifestyle:[12] 'the Twa of Rwanda are part of a larger grouping of Twa Pygmies. They were historically specialist hunter-gatherers adapted to the mountain forests of the region. They are the indigenous people of the Great Lakes Region' (Lewis 2000: 2). The claim of a distinct way of life or place in society receives support from the traditional oral culture of the region. Chrétien notes the existence of a belief in groups defined by socio-economic vocation: where the Batutsi are associated with the cow and the Bahutu with the hoe, the Batwa are associated with hunting and pottery (2003: 77).[13] A forest-dwelling, hunter-gatherer lifestyle also tended to entail physical apartness from agriculturalists and pastoralists, who lived interspersed across Rwanda's hillsides – a physical separation that grew as the expansion of agriculture pushed Twa deeper into the remaining forests (Taylor 2004: 361). The narrative of Twa as forest-dwellers and as hunter-gatherers also portrays

[11] Lewis writes, 'The Batwa ritually "licensed" later arrivals to use the land' (2000: 7).

[12] The term *-twa* in Bantu languages refers to hunter-gatherers, according to Lewis (2000: 5). Bahuchet (2012: 14) suggests, however, based on linguistic evidence, that Pygmy lifestyle more generally was 'highly variable'.

[13] Various versions of stories exist in which children are tested by a mythical king and, depending on their success, secrets are revealed and functions allocated to them. See also Vansina (2004). Note, however, Vansina's warning about reading old tales as history (2000).

Twa as living in harmony with nature, and of possessing unique and 'original' knowledge of the forest eco-system (Lewis 2000: 3). This is contrasted again with the agriculturalists and pastoralists, who are accused of destroying the forests for farmland and for grazing land.

This narrative also occasionally draws upon physical distinctiveness to mark a boundary with the majority. The Twa are widely noted as belonging to a larger regional grouping of Pygmy people in Equatorial Africa, and the reader is most commonly left to draw their own conclusions about the extent to which membership of this group has led to physical distinctiveness from the majority populations.[14] The *Encyclopaedia Britannica*, however, is explicit, and tells us that the Batwa are 'one of the best-known of the many Pygmy groups scattered across equatorial Africa' and that they average about 5 feet (1.5 metres) in height.[15] This inscribing of race into physical characteristics is of course a common phenomenon. As Weismantel explains, 'the construction site [of race] is the zone of interaction between our skin, flesh, bones, and the world around us' (2001: 188). Where differences in skin colour cannot function as an index of racial difference, other physical characteristics are imbued with an immutable character and an explanatory power. Canessa has explored a similar phenomenon in the Bolivian Andes, where race is inscribed as 'short stature (due to malnutrition), tanned skin, and poor teeth, and the muscles that carry, feet that tread, and backs that bear loads' (2012: 24). There is, however, a reluctance to note any physical distinctiveness of the Twa in institutional or scholarly accounts, likely as a result of colonial narratives of physical inferiority and race.[16]

In addition to a separate way of life based on a connection to nature and a separate physiology, this first narrative also claims a culture distinct from the majority (UNPO 1994; Lewis and Knight 1995). The Twa were Rwandan society's entertainers, performing dances, songs, and acrobatics at rituals and celebrations. In addition to hunting and to income from performing, Twa engaged in pottery. As with forest-dwelling, earth or clay is used to index ethnic difference. These elements are emphasised and claimed as creating a unique culture with distinctive values, despite the

[14] As Ndahinda notes, the tendency to equate Twa with Pygmies and to fuse this 'seemingly anthropologically exotic' identity with a surviving group of historic hunter-gatherers is by no means an unchallenged historical fact (2011: 228). See also Vansina (2004), who notes the degrees of inter-marriage between all groups of Rwandan society. Also, Hurlbut (1894) took pains to distinguish the Batwa of Rwanda from 'the equatorial dwarf tribes of the same name' (cited in Ndahinda 2011: 221).

[15] www.britannica.com/topic/Twa.

[16] For example, the UNPO report notes that there are no distinct physical characteristics (1994: 9).

language, religion, and practices that Twa shared, and continue to share, with their neighbours. The nature of the Twa traditional lifestyle has also led to claims of cultural features that are not shared with the majority: Twa culture has been lauded as 'demand-sharing' and therefore enjoying a high degree of social equality. Likewise, gender relations in traditional Batwa culture are said to be 'among the most egalitarian known' (Lewis 2000: 8).

This tale of apartness has a darker side, however. By the nineteenth century, the Twa had been set apart from the rest of society by specific forms of social exclusion, known as *kuneena batwa*. This code comprised a set of cultural practices that included all forms of social interaction, such as relationships, work, production, consumption, and the body. For example, Twa were not allowed to till the soil or to marry outside their group. They consumed foods considered unclean by other groups, such as mutton, and, as a consequence, they were not allowed to share utensils with or drink from the same pot as non-Twa. Although Taylor suggests that the Twa were also feared for their military skills, which they demonstrated in raids on settlements before disappearing back into the forest (2011: 196), *kuneena batwa* undeniably characterised Twa negatively: as wild, disgusting, and impure, and their contact as polluting. According to Taylor, 'Twa bodies were considered to be permanent repositories of impurity in early Rwanda' (2004: 366). Avoidance and scorn, according to Vansina, characterised relations between Twa and all others, although he notes that the hostility was perhaps mutual (2004: 36).[17] Moreover, there is a suggestion that the *Impunyu* among the Twa – the deep forest-dwellers – were scorned even by other Twa, thus constituting the lowest of the low (UNPO 1994: 9).

The embeddedness of Twa exclusion can be seen in the oral culture of the region. These old stories work to explain the social order but also to legitimise it. In Rwanda, hierarchy has traditionally been based on moral value, as denoted by economic practices, with Batwa at the bottom of the scale. One of the versions of the mythical challenge alluded to earlier involves having to kill a brother; in this tale, only the Mutwa accepts, demonstrating his depraved nature, and thus as deserving of sanction and exclusion (Chrétien 2003: 78; Vansina 2004). This social disgust has also manifested itself as sexual violence. Canessa, building on Wade's work, has noted the close connection between fear and sexual desire,

[17] Bahuchet, too, notes that Pygmies have been given a semi-supernatural symbolic status that gave 'rise to a form of respect and fear that often goes together with admiration and despisement [*sic*]' (2012: 17).

suggesting that power and sex are 'merely refractions' of the conjoining of desire and fear (Wade 2009; Canessa 2012: 30). In the case of the Twa, stories of non-Twa men seducing Twa under-age girls and then abandoning them and any offspring are sufficiently widespread to be a recognised social phenomenon. The refusal to care for the children produced by these rapes is based on disgust at fathering a Twa child. It is a practice that our field research suggests continues, although it appears to be much less common than it once was.[18] The rigid patterns of hierarchy and exclusion that produced such practices are thus understood to long predate the arrival of the European colonial powers; as such, hostility towards the Twa is 'home-grown' (Vansina 2004: 36; Taylor 2011: 196).[19]

These efforts to assert a narrative of distinct identity and separateness must necessarily confront the fact that Twa speak the same language as the majority and participate in a shared culture. While Twa may have had specific, and sometimes undesirable, roles to play in Rwandan culture, these roles nonetheless denote participation in shared webs of meaning. Thus, while strong proponents of the first narrative of apartness stress the distinctness of the Twa, they also characterise them as a 'fundamental constituent of Rwandan society and culture' (Lewis 2000: 3). Twa figure prominently in the mythical narratives and rituals of early Rwandan clan and kingship dynamics. Separately, their talent as performers – musicians, singers, dancers, acrobats, and clowns – is widely recognised and integrated into Rwandan culture and societal relationships. Twa were an accepted part of society: they had a role, both economically and socially, albeit the role was often one of extremes.

It is also worth noting – as highlighted in Chapter 1 – that pre-colonial Rwandan society was highly complex and what are viewed today as ethnic groups did not form the only, or perhaps even the main, lines of distinction or identification. Rather, traditional clan structures transcended ethnic groupings. According to Ndahinda, 'in a society traditionally divided

[18] In the early part of the project, when we were meeting with many groups and individuals to get a sense of what they viewed as the main barriers to Twa social inclusion, this issue of non-Twa men impregnating Twa schoolgirls was broadly flagged as a key issue (see also Zephyrin 2003: 54). However, we were told of only a handful of cases of pregnant schoolgirls during fieldwork and in half of those, the man's family was supporting the resulting child. We were also told many stories of inter-marriage between Twa and non-Twa communities.

[19] This is not to say that it was not reinforced and/or exacerbated by European racial theories, which placed Pygmies at the bottom of the racial hierarchy. See, further, Ndahinda (2011).

into families (*inzu*), lineages (*imiryango*) and clans (*amoko*), the latter category brought together Hutus, Tutsis and Twas in single clans, despite the fact that, like families and lineages, clans were said to be initially descent-based' (2011: 226; also C. Newbury 1978; D. Newbury 1980; Vansina 2004).[20] Belonging in clan-based networks of obligation and protection co-existed and interacted with other forms of belonging to create multifaceted forms of social hierarchy. Within these clan structures, there is evidence of ethnic identification being fluid; that is, individuals and families being able to move up from Twa to Tutsi.[21] Notably, however, the Twa were – with a few exceptions – generally at the bottom of this hierarchy (Taylor 2004: 362).[22] It is this – the pre-colonial practices of exclusion and claims to first-inhabitant status – that narratives of long-standing Twa distinctness emphasise.

2.1.2 Displacement, Dispossession, Discrimination

The second half of this narrative of distinctness turns from a history of exclusion to the more recent past and to the present. It is a tale of suffering – of dispossession, displacement, and discrimination – across the twentieth and twenty-first centuries that sees Twa buffeted by economic and political-social developments. In part, this half of the tale is an explanation of an unrealised distinctiveness, or of why the Twa are no longer living a forest-dweller's way of life.

In this part of the tale, in a pattern familiar from settler societies, Twa have suffered the dispossession of their forest land over the centuries as the land was cleared and claimed, first for metal production, and then more broadly for agricultural purposes (Vansina 2004). In the twentieth century, deforestation continued apace as the population grew and industrialisation developed. Following dispossession, the Twa have also been displaced from the forests that remain, with the creation of conservation areas and national parks. Under the rules of global conservationism, the creation of parks entailed the emptying of the forests of

[20] Footnotes omitted. Ndahinda is drawing on the work of the Rwandan writer and scholar Alexis Kagame.

[21] This is not surprising as sociologists have documented ethnic fluidity in other contexts; e.g., how Irish immigrants became white in the United States. See Ignatiev (2009).

[22] Taylor (2004) argues that the practices of *kuneena batwa* entailed that while membership of other categories was fluid and one's status could change, there was in practice little possibility of Twa changing their categorisation. He notes, however, the existence of stories of whole Twa families being raised to Tutsi status by the king.

remaining dwellers and Twa were displaced to the edge of the new parks or to elsewhere within the country (UNPO 1994; ACHPR/IWGIA 2005; Ndahinda 2011).[23] These processes of dispossession and displacement have left the Twa unable to provide for themselves. Without access to land for agriculture, Twa were left reliant on pottery, day-labouring, and begging in order to survive (Lewis 2000). The increasing economic unviability of pottery, the increasing inaccessibility of clay as a result of land reforms, and the loss of the social structures that supported Twa's traditional role as entertainers left begging as the main option for survival. The socio-economic practice of begging fed into the traditional stories about the Twa as disgusting and immoral, reinforcing their social exclusion – as did the physicality of their poverty, such as being dirty. Moreover, the loss of pottery as a viable means of income has not only meant further economic vulnerability but has also affected the sense of community: pot production is a social process, involving all members of the community. The decline of this economic practice has therefore also impacted on community cohesion (Lewis 2000: 10).

In addition to losing access to the forests and thus to a traditional way of life, the Twa continue to suffer from social exclusion. According to this tale, Twa suffer from widespread discrimination, both from officials and from neighbours. Lewis writes, 'in all places they are discriminated against' (2000: 6). Indeed, Lewis claims that discrimination is the biggest issue Twa face in Rwanda, as they continue to endure negative stereotyping as backward, childish, and immoral (2000: 13). Similarly, growing recognition of the importance of environmental conservation has also seen the Twa denigrated both nationally and internationally as poachers and encroachers on the conservation zones of the national parks (Lewis 2000: 9).

At the same time, Twa are frequently described as 'ignored' (Lewis 2000) or 'forgotten' (Willis 2005) or 'invisible' (Thomson 2009).[24] This loss of lifestyle and of relegation to the margins of society have led, according to Lewis, to a 'crisis of identity' (2000: 4). Such is the position of Twa today that they have been described as 'one of the most marginalized groups *anywhere* – threatened by modernization in their traditional world, by conservation in the forests they have helped preserve, and by discrimination in societies in which they do not count' (Willis 2005: 130;

23 This is drawn out in more detail in the next chapter.

24 The discourse of invisibility is common to reporting on indigenous peoples: see the 2015 UNPO report, 'Indigenous Peoples – Invisible Peoples': unpo.org/article/18575.

emphasis his). This experience is then said to be 'typical of many marginalized indigenous groups in Africa' (Willis 2005: 133). This second part of the narrative thus highlights suffering as the basis of a distinct identity.

This story of suffering and of invisibility also draws upon the position of Twa during the 1994 genocide. It is not known how many Twa killed or were killed during the genocide, but figures are cited to suggest that around a third of the entire Twa population was lost during that time (Ndahinda 2011: 234). However, in the aftermath, in which Tutsis are commemorated as victims and Hutus are labelled as perpetrators, many commentators suggest that the Twa's role of suffering during the genocide is not explicitly acknowledged in official narratives (Willis 2005: 136–138; Thomson 2009). Indeed, as further explored in Chapter 5, the Twa are not included in the binary form of genocide accounting that Doughty has labelled 'genocide citizenship' (2016).

While the first part of the tale asserts a factual claim to indigeneity, the second part of the tale – by framing Twa as both suffering and ignored – sets up the political demand for recognition. This claim to recognition as Twa entails recognition as an indigenous people (Thomson 2009; UN 2011). To be Twa, then, is to be indigenous. This conclusion is substantiated by repeated references to the numerical minority of Twa in Rwanda and to a declining population. UNPO has asserted, for example, in a 2016 submission to the UN Expert Mechanism on the Rights of Indigenous Peoples, that Rwanda's Twa population declined by 40 per cent between 1978 and 1991, where – during the same period – the Rwandan population grew by 50 per cent (UNPO 2016: 2).

This narrative of a people apart and forgotten builds up to the fear that Rwandan Twa are disappearing as a consequence of loss of culture and of (forced) assimilation; indeed, it is viewed as a 'legal erasure' (UNPO 1994), an argument that flows not only from the 'refusal' to acknowledge Twa as indigenous and thus possessed of indigenous rights but also as a consequence of the legal framework enacting Rwanda's unity and reconciliation policies – notably Law N° 47/2001 criminalising divisionism. This fear of disappearance has also been explicitly named by a former director of CAURWA and Senator Zephyrin Kalimba in the Rwandan parliament. Willis quotes Kalimba as stating that 'the contribution of the Twa in the development of our country remains negligible and consequently our community is heading towards extinction' (2005: 127). Willis continues on the same theme, attributing the disappearance of the Twa to the displacement from the forests and quoting a biologist as stating that 'the real story of genocide in Rwanda is what has happened to the Batwans [*sic*]' (2005: 135). Similarly, although less dramatically, Ndahinda notes that in the increasing polarisation between Hutus and Tutsis across the twentieth century, Batwa became not only the 'perpetual victims' of this conflict but also suffered 'political and social annihilation' as all aspects of social, political, and economic life gradually came to be viewed through the polarity of Hutu–Tutsi relations (2011: 234). The narrative of apartness, rooted in the far distant past, thus culminates in the present in an existential threat that only recognition of the Twa as an indigenous people can remedy.

2.2 The Second Tale: A Historically Marginalised People

In this tale, Twa are made legible not as indigenous or as Twa but as members of a marginalised community. This second contemporary narrative sees the Twa community renamed and repositioned by the state as not-yet national development subjects. It does so by reframing the global development narrative, notably poverty reduction and inclusive development (considered in more detail in Section 2.3 as the third tale), through the lens of 'home-grown' solutions. This sees Twa categorised within government policy as 'historically marginalised' in comparison to other groups within society, stressing limited access to education and 'low social status'.

The state's location of national unity as the highest priority, legally enshrined in the 2003 constitutional reforms, does not allow for the recognition of Twa as an indigenous people. Moreover, Article 54 of the Constitution prohibits political organisations that are based on 'race, ethnic group, tribe, clan, region, sex, religion or any other division which may give rise to discrimination' (2003 Constitution, amended 2015). However, if the state's narrative of 'only Rwandans' is to have traction, it needs to account for the continuing marginalised position of Twa within society that the first narrative draws so heavily upon. It does so by confining this marginalisation to history – the Twa are a *historically* marginalised people – and it is therefore the consequences of these past acts that continue to reverberate today. This tale of historical marginalisation not only explains continuing differences as negative but also further works to neutralise the claim of indigenous status by attributing the introduction of ethnic differentiation among the Rwandan population to colonialism, in contrast to the authentic Rwandan culture of pre-colonial social harmony.

The HMP (Historically Marginalised People) label emerged during the 2003 constitutional reforms: Article 80(2) of the 2003 Constitution stipulates that the president will appoint eight senators to represent the 'historically marginalised', including those of 'special national interest', although only where 'particular consideration [is given] to the principles of national unity' (2003 Constitution, amended 2015; Ndahinda 2011). It is thus not a category unique to Twa but is one they share with women and people with disabilities and 'all Rwandans left behind by history' (Collins et al. 2021: 583). According to Ndahinda, the question of whether Twa were intended to be included as 'historically marginalised' is settled by an unpublished 2007 report of the Rwandan Senate (2011: 246).[25] The language of historic marginalisation highlights not only that the Twa are the 'poorest of the poor' but also that 'Twas have, more than others . . . suffered from patterns of exclusion and individual as well as community disempowerment' (Ndahinda 2011: 240).

However, while it is assumed that Twa are part of the HMP category – indeed, our experience was that the term was widely, if not exclusively, used to refer to the Twa[26] – Twa are not named in the Constitution.[27] Instead, Article 51 recognises the special welfare needs of those with disabilities, and included in the last paragraph of this article is reference to 'other vulnerable groups'. This paragraph provides: 'The State has also the duty, within the limits of its means, to undertake special actions aimed at the welfare of the indigent, the elderly and other vulnerable groups.' The Twa are thus included in the Constitution for their vulnerability rather than any distinct identity. This is despite a Working Group of the Conference on Constitutional Development in Rwanda, held in 2001, outlining a need for minorities to receive special protection within the new Constitution (Wing and Johnson 2002: 307). This subsumption

[25] Senate of the Republic of Rwanda/Committee on Social Affairs and Human Rights, 'Report on Some Historically Marginalized Rwandans', July 2007 (unpublished).

[26] For example, our research permit, issued in 2014 by the then-Minister of State in Charge of Community Development and Social Affairs, gives 'authorization to conduct a research on the inclusion of HMPs in development in Rwanda'; and it was clear in the project description that was part of our permit application that our research focused on Batwa. Similarly, in 2018 the Rwanda Senate created an ad hoc committee to investigate the continuing challenges facing historically marginalised peoples that focused solely on the Batwa: www.parliament.gov.rw.

[27] It is also not clear to what extent, if any, Twa individuals played a role in the Constitution-making process begun in the Urugwiro Process.

into a general category of vulnerability is continued in the most recent document laying out Rwanda's development plan: Vision 2050. While women, youth, and persons with disabilities are listed as distinct stakeholders, Twa do not feature as a separate group, even as HMPs. Instead, they are included in the 'all Rwandans' category that the vision defines as 'actors of sustainable development' (MINECOFIN 2015: 7). This tale is thus a rather ambiguous one, which is perhaps accounted for by the fact that it is a negative tale that state development and unity policies aim to overcome.

As the name suggests, portraying Twa as historically marginalised is based on an interpretation of history, but not one that privileges the Twa as first inhabitants. According to Doughty, the government's 'master narrative of history' is designed to counter and replace the Hutu-power narrative that saw Tutsi as foreign invaders that had exploited and oppressed Hutus for generations (2016: 53; Eltringham 2004). This Hutu-power historical narrative, which portrayed Hutus as indigenous Rwandans in contrast to foreign Tutsis, played an important role in rallying the masses to genocidal violence (Sanders 1969: 521; Newbury 1998; Mamdani 2001; McDoom 2020). In its place, the official post-genocide history lays the blame for the creation of distinct ethnic groups – whose relations were marked by hostility, oppression, and violence – on the shoulders of outsiders. President Kagame, in his commemoration speech to mark the tenth anniversary of the genocide, stated that 'the genocide in Rwanda stems from the colonial period when the colonialists and those who called themselves evangelists sowed the seeds of hate and division' (cited in Doughty 2016: 59). Blaming the colonial powers and foreigners more generally for the post-colonial discord and violence allows the Rwandan state to do a number of things: firstly, it absolves Rwanda's past leaders and elites of their part in creating and perpetuating an exploitative and unstable system of rural governance (C. Newbury 1978). Secondly, and most obviously, it denotes the division of Rwandans into ethnic groups as a foreign invention and not in any way a 'natural' part of Rwandan culture.[28] Thirdly, it allows the state to assert control and ensure its own legitimacy (Pottier 2002; Lemarchend 2009; Reyntjens 2011; Doughty 2016).[29]

[28] This tactic falls into the pattern of what Gilbert has labelled the 'colonial approach' under which all Africans are labelled indigenous or native (2017: 661).

[29] It should come as no surprise that Rwanda's history is contested or that the post-genocide state has made use of history in its national rebuilding efforts. The use of history also needs to be understood within a post-colonial framing; see Mamdani (1996). Moreover,

In this tale of the Twa as HMPs, pre-colonial Rwandan society was marked by social harmony until the arrival of the Europeans. This story of pre-colonial harmony is explicitly a national one; that is, where outside influence has been malign, the solution is to come from within. The mandate to find solutions from within is so central to the Rwandan post-colonial state that it is laid down in the Rwandan Constitution, notably Article 11.[30] This technique of portraying the outside as a source of division and instability has determined how Twa can be framed within the national context. By laying Twa marginalisation at the door of colonialism, the causal connection drawn by the indigenous rights discourse between marginalisation and the denial of recognition can be rebuffed (Ndikubwimana et al. 2024). Moreover, the notion of historical marginalisation enables the government to portray indigenous rights as an external narrative that is used to sow division between Rwandans when unity is essential for the stability of the country.[31] Twa are thus denied indigenous status, with all that this entails for any political representation or cultural claims they may seek as a distinct group or ethnic community.[32] This denial is reinforced by the criminal legal framework, which criminalises both individuals and organisations that promote 'divisionism' or that discriminate on the basis of ethnicity (Reyntjens 2024: 184). This interpretation of history that sees ethnicity as produced by outsiders, which in turn was directly responsible for the violent breakdown of society, determines that the solution will be a Rwanda without ethnicities and cannot be one that tolerates the privileging of a distinct and separate ethnic identity in its midst.[33]

that the government is wary of endorsing or encouraging claims based on ideas of indigeneity, or 'firstcomer' status, needs to be seen against the background of the 'Hamitic Hypothesis' and the violence it inspired. Others, however, have suggested more cynical reasons for the government's refusal to accept Twa as an indigenous people, notably that such acceptance might lead to land claims to 'lucrative national parks' (Collins et al. 2021: 584).

30 Article 11 reads: 'In order to build the nation, promote national culture and restore dignity, Rwandans, based on their values, initiate home-grown mechanisms to deal with matters that concern them.'

31 The portrayal of indigeneity as a foreign import is a tactic used by African states more widely; see Ndahinda (2011).

32 For a history of Rwandan Twa's claims to recognition as indigenous, see Ndahinda (2011) and Chapter 5, Section 5.2.2 of this book.

33 At the same time, as Doughty and others have noted, the unity narrative underpinning this characterisation of Twa nonetheless promotes belonging along ethnic lines by reserving victim status for Tutsis and labelling Hutus as perpetrators who must atone for their crimes, regardless of whether they were implicated in the violence or not

This tale of foreign intervention and home-grown solutions – that sees ethnic groups, at worst, as a foreign barrier to national unity and reconciliation and, at best, as an historical anachronism – works to de-ethnicise and renationalise the Twa. In addition to not being viewed as part of a global community of indigenous peoples, the Twa, in being categorised as Historically Marginalised, are disconnected in this tale from the regional grouping of Twa in Burundi, Uganda, and the Democratic Republic of the Congo.[34] Instead, this tale positions Twa as historically marginalised Rwandan subjects. The past of Batwa exclusion is not denied, but it is assigned to the (colonial) past. Such historic marginalisation – the when, what, and how of this historic marginalisation – is not, however, explained in detail anywhere. It also does not lead to special protection, such as additional rights or access to allocated resources, or to group-based targeted efforts to address past wrongs. Moreover, the political representation of Twa as part of the HMP category of senators specially appointed by the president is, it seems, no longer being granted since Senator Zephyrin Kalimba stepped down in 2020.

In addition to referencing historical marginalisation, the HMP category also denotes a 'mind-set' problem in the present. We were frequently told by local leaders that the main issue in overcoming historical marginalisation for Twa was one of 'mind-set', which suggests a 'self-marginalisation' in addition to a historical one. This explanation is also used at the very top: at a 2019 hearing of the Senate to question the government on why the problems of HMPs had not yet been solved, the Minister of Local Government, Professor Shyaka Anastase, reported that while the government has invested a lot of energy in assisting HMPs, 'the reasons why different programs have been unable to change the lives of people in this category are related to the mindset'.[35] Mind-set problems relate to one of the key organising principles of Rwanda's rebuilding efforts: *agaciro* – translated as dignity or self-reliance.[36]

HMP is best understood, therefore, as an explanatory category – historical and psychological – for the physical fact of continuing

(Reyntjens 2011; Vandeginste 2014b; Doughty 2016). This is considered in more detail in Chapter 5.

34 Doughty has suggested that the government's historical narrative works more broadly to deny the regional connections that underpin group dynamics in Rwanda, with family networks across Burundi, Uganda, and the broader Great Lakes region (2016: 63).

35 Rwandan Parliament Press Release, 'The Senate dissatisfied with oral explanations of the Minister of Local Government on the problems of the category of Historically Marginalized Rwandans', 14 February 2019.

36 The relationship between mind-set and *agaciro* is explored in Chapter 4.

socio-economic difference from the rest of the population. In this way, while Twa may have been historically marginalised, it does not follow that indigenous status is necessary or appropriate to address their needs. Nor does it necessarily imply that Twa are subject to (ethnic) discrimination or stigmatisation by the rest of the population. By framing Twa existence negatively as marginalisation – by a past society and in their own minds in the present – this tale sees their presence in society as a challenge to be overcome rather than an identity to be preserved. Yet, while viewed negatively in this tale, Twa are still seen. In being 'nationalised' as a special type of Rwandan citizen based on their marginalisation or vulnerability, they disappear as a distinct identity at the same time that they are legible as HMPs to state actors, local actors, fellow Rwandans, and international actors. This form of subjectivity is, however, only a staging post in the national story of the journey towards their destination: the good Rwandan development subject.

2.3 The Third Tale: The Model Rwandan Development Subject

As with the second tale, the third key framing of Twa is as a national development subject. This positioning continues the process of nationalisation but looks forward to the moment that the historically marginalised will disappear by ceasing to be economically and socially marginalised. Instead, they will have become model Rwandan citizens. This is the future envisioned by Vision 2050 and the Itorero programme, neither of which make any reference to Twa or HMPs, instead casting all Rwandans as development actors (MINECOFIN 2015).

This third narrative can be distinguished from the previous accounts of the place of the Batwa in Rwandan society by its disinterest in the past. Instead, the emphasis here is on the future and on an imagined model citizen. In this tale, Twa are thus 'simply' poor and are the targets of state-led development efforts because they are most often the poorest of the poor. That is, while the third tale told of the Twa has a similar end goal or vision of the future to that of the second tale – economic inclusion and material progress – the starting point is different: contemporary poverty rather than (historical) exclusion.

One of the key missions of the Rwandan state is poverty reduction and improving the well-being of its population (MINECOFIN 2002). While national unity is the core state policy, development is seen as crucial to achieving it (NURC 2016). Rwanda has a number of structural economic disadvantages – inter alia soil erosion, high population density, being landlocked – in addition to the ongoing legacy of genocidal devastation. However, despite these disadvantages, Rwanda has made considerable strides in addressing poverty: between 2000 and 2013, the poverty rate, as measured by the World Bank, declined from 75.2 per cent to 52 per cent, with the poorest benefitting most.[37] This has been possible because of clear priority setting and focused service provision. As part of this progress agenda, household wealth in Rwanda was categorised in 2000 into four levels, or *ubudehe* categories, so as to prioritise the targeting of welfare and development assistance. Up until 2020, these levels were numerical, with 1 denoting the poorest. In 2020, the scheme was reformed, re-labelled with letters, and a fifth level was introduced (Havugimana 2023). The new level E is a special category to denote households that are especially vulnerable due to either age or lack of ability or skills to work (LODA 2022). As development subjects, therefore, Twa are seen through the lens of *ubudehe* categories.

This tale of the Twa draws heavily upon the global development discourse, with its focus on poverty reduction and inclusive development. The commitment to poverty reduction and its now centrality in mainstream global development thinking is evidenced by the prominence given to ending extreme poverty as Sustainable Development Goal (SDG) 1. The commitment to poverty eradication has renewed the focus on inclusive growth, where inclusion is understood as access to the economic mainstream as measured by median income and consumer purchasing power (Suryanarayana 2013). In contrast to the purely economic focus of poverty reduction and inclusive growth, inclusive development denotes a broader understanding of development. The concept brings together concerns with poverty reduction, empowerment, gains in human capital, gendered development, and social protection (Gupta et al. 2015). Inclusiveness is here understood as a combination of material, social-relational, and psychological well-being (Gough and McGregor 2007). For Rwanda to be able to achieve this broad understanding of inclusiveness, it is necessary for it to focus resources on the poorest, the most vulnerable, and the most marginalised. This is reflected in the *ubudehe* categories. It is also necessary for development to be inclusive to ensure that the knowledge and desires of those targeted for inclusion are taken into account in the development process, whatever forms that takes (Dekker and Pouw 2022). Inclusive

[37] World Bank Rwanda overview, updated 21 September 2023: www.worldbank.org/en/country/rwanda/overview#1. It is worth noting, however, that although World Bank data suggests that inequality is declining, Rwanda has a higher Gini co-efficient (0.43) than neighbouring countries. See also McKay and Verpoorten (2016).

development, then, requires participatory mechanisms that are capable of giving voice to those at the bottom and of translating their knowledge and aspirations into policy-making (Goodwin 2022). Within global development discourse, this inclusivity is often reduced to legal mechanisms, such as the existence of non-discrimination norms – on ethnicity, gender, and disability. This is echoed in strict non-discrimination laws in Rwanda; however, development inclusion is here primarily connected to national unity and reconciliation and finds expression in the forging of the good Rwandan citizen through programmes such as Umuganda – a community-based public works programme – in which Twa participate as local residents (UNDP 2020) or in the Itorero programme, designed to create model Rwandan citizens (Purdeková 2015; Sundberg 2016). While gender, disability, and youth are explicitly recognised as specific targets of inclusion in Rwandan development plans, ethnicity is not.[38] Twa are instead located in this broader understanding of inclusive development simply as potentially active development subjects.

This tale is thus based on global development imperatives that are then reframed by the Rwandan state to remove ethnicity as a category requiring inclusion. In this, they are supported by other development actors. The World Bank is an important provider of finance and support for the Rwandan government's social protection programmes; the goal of this collaboration, according to the World Bank, is 'to reduce social vulnerability and to ensure that the most vulnerable Rwandans also benefit from growth'.[39] Although Twa are not named anywhere on the World Bank webpages on Rwanda or in the project reports, projects that focus on reducing the poverty and improving the health and well-being of the poorest Rwandans will inevitably target Twa individuals. The decision by the World Bank not to name Twa in development projects is more marked because of its focus on other groups that fall within the government's categorisation of 'historically marginalised populations'. For example, the World Bank has provided financing through its Inclusive Education Initiative for the rebuilding or renovation of more than 22,000 classrooms across Rwanda in order to facilitate the inclusion of children with disabilities in education.[40]

[38] This follows, of course, from the Constitutional and ordinary legal provisions that prohibit the use of ethnicity as a basis for categorisation or distinction (Article 33 prohibiting the propagation of ethnic division; 2013 Constitution, amended 2015). See further Chapter 5.

[39] See note 37 of this chapter.

[40] See www.worldbank.org/en/news/immersive-story/2022/02/15/an-accessible-future-for-persons-with-disabilities-what-does-it-take.

Rwandans with disabilities can be named and explicitly targeted for support. Similarly, the UNDP in Rwanda pays special attention to the most vulnerable, who are firstly those with disabilities and secondly the extreme poor (UNDP Rwanda 2022: 7–8). In addition, special focus is given by the UNDP to Rwandan youth and to women.[41] The Twa are not mentioned by name in any of these projects. They are, thus, subsumed into the category of poor development subjects and made into general targets of development intervention.

The broad adoption of this tale of the Twa – a tale of general poverty – by development actors is pragmatic. It enables international actors and researchers to side-step the question of Twa identity by focusing on their poverty; this allows such actors to work in Rwanda on poverty alleviation without falling foul of the legal prohibition on ethnic separatism. However, as will be drawn out further in Chapter 4, the focus on poverty eradication within development is also an ideological move that works to depoliticise the development agenda (Ferguson 1990; Pahuja 2011; Escobar 2012). At the level of the global development discourse, poverty eradication and inclusion support an understanding of development as economic growth, which is the responsibility of each state. It is a vision of development that does not challenge the capitalist model or the construction of the post-colonial world order but is instead a means to mitigate their excesses (Adelman and Paliwala 2021). In this way, poverty reduction is a measurement of successful economic and trade policies rather than an assertion of national home-grown solutions. This depoliticised narrative of global development fits nicely with the Rwandan state's efforts to depoliticise the Twa and renationalise them as poor Rwandans.

2.4 Bringing Agency Back In

The UNPO has accused the Rwandan state of the 'legal erasure' of the Batwa (1994). Yet what these tales demonstrate is how the Twa are formed as subjects through the encounter of different narratives and regulatory forces, such as the national prohibition on ethnic divisionism or global development, which construct their subjects as poor and in need of inclusion, or global indigeneity that forms Twa as separate and distinct subjects. These tales are told for different purposes and are

[41] This focus is shared by one of the larger NGOs operating on the ground in Rwanda, Care International. Their Rwanda webpage states that their focus is on improving the 'incomes and status of vulnerable and marginalized groups, particularly women and children': www.care.org/our-work/where-we-work/rwanda.

directed to different audiences, such as a claim to recognition targeted at international human rights institutions, or a mandate for inclusion and national unity directed towards local communities. Within the global human rights framework, the tale of indigeneity dominates, while in Rwanda, the tale at the national level is of Twa as development subjects, with the tale of HMPs having greatest resonance at the local level. However, the point is not to suggest that these tales can be characterised as 'global', 'national', and 'local'. Rather, the aim here has been to suggest that these tales of the Twa are best understood as narrative encounters that are constructed and co-constructed by a wide variety of actors across a range of locations for a variety of purposes, both ideological and pragmatic, and, crucially, through the encounter with global legal discourses. These tales, although they construct different subjectivities for the Twa, nonetheless co-exist in the same space and interact with one another; that is, we should not conceive of the tales as entirely distinct from one another, or necessarily as competing, but rather as forming part of the spaces in which different stories resonate or do not and which shape the space of agency. Moreover, the Rwandan state plays a key role in the form that these narrative encounters take through its engagement with the different global discourses; that is, through refusing or reframing each of their different narratives through legal and programming means.

At the core of each of these tales is a positioning of Twa as vulnerable. That is a choice about how the tales are told: the narratives in themselves do not need to position the Twa as, in the words of the IWGIA in their 2001 Indigenous World Report, 'the marginalised and impoverished indigenous Twa people' (IWGIA 2002: 392). An indigenous rights narrative, although traditionally emerging out of discrimination and threats to a distinct way of life, is more commonly portrayed as empowering (e.g. Engle 2010; Sieder and Barrera 2017). The indigenous tale told of Rwanda's Twa is, however, less one of self-determination and more about overcoming marginalisation; less a political choice or claim – that is, an expression of political agency – than an essentialist-based demand that indigenous recognition should be granted because of 'what they are' and because of what they have suffered.[42] Likewise, the tales of Twa as HMPs or as ordinary development subjects situate them as

[42] For example, 'Their [Twa] ability to resist expropriation, exploitation or violence diminishes and they descend into a spiral of increasing insecurity, marginality and poverty. Their lowly status, small numbers and the dispersal of their communities have contributed to their extreme political weakness and the serious difficulties Twa have in asserting their rights' (Lewis 2000: 5).

marginalised and extremely poor, albeit they stress these characteristics differently and give them different explanatory power.

In doing so, all these tales position Twa as passive: the objects of development interventions, or of discrimination and exclusion by those around them. Even in the tale of indigenous identity, the Twa are conceptualised less as actively claiming indigeneity than as needing that status for basic survival. In none of these stories are Twa portrayed as agents, as actively navigating their own societal positioning within the legal and material constraints present. This can be read as a response to the material realities and legal constraints in which Twa live. Very many Twa are extremely poor, even by the standards of their neighbours; and while our data suggests that societal discrimination against Twa is declining, it certainly still exists. Moreover, since 2003, and Article 33 of the 2003 Constitution in particular, there has been no space for active political claims for indigenous rights within the Rwandan political landscape. While Rwandan Twa were among the earliest of African groups to adopt the indigenous rights discourse and participate in the various international forums dedicated to indigenous rights, COPORWA has had little choice but to switch its focus to socio-economic marginalisation and away from political claims (Ndahinda 2011: 234). The notion of HMPs provides a space in which COPORWA can still operate, but it is necessarily as an NGO working to address socio-economic marginalisation rather than as a political actor seeking to preserve and facilitate Batwa identity. These realities, as much as the tales told about them, condition the space in which Twa have to navigate their lives.

This positioning of Twa as passive arguably draws on a thin notion of agency that views it statically as either absent or expressed as resistance. Instead, following Page, the aim here is instead to situate agency as 'a capacity for action mediated through situated capabilities, struggles and desires' (2018: 281; also Menzel 2020). Seen in this way, agency is 'connected to political, cultural and historical forces that impinge upon bodies and subjectivities and direct activities and energies through multiple demands, obligations, and desires'. Likewise, vulnerability, instead of being defined as a condition of existence or a relation to others, is understood as 'interwoven through lives as elements engaged within layers of agential capacities' (Page 2018: 295).[43] Thus, while these tales position Rwanda's Twa as passive, Twa do not encounter these stories

[43] See further Chapter 1 for a deeper explanation of how agency is conceptualised in this work.

about themselves passively. They are, as we shall see in subsequent chapters, actively engaged in the reworking of these stories, albeit necessarily within the constraints of the narrative nexus, legal subjectivities, and the socio-economic conditions in which they live. They exercise their agency in specific contexts, at specific moments, and in different ways.

How Twa position themselves in relation to the global discourses of indigeneity, conservation, and development in the context of Rwanda's legal, socio-economic, and cultural dynamics is the subject of the remaining chapters.

3

A Different Kind of Dirt

On Survival International's website, the page on Forest Peoples opens with the tagline 'Guardians of the Rainforest'.[1] The page, drawing connections between Forest Peoples all over the world, has a scrolling box dedicated to 'Pygmies', including the Twa. A Congolese 'Pygmy' is quoted as stating, 'We love the forest as we love our own bodies', and the remaining text suggests that, despite speaking different languages, the 'distinct forest peoples living across Central Africa, such as the Baka, the Twa, the Aka and the Mbuti', have 'one word [that] is common to many of them: jengi, which means the spirit of the forest'. Similarly, Dowie notes that many 'Pygmy' groups share a common creation myth: 'Pygmies were God's forgotten people. When they realized their fate, the myth says, they kneeled together before their creator and said: "You have given something to all other peoples – pastures to the pastoralists, savannahs for the bushmen, flocks and herds to the hunters and fruits to the gatherers. What have you for us?" And God gave them the forest' (2009: 65).

These expressions of connection are a reflection of the now common understanding of the centrality of land – in this case, a very particular type of land – to the cosmovision of indigenous peoples (Daes 1997; Engle 2010: 146). It is an understanding that roots indigenous identity in a unique physical, material, and spiritual connection to nature and thus to the place in which that nature is located. From this unique connection – a form of spiritual symbiosis with the land or, here, forest – it is a small step to viewing indigenous peoples as the best guardians of nature.[2] Lewis has noted of the Twa: 'In contrast to later-comers, the Twa used the environment without destroying or seriously damaging it. It is

[1] www.survivalinternational.org/galleries/forest-peoples.

[2] For example, Survival International uses the tagline 'Indigenous People are the best conservationists' on their website and there is a swathe of academic literature that makes similar claims, e.g. Blaser (2004).

only due to their long-term custody of the area that later-comers have good land to use' (2000: 7).

The claim to a distinct and special relationship with the equatorial forests forms an important part of the basis of the claim to indigeneity for Twa and other Pygmy groups. It is a claim that is rooted in the past but has clear implications in the present: where a connection to the forest makes a group distinct, the relationship must be protected, restored, or compensated. That is, in the context of global indigenous narratives, the connection to the forest should determine what policy solutions are offered in the here and now. However, while Engle has suggested that the notion that indigenous peoples have a special connection to land is a 'relatively uncontroversial political claim' (2010: 147), this is not the case in Rwanda and arguably not across much of the African continent (Hodgson 2011; Ndahinda 2011). The strong emphasis by indigenous activists that redress for wrongs done to the Twa must be a return to the forest sets up a clash not only with the national identity project in Rwanda but also with an alternative global discourse, that of conservationism. In a panel organised by the Forest Peoples Project at the turn of the century, a Maasai spokesperson was commenting on the situation of the Twa in Rwanda, particularly their eviction from protected forests, and he stated: 'you cannot talk about Batwa without talking about the forest' (quoted in Kalimba 2003: 85). Such an approach appears to position Twa between a rock and a hard place: they have no identity without the forests, yet that relationship is prevented by both the national legal framework (explored in Chapter 5) and the implementation of global conservation imperatives. This chapter explores how the space of nature has been created in Rwanda. It examines the jurisdictional encounter of global conservation norms, of indigenous claims, of promises of development, and of inclusion in shaping the space of nature for Rwandan Twa, as well as in conditioning their access to resources such as land.

3.1 Rwandan Forest Governance

Rwanda is home to forests of global significance, notably the mountain forests in the north of the country and the rainforest in the south. Rwanda's forests are governed by a series of interlinked plans which are brought together in the National Forestry Policy, most recently updated in 2018. At the heart of the Policy is the restoration of biodiverse forest cover from the current 11 per cent of the total national area to 30 per cent forest cover by 2020 (Ministry of Lands and Forestry 2018). This was achieved as of 2019, according to the Ministry of Environment website.[3] As part of the African Forest Landscape Restoration Initiative, the government committed in 2011 to restoring 2 million hectares of forest, the largest proportional commitment of any country. The National Forestry Policy and the government's ambitions to protect and restore the country's natural forests have been hailed internationally as global leading.[4] In addition, Rwanda is one of the World Bank's core implementing countries within the Nature Capital Accounting project (World Bank 2015; Ministry of Lands and Forestry 2018). It is also a key part of the Green Amayaga Initiative – supported by the United Nations Development Programme (UNDP), funded by the Global Environmental Facility, and implemented by the Rwanda Environment Management Authority and the Rwanda Forestry Authority – to restore depleted eco-systems, focusing on afforestation (UNDP 2022: 5). Rwanda currently has nine protected areas, ranging from forests to wetlands and marshes; seven of these are nationally designated areas and two are internationally designated.[5] These areas cover 9.11 per cent of the country's total land area, some 2,317 square kilometres (UNEP-WCMC 2023).

The National Forestry Policy is authorised by Law N° 47bis/2013 on the Management and Utilisation of Forests in Rwanda, which itself is located within a broader approach to land governance, which – in turn – is determined by the Organic Land Law (Law N° 8/2005).[6] Article 3 of the Organic Land Law declares that all land is 'the common heritage of all Rwandans', and thus 'the State has supreme powers to manage all national land'. This includes the right to expropriate private land for public purposes but also allows for the private ownership of conservation zones. Rwanda's national parks are currently publicly owned, although private management is encouraged (McAuslan 2013; Ministry of Lands and Forestry 2018).

[3] The website gives coverage of 30.4 per cent in the 2019 forest cover map: www.environment.gov.rw/mandate/forestry-resources-management-for-economic-growth.

[4] For example, in 2011 Rwanda was awarded a 'Gold Future Policy Award' in recognition of its National Forestry Policy being 'the world's most inspiring and innovative forest policy'; www.futurepolicy.org/forests/rwandas-national-forest-policy.

[5] The latter are the Ramsar Site as a Wetland of International Importance and the international designation of the Volcanoes National Park as a UNESCO-MAB Biosphere Reserve (UNEP-WCMC 2023).

[6] The rules on land governance were updated in Law N° 43/2013 and, again, in Law N° 27/2021.

Rwanda's conservation efforts are entwined with development and are seen by the government as central to achieving its vision of development for two core reasons: the first is that the Rwandan economy remains significantly dependent on agriculture, and soil erosion and land degradation, together with climate change, pose a significant threat to continued economic development. Rwanda was ranked 153rd in the world in 2021 by the World Bank for climate change vulnerability, mainly relating to soil erosion. The second reason for Rwanda to invest heavily in conservation is that conservation tourism is an important part of Rwanda's economy. Between 2000 and 2019, the number of foreign visitors to the national parks grew by more than 2,800 per cent, with the generated foreign exchange earnings of these visits amounting to double the income of the earnings from tea, coffee, and mineral exports combined (Ministry of Lands and Forestry 2018; Benitez et al. 2021). Conservation in Rwanda thus goes hand in hand with development.[7]

Conservation projects began in Rwanda under the Belgian colonial administration, with the formation first of the Volcanoes National Park in 1924, then with its incorporation into the new Albert National Park in 1929, which straddled the Rwanda–Congo border (Kalimba 2003). Following independence, this park was renamed and divided into the Virunga National Park on the Democratic Republic of the Congo side of the border and the Volcanoes National Park on the Rwanda side. The Nyungwe and Gishwati Forest Reserves, as well as the Akagera National Park in the east of the country, were all created in the 1930s (Kalimba 2003: 57). However, the designation of these sites as nature reserves did not protect them from deforestation. The pressure for land for subsistence farming caused by population growth, as well as economic pressures to grow cash crops, mean that the forest reserves were chipped away at even as they were formally protected (Ministry of Lands and Forestry 2018). For example, according to multiple sources, Gishwati Forest was largely cleared in the early 1980s to create tea and eucalyptus plantations and new pastureland, as required by the World Bank (UNPO 1994). According to Musahara and Huggins (2005: 301), Gishwati has lost 86.4 per cent of its size since the 1930s; and the Mukura Forest reserve, designated in 1951, has lost almost 50 per cent of its size. Similarly, where the original Volcanoes National Park comprised an area of 30,000

[7] Rwanda's national development vision is explored in Chapter 4. Essentially, Rwanda's vision of development most closely models understandings of inclusive development, in which development is based on economic growth but where poverty reduction is a key objective.

hectares in the 1920s, by the beginning of the twenty-first century, it had already been reduced by significantly more than half its size. The remaining parks have shrunk by smaller but still significant amounts.

At independence in 1962, the management of the parks passed to the newly created Ministry of Agriculture and Livestock until 1973, when the Rwanda Office for Tourism and National Parks was formed. In 1974, new rules came into effect to protect the natural resources of the parks from private citizens, which prohibited the hunting, fishing, and trapping of animals, the cutting of trees or any other plants, and any activity likely to threaten nature and the ecosystem, and which also created a mechanism of monitoring the enforcement of these new laws (Kalimba 2003). Today, the Rwanda Environment Management Authority (REMA), created under Law N° 63/2013 and under the supervision of the Ministry of Environment, takes the lead on national environmental protection, including conservation. Responsibility for the management and protection of Rwanda's forests is further delegated to the Rwanda Forest Authority, established in 2020 under Law N° 72/2019.

In addition, Rwanda is a party to the 1995 Convention on Biological Diversity (CBD), which it implements via its National Biodiversity Strategy and Action Plan (2016). Protection of the parks is, as noted, provided for in Law N° 47bis/2013, in Law N° 1/2023 authorising the conversion of private land to parks and allowing for private management of parks, as well as in Law N° 17/2008 establishing the National Forest Authority (NAFA). This legal framework is implemented by, inter alia, the 2018 National Forest Management Plan and Vision 2050 (MINECOFIN 2015), which establish the government's overarching development plan for Rwanda 2020–2050, and includes its Green Growth and Climate Resilience Strategy (GGCRS). While the government has stated the need to understand the important role that forests play in subsistence farming and in poorer households, it is committed to protecting the remaining forests and to reversing some of the deforestation (Mutandwa and Kanyarukiga 2016; Article 4 Law N° 1/2023). For example, the government announced in 2022 that the Volcanoes National Park will be expanded from its current 13,000 hectares to 23,000 hectares, with a further 6,200 hectares creating a buffer zone between the expanded Park and agricultural land (Ngounou 2022).[8] As

[8] Agroforestry will reportedly be permitted in the buffer zone, meaning that agricultural land will not be confiscated; www.matadornetwork.com/read/following-gorilla-rejuvenation-rwanda-volcanoes-national-park-expanding.

such, Rwanda's commitment to conservation is fully aligned with global discourses on conservation, sustainability, and biodiversity.

3.2 Global Conservationism

Where European imperialism gave shape to the first form of nature conservation as a global narrative, capitalism determined the second – from commodification to the belief that private actors are best positioned to protect nature by extracting value from it as wilderness.

3.2.1 Global Enclosure

From the mid-twentieth century onwards, biologists began to sound alarms about the loss of biodiversity. This creation of the notion of biological diversity, begun as a political movement in the US in the 1980s, has led to a broad global consensus that the world is in a biodiversity crisis (Takacs 1996). It is out of this understanding that the global conservation movement has emerged, the central strategy of which is the creation of protected areas (Dowie 2009). Protected areas have since seen a rapid proliferation, with a 50 per cent increase in global protected areas since 1996.[9] In Africa, however, in less than thirty years from 1960, according to Neumann, the amount of land under strict conservation measures had doubled (1998: 4). The global conservation agenda has since been given fresh impetus by the growing awareness of human impact on the natural world. In the context of climate change, protected spaces have taken on a new importance: not only are they viewed as essential for preserving biodiversity but they are also increasingly viewed as being on the frontline of climate change mitigation efforts.

To designate an area as demanding conservation entails a transfer of a set of resources, including land, from one group to another, with all the profound social implications that follow (Garland 2008). The widespread creation of nature reserves across all continents has led to displacement and dispossession of land, creating in turn waves of 'conservation refugees' (Medina 2015). Those dispossessed or deprived of access to traditional resources, often without consultation or compensation, need then to be forcefully kept out of the protected spaces, leading to the creation of wildlife guards – a model that has been widely dubbed

[9] See the World Databased on Protected Areas (WDPA): www.protectedplanet.net/en/thematic-areas/wdpa?tab=WDPA.

'fortress conservation' (Luoma 2022). This follows from what Neumann has suggested is the 'national park ideal' that sees wilderness as peopleless, with human activities viewed as despoiling nature rather than being part of it (1998).[10]

This reification of wilderness has its roots in the colonial construction of nature. As Escobar has put it 'very schematically':

> the main features of the coloniality of nature, as established by myriad discourses and practices in post-Renaissance Europe and beyond, include classification into hierarchies . . . with nonmoderns, primitives, and nature at the bottom of the scale; essentialized views of nature as being outside the human domain; the subordination of the body and nature to the mind . . . seeing the products of the earth as the products of labor only, hence subordinating nature to human-driven markets; locating certain natures (colonial and third world natures, women's bodies, dark bodies) outside of the totality of the male Eurocentric world; the subalternization of all other articulations of biology and history to modern regimes, particularly those that enact a continuity between the natural, human and supernatural worlds.
>
> (2008: 121)

Neumann has, further, argued convincingly that the creation of parks is an integral part of a particular historical narrative of European imperialism. This narrative sees colonialism and the global expansion of European economic and cultural hegemony as transforming empty wilderness into the productive space of fields, factories, and cities. As Neumann writes, 'In the imperial European conceptual map of the world, Europe was culture and the colonies were nature . . . parks are but one aspect of the portrayal of global history as the history of Europeans, with the rest of the world frozen in some primeval state' (1998: 32–33; also Nandy 1983). National parks represent here remnants of a 'pre-European landscape' that must be saved (the so-called Eden complex) (Neumann 1998: 29–30). This impulse played a particular role in settler states, where parks helped to conceal the violence of conquest and where the encounter with wilderness could form an important symbol of a national identity cleansed of the primitive 'Other'.[11] In Africa, it saw conservation efforts driven by 'European ideals of the scenic African landscape' (Neumann 1998: 3) and the romance of the 'out of Africa' relationship between saviour conservationists and ignorant locals – this despite the fact that much of the now protected land

[10] This approach draws on US legislation, which defines wilderness in the 1964 Wilderness Act as 'an area where the earth and its community of life are untrammelled by man'; cited in Dowie (2009: xvi).

[11] More broadly, Radkau suggests that the forest is a locus of imperial power (2008: 233).

created as conservation zones was not ‘unspoilt’ wildernesses but had long histories of human occupation and use.[12] This need to cleanse the wilderness of human presence entailed that early conservationism took the form of a globalized enclosure.

However, although nature was to be cleansed of human presence, it was not immune to the imperatives of capital. As Peluso has noted, nature is always produced and historically situated (2012: 84). In our era, it is capitalism, more specifically neo-liberalism, that determines how nature and knowledge about nature is given form (Peluso 2012). Whereas the construction of nature as pristine and wild was concerned in the nineteenth and early twentieth centuries with colonial superiority and national identity, in our era nature is produced as a socio-natural commodity. Conservationist capitalism sees an ideal of wilderness now packaged for Western consumer consumption.

The debt crises and structural adjustment mandates of the 1980s and 1990s meant that available state revenues of countries in the Global South were dwindling just at the moment they were expected to invest heavily in nature protection (Brockington and Igoe 2006; Ferguson 2006). The solution was to commodify nature in order to fund its own protection, what Brockington and Scholfield have labelled a ‘conservationist mode of production’ (2010). This crowning of market mechanisms as the means to fund nature protection came about despite the awareness within global conservationism that capitalist exploitation constituted the biggest threat to nature (Peluso 2012). Yet, (eco-)tourism was suddenly viewed as the magic wand that could resolve the conservation burden placed on poorer countries: not only could tourism fund the management and guarding of protected spaces but, crucially, it could also – by attracting wealthy Northern tourists – provide the foreign currency exchange necessary to pay foreign creditors. Nature was thus repositioned and re-packaged to service capitalism. Moreover, attracting foreign tourists would provide jobs and income to local communities negatively affected by a reserve’s creation. (Eco-)tourism was thus understood as creating a win–win situation (West et al. 2006), despite the well-documented fact that there is little that is sustainable about such tourism (Peluso 2012). Indeed, such is the entwinement of capitalism and conservation in modern environmental governance that Brockington and Scholfield have noted, ‘it

[12] See also Sharon Tshipa, ‘Environmental protection is deeply-held practice in African spirituality. What happens when it is re-shaped by Christianity and capitalism?’, Africa Is a Country, 15 November 2023: africasacountry.com/2023/11/god-ancestors-and-nature.

[conservation] is produced by it [capitalism], and thoroughly integrated into it, such that capital and conservation become two core complementary and mutually enforcing processes in the contemporary production of nature' (2010: 552; Polyani 1944). This production of nature is a global narrative. Indeed, it is this that constitutes the current hegemonic global discourse of nature conservation or 'mainstream conservation', which has – at least for the moment – pushed out alternative conceptions of nature and of nature protection activities to the fringes (Brockington, Duffy, and Igoe 2008: 9; Igoe et al. 2010).

And global conservationism is big business. According to a 2020 OECD report on global conservation funding, in the period 2015–2017, some 78–91 billion US dollars was spent annually on conservation efforts. More than half of this finance is given to just five global conservation actors (Dowie 2009). However, a 2022 UN report, led by the UN Environment Programme (UNEP), the World Economic Forum (WEF), and the Economics of Land Degradation (ELD), found this figure to be woefully insufficient; their report calls upon G20 nations to commit to tripling their spending on 'nature-based solutions' to 285 billion US dollars by 2050 (UNEP 2022). Moreover, this additional funding is just a beginning to close what the report has identified as a 4.1-trillion-US-dollar funding gap in these same 'Nature-based Solutions'.[13]

However, while the main form of commodification and value extraction in conservationism is (eco-)tourism, it is not the only form that such extraction of value takes.[14] For example, protected spaces that are not tourist destinations can be utilised for fundraising, for education or research purposes, or to produce value via mediarisation as a location for documentaries (Igoe 2010; Igoe et al. 2010: 497–498). Pristine spaces also have non-tourist value as offsetting carbon use. This extraction of value for the benefit of Western tourists and donors has led to a generification of nature (West et al. 2006), whereby both nature and people are made less complicated in order to make them legible to faraway conservationists and managers (Igoe 2010). For example, unique spaces are brought into line via labels such as 'wetlands' that must meet certain criteria to be designated as internationally significant depending on their 'authenticity'; that is, the extent to which they are deemed to be pristine natural

[13] The report defines 'Nature-based Solutions' as 'a category of assets in which businesses, governments and citizens can invest in order to work with nature instead of seeing it as a barrier to economic development and progress' (UNEP 2022: 3).

[14] See also, e.g., the Green Living Project: www.greenlivingprojects.com.

spaces or have been degraded by human activity according to Western criteria (West et al. 2006; Igoe 2010). The International Union for the Conservation of Nature (IUCN) has created a worldwide categorisation of types of protected areas and requires national governments to make their protected spaces fit their criteria, with little regard to local ways of knowing the space (West et al. 2006). As Igoe et al. note, the value of protected spaces as a currency of global conservationism is that they are 'discrete, measured and eminently countable' (2010: 495). This abstract quality of protected spaces and their exchangeability has allowed nature protection, as a particular form of global environmentalism, to maintain a core place in this movement as it reorientates from protection to climate change mitigation. The exchangeability of protected spaces fits with mitigation strategies that allow the degradation of the environment under capitalism's extractive logic to be offset by the creation of pristine wild spaces (Anderson and Berglund 2003; Igoe 2010; Igoe et al. 2010: 495). In this way, global wildlife conservation is not the sort of environmentalism that is rooted to a particular place (Brockington 2008), in contrast to indigenous connection to place; instead, it is dependent on distant connections. Local places are thus necessarily transformed into global spaces and are detached from their locality (see also Natarajan 2022).

Moreover, Igoe has suggested that the performance of conservationism – what he terms the 'spectacle of conservationism' – repeatedly invokes a global community: we, all of us, our planet. This is encapsulated, for example, in the Conservation International slogan 'lost there, felt here' (Igoe 2010; Kneas 2017). This celebrity-backed campaign pushes a global narrative in which 'they' do the damage and the effects are felt by us. It is a narrative which grants moral superiority to those that recognise the importance of pristine nature. For those that do not share this vision of nature as spaces cleansed of human activity, education projects are necessary to overcome ignorance (WB 2022). As such, nature protection continues to be part of a (neo-)colonial project, which becomes visible at such moments.

Yet it is important to note as well that decisions to establish protected spaces are not only the result of market logics and neo-colonial global imperatives. Brockington and Igoe highlight that 'there is clear evidence of locally driven, national prerogatives and priorities at work in protected area evictions', whether in pursuit of socialist-inspired policies of collectivisation, intolerance of indigenous peoples, or disputes over land for agricultural production (2006: 444). As Peluso reminds us, how nature and capital come together at local sites is always ambiguous, 'even in this most neoliberal of ages' (2012: 99).[15] In Rwanda, the demands of conservationists for nature protection coalesce with the national vision on development, which is drawn out in detail in the following chapter, and both are folded into the bigger goal of national unity, whereby nature reserves and the wildlife therein are 'nationalised' and presented as both a source and symbol of national pride.[16] At the same time, this transactive or commodification process, via the funds from eco-tourism, creates the possibility for development and for the transformation of Twa into development subjects.

3.2.2 *Conservation's Subjects: Poachers, Protectors, Managers, Indigenous Peoples, Local Communities*

The commodification of enclosure – this entwinement of colonial ideas of wilderness with the capitalist imperative – that forms the basis of nature protection law has in part been so successful because of its ability to assert its positioning of actors, or their subjectivisation, via a clear assignment of roles.

The dislocation of nature by means of the generification or standardisation of nature according to global norms and metrics allows local community reliance on park resources to be packaged for global consumption as poaching, which is made possible by the discursive separation of nature and culture (Stegeborn 1996; Freedman 2002; Roth 2004).[17] The establishment of parks and other protected areas has criminalised communities' customary use of land and natural resources and, as a consequence, protected areas have become areas for conflict over

[15] See Takacs (1996), esp. chapter 2 on 'The Making of Biodiversity'. Also see Tsing's observation in her study of conservationism of the Indonesian rainforests that conservationism has always argued that nature has a value that transcends all things (2005: 97–99). See further Dowie's reporting of conservationists who reject the logic of economics in relation to conservation as immoral, and who regard economic development and conservation as mutually exclusive goals (2009: 82–83).

[16] A clear example of this is the annual national naming ceremony for newborn gorillas, 'Kwita Izina', which receives widespread national media coverage and is reported on in the compulsory village meetings: visitrwanda.com/kwita-izina. Our interviewees frequently mentioned the gorilla naming ceremony as attesting to the gorillas' importance to the nation.

[17] Although, following Radkau, this discursive move was only possible once Europeans begin to see Africans as fully human; prior to that moment, they were not perceived as foreign bodies in nature but as part of that nature (2008: 163).

resources across many countries (Neumann 1998). Moreover, these are conflicts with high stakes, both economically and ecologically.[18]

A consequence of this is that conflict is at the core of the establishment and maintenance of protected spaces (West et al. 2006: 260), as poachers, like pirates before them, are outlawed and hunted down by militarised guards (Heller-Roazen 2009; Igoe 2010; van Beemen 2024b). They are placed outside the global community that global conservationism brings into being (Lindahl 2018). Unsurprisingly, the drawing of these conflict lines also has a racial charge. Nature conservation, particularly on the African continent, can be viewed as a part of what da Silva has described as the 're-racialisation of the globe' (2007). Similarly, Garland's work has suggested that the conservation movement is a means of value appropriation of African nature for Northern enjoyment and capital accumulation; she contrasts, for example, the 'hidden' work of Black conservationists with the value-generating exploitation of white conservationists, dubbed 'conservation entrepreneurs' or 'conservation heroes' by Brockington and Scholfield (2010: 552; Garland 2008: 52, 74–78; Peluso 2012; van Beemen 2024a). This discursive technique is brought into sharper focus by the profiling within conservationism of trophy hunters, usually white and Northern, as nature lovers (Neumann 1998); the same point could be made of eco-tourists who travel by plane to visit nature reserves far away and who view themselves as environmental protectors, in contrast to the locals who are immersed in that environment but who are nonetheless required to repeatedly demonstrate their conservationist convictions.[19]

Another key feature of global nature protection is the delegation of state responsibilities for the management of nature to civil society actors and/or the private sector (Medina 2015: 273). The number, size, and

[18] The impact of the dominant conceptualisation of the relationship between humans and nature on the social, economic, and cultural well-being of communities was recognised in the Durban Action Plan produced by the fifth World Parks Congress in 2003, which convened under the banner 'Benefits beyond Boundaries' – an explicit recognition of the impact that nature conservation has on many and on the unequal sharing of its costs.

[19] I have encountered this anecdotally: towards the end of a tourist hike up Mount Bisoke in the Volcanoes National Park in May 2024, as we exited the park, a troop of golden monkeys dropped down from the forest to rampage across the farmland that butts up against the park boundary. The monkeys pulled up crops and generally caused havoc. While a farmer and his children attempted unsuccessfully to chase the monkeys away, their efforts were met with blank indifference by our guide and the accompanying porters. In this moment, the practice of conservationism appeared as an all-or-nothing binary, in which empathy with the farmer would tarnish their conservationist credentials.

influence of conservation NGOs or not-for-profits have risen dramatically from the 1980s. According to Medina, 'by the 1990s, the devolution of management responsibilities for protected areas had become the norm' (2015: 273). This sees private actors, often global NGOs or foreign not-for-profits, become the trusted partner of governments in managing their nature reserves and parks, a relationship extending as far as the possibility of privately owned nature reserves (see, e.g., Article 9 Law N° 1/2023, which allows for a private individual to own a nature reserve). This apparent withdrawal of the state is better understood not as de-regulation but as a form of re-regulation, whereby the state ostensibly delegates responsibility to private actors but nonetheless continues to assert its priorities through these partnerships and via the allocation of resources (Igoe et al. 2010: 496). Brockington and Scholfield see these private actors as having become 'vital brokers' in the production of value from nature (2010: 562), but they are more than brokers. The management of 'nationalised' spaces of nature have been outsourced and effectively privatised by contract (Affolder 2018; van Beeman 2024a).[20] That external, often (white) foreign, actors, divorced from the local context, are entrusted with the task of managing a nation's natural assets speaks to the power of the discursive separation of nature and culture and of the positioning of (Black) locals as the main threat to nature protection.

Indigenous people have become a partial exception to the separation of nature from human activity explicit in nature capitalism, but only when envisioned as the noble savage and thus as not fully cultured human beings (West et al. 2006: 256).[21] This exception has, however, rarely protected indigenous peoples from relocation, as Dowie has extensively documented: for example, the Batwa of Uganda were officially designated as 'encroachers' before being removed from the Bwindi Impenetrable National Park in the 1990s (Dowie 2009: 66–67). As West et al. note, 'the imposition of this putative nature/culture dichotomy has

[20] Africa Parks, a South African-based not-for-profit actor, took on the management of Akagera National Park in 2011, together with the Rwanda Development Board (RDB). According to Africa Parks, the success of this collaboration led the Rwandan government to sign a twenty-year agreement in 2010 for the management of Nyungwe Forest Reserve; www.africanparks.org/the-parks/akagera. Similarly, the Volcanoes National Park is managed by a consortium of the Dian Fossey Gorilla Fund, the Karisoke Research Center, and the International Gorilla Conservation Programme, together with the Office Rwandais du Tourisme et des Parcs Nationaux (ORTPN).

[21] It is perhaps worth noting that the assumption that indigenous peoples are those most harmed by the enclosure of protected spaces is not supported by the evidence and produces, according to West et al., fundamental inequalities (2006: 259).

had significant material and social impacts, either by forcefully excluding people from their land or holding them to discursive standards that are nearly impossible to live up to in practice' (2006: 256; Engle 2010). Moreover, this is particularly the case for forest reserves. Radkau notes that 'the forest runs like a leitmotif through all of global environmental history', becoming, 'in popular consciousness, the embodiment of the natural world in need of protection against exploitative private interests on behalf of the common interest in the future' (2008: 212–213).[22] Thus, while the environmental movement more recently has begun to enthuse about the value of traditional knowledge of eco-systems as a basis for environmental protection, in practice, global conservationism is designed by market forces to align with fortress conservation rather than inclusive processes (Escobar 2008).[23] Indigenous peoples are to be consulted and participate in decision-making and their traditional knowledge is to be preserved, but this is not the same as accepting indigenous or otherwise local communities as integral to the nature that is to be protected and including them in the notion of protected spaces; nor is it an acceptance of alternative epistemologies (Natarajan 2022; also Hodgson 2011). This contrasts with the private actors aligned with or part of the global conservation movement, who are to be trusted with the protection of nature.

There is, according to Brockington and Igoe, however, little detailed scholarship on the impact of globally designed conservation projects on local communities or on how such projects have affected the relationship of local communities to nature (2006). Others, though, have suggested that the impacts are frequently profound, alienating communities from land and changing social relations. For example, conservation zones have fuelled conflict between groups, disrupting local power relations and altering gender relationships within households and communities (West et al. 2006). Moreover, 'whereas rural peoples' previous interactions with plants and animals were unique social ways of relating to their surroundings, these plants and animals' instillation into economic valuation erases local ways of seeing and being' (Tsing 2003; West et al. 2006: 263). In addition to creating resistance, however, some studies have shown the contrary, that the language of conservation has instead permeated local language and practices as local people seek to claim some of the benefits

[22] The turn to the private sector to protect nature from the actions of the private sector does not, however, remove the public sphere from the equation.

[23] Indeed, all the major conservation organisations now state their commitment to the traditional and sustainable use of protected areas (Dowie 2009).

(Pfeffer et al. 2001; West et al. 2006; Medina 2015). While on one level this can be read as an instrumental adaption to powerful changes to lived circumstances, there is also evidence that the adoption of the language of conservation has worked to change local peoples' understanding of their relationship to their surroundings (Pfeffer et al. 2001; Agrawal 2005).

Neumann noted almost twenty-five years ago that the pushback against the demands of conservation by local populations has birthed two mainstream explanations as to why local people have not given themselves over to the conservation imperative. The first is that population increase is creating ever greater demand for land; and the second is a lack of understanding among local people of conservation, which requires education so that they are able, in the phrasing of a Serengeti management plan, to 'appreciate the wildlife spectacle' (cited in Neumann 1998: 8). In this way, 'national parks are treated as threatened by land-hungry populations rather than as being historically complicit in the creation of conditions of land and resource scarcity' (Neumann 1998: 8). Both these explanations are clearly present in the Rwandan government's approach to natural resources and forest management (Ministry of Lands and Forestry 2018).

Moreover, Rwanda has fully incorporated the global conservation discourse into its approach to nature protection, whereby nature is understood as resources that must be managed (Law N° 1/2023); where the protection of nature is fully aligned with market principles (MINECOFIN 2015); and private actors are embraced as one of the core principles for the management of its natural resources (Ministry of Lands and Forestry 2018).[24] At the same time, Rwanda has embraced the more recent shifts within global conservationism towards 'local participation' and 'community development' as key to achieving nature protection (Republic of Rwanda 2020; Ministry of Lands and Forestry 2018; Articles 4 and 7, Law N° 1/2023). This is in line with the terms of Article 8 of the CBD, which requires state parties to 'respect, preserve and maintain knowledge, innovations and practices of indigenous and local communities'.[25] This requirement, however, is caveated by the need to do so only in accordance with national legislation. The government's refusal

[24] In addition to the outsourcing of the management of Rwanda's natural resources to private actors, the latest Rwandan National Report to the CBD (2020) was produced, according to the acknowledgements section, by the International Union for the Conservation of Nature (IUCN) rather than by a government ministry or agency (CBD Report 2020).

[25] Convention on Biological Diversity, entered into force 29 December 1993; 1760 UNTS 79.

to view Rwandan Twa as indigenous or to accord Twa a special status in relation to forest management is not therefore a breach of its international obligations, albeit it sits awkwardly with the current trend in global conservation to acknowledge that indigenous peoples have special knowledge of nature. Instead, Article 7 of Law N° 1/2023 acknowledges the importance of community-based conservation.

The formation of Rwanda's national parks has had a considerable impact on the Twa. Batwa hunting and all other activities were proscribed in the new parks, with the rules further tightened after independence. According to Kalimba, the effect of the creation of the Volcanoes National Park was to deprive some 4,500 Batwa, who relied on the forest for food for subsistence and barter, of their means of survival. According to these accounts, although none give a source for the information, the forests were closed off to the Twa without consultation or compensation for the loss of their livelihood (Kalimba 2003; Willis 2005: 134). Prior to the genocide, the Association pour la Promotion Batwa (APB) estimated that there were some 3,000 Batwa living a traditional way of life in Rwanda's forests (UNPO 1994) from a population that they estimated at 29,000. As Ndahinda has noted, 'Twa entitlement to, and occupation of lands became more and more precarious and, eventually, it was somehow terminated' (2011: 207). This physical displacement took place almost entirely before the current Rwandan regime came to power in the aftermath of genocide. This means that the physical loss of connection to the forest was not a product of the laws and policies of national unity; that is, it was not a consequence of legal tools prohibiting divisionism and the subsequence refusal to recognise Twa as a distinct and/or indigenous group. Instead, it came about because of the jurisdictional encounter between global conservation norms and of neo-liberal capitalism, which produced ideas of development that were rooted in economic growth, and which also saw the commodification of nature as lush wildlife reserves packaged for Northern consumption.

Willis has stated that, 'the Batwa, or Impunyu (forest people), are a forest people without a forest' (2005: 134). It is clear that the Twa of Rwanda are no longer forest-dwellers, although, as with other parts of the population that live on the fringes of the parks, they almost certainly continue to draw on the forests for some part of their sustenance. This is widely viewed in human and indigenous rights reports as an 'expulsion' from their traditional way of life – one which has forced Twa individuals and communities to adopt the sedentary lifestyle of their neighbours without support to find alternative employment or gain access to land

and with the attendant loss of traditional culture and way of life (e.g. ACHPR/IWGIA 2005; Willis 2005: 134). Such an understanding sees the Twa as having suffered a double erasure: a physical displacement from their connection to the forest, as so many communities have been worldwide, as well as a socio-cultural displacement that denies them a place in national memory-making as forest-dwellers. What, though, does that mean to them?

3.3 Twa Relationship to the Forest Today

'Nature' did not form a core part of our research project: in investigating what Twa understood to be barriers to their inclusion in society, we did not view their relationship to and understanding of nature as a key question. We included it because it is part of Nussbaum's ten central categories of capabilities that are necessary for human flourishing: being able to live with concern for and in relation to animals, plants, and the world of nature (2011: 33–34). Nussbaum's notion is rooted in a spiritual or emotional connection that humans have or need to have with nature. This, it turned out, did not resonate with our stakeholders or our local team members who carried out the interviews; and the struggle to communicate this idea is visible in how they asked questions about nature. Although the interviews were loosely structured around the invitation to 'tell me about your life', several of the interviewers had a tendency to follow up any mention of the environment with the question, 'what does nature mean to you?', which generally elicited an instrumental response. However, while the framing of the question, it could be argued, brought the instrumental response, even where our interviewers persisted with open questions, the response was an instrumental understanding of nature. That is, they viewed nature as a resource to be used in their everyday lives or to be conserved in order to bring in foreign money. Nature was thus perceived primarily as having instrumental value but no intrinsic value.

Moreover, there was no suggestion that our interviewees understood themselves as having a special connection to nature or to the forests more particularly. Their responses instead locate them, firstly, as ordinary villagers focused on subsistence farming and on survival; and, secondly, as Rwandans, for whom cultural norms surrounding land and cattle had deep resonance. Thus, although it was repeatedly suggested to us by our national and international contacts – indeed, on one occasion, forcefully argued by a member of COPORWA at one of our team visits to Burera district[26] – that the Twa wished to reclaim their forest lifestyle, our findings were that the overwhelming approach to nature among our interviewees was not one of longing for the past or of emotional connection in the present. They saw the environment as important for practical reasons related to their physical well-being, either as a provider of resources, such as firewood, or for its role in the climate, or for security. All of our respondents, with the exception of one or two that I draw out later, had a clear understanding of how the environment is important to them in this instrumental way, both directly and indirectly, and gave elaborate answers on what they think the environment is and the role that it plays in their lives.

The environment is important directly via, for example, animals to sell or eat, milk to drink, or wood as firewood or for house-building.[27] In considering the role that the environment plays in their lives, our interviewees did not distinguish between domesticated nature, such as cows or goats, and what we might term 'natural resources'; instead, the non-human or 'natural world' was understood entirely as natural resources, with the distinction being the degree of utility[28] or the risk that one takes in accessing it. In addition to the direct utility of the environment for their own daily survival, our respondents also frequently drew an indirect connection between nature and their personal well-being; for example, between the forests and the climate. A gentleman in Rusizi district, Karangiro cell, stated: 'trees bring rain, which is important for crops, even if I have no crops' [B1].

Further, the responses of our interviewees disclose that the government has formulated clear messages about nature conservation and that these messages are taught in schools and village meetings.[29] The lessons, as related to us, focus on the importance of protecting the forests for rain, clear air, and preventing soil erosion; of the gorillas for both the image of Rwanda and the development of the country; and also on the beauty of

[26] Personal fieldwork notes, 17 May 2017.

[27] For example, 'With no access to the forest, it is difficult to get firewood' [E1], Gatsibo district, Nyabisindu cell.

[28] G7 (a middle-aged man in Rusororo district) distinguishes between animals not based on notions of domesticated or wild but on whether they can be eaten or not. Crocodiles and hippopotamuses, he stated, cannot be eaten.

[29] G10 stated explicitly that she was taught at school about the importance of forests in bringing rain. Similarly, D1, a woman in Nyaruguru district, Bunge cell, told us: 'There are some people who do cut trees in the forest but the state is against it. The forest is important because, *we are told*, that the good air that we breathe is because of the forest.'

the country. Messages about the importance of the forest for wind and rain were repeated back to us irrespective of where in the country the interview took place and are seemingly thus part of a general education programme (see, too, Ministry of Lands and Forestry 2018). Similarly, nearly everyone was aware that foreigners come to Rwanda to see animals and they bring in lots of money. For example, an elderly woman in Kigabiro sector told us: 'Their [wild animals] importance is to generate income for the government. If white men come to visit them, they take photos and we can see them on TV and in movies' [G15]. There is also a clear understanding and acceptance of the connection between wildlife protection and development; that is, the commodification of wildlife for economic development. As a woman in Gakenke district noted, 'Gorillas and other animals in the parks give a good rank to our country. They attract tourists and are a source of income to our government, and we can then have infrastructure like roads, water and we can have the support for roofing iron sheets' [G10]. As these comments also suggest, the messaging about Rwanda's wildlife is not only instrumental but also aims at creating a sense of national pride and thus forms part of the broader national cohesion efforts: the gorillas give 'good rank' or national status. This sense of pride was shared quite widely.[30]

However, government conservation messaging does not only educate in relation to the positive benefits of the natural environment for Rwandans but also the criminal sanctions attached to, for example, harming wildlife. Our respondents were very aware that 'forest animals are the property of the government' [G7] and understood the criminal sanctions for harming them. As a woman in Nyamasheke district told us, you can be arrested and jailed for killing a wild animal, 'because you have done evil to it. You have harmed the environment' [G2].[31]

It is thus clear that the Twa, alongside other Rwandans, receive the government's environmental messaging and accept the core elements of it. Some of our interviewees were enthusiastic supporters of the government's policy, such as an elderly man from Kicukiro district [J2]. There

[30] For example, a woman in Kayonza district in the east of the country told us that foreigners coming to Rwanda to visit the wildlife 'is part of our dignity' [K11]. Likewise, a young woman in Gasabo district stated: 'All those things [animals, forests, volcanoes] make up the beauty of Rwanda' [G8].

[31] Hunting protected animals and harming the environment are indeed prohibited under Law N° 48/2018 on the environment. Article 58 of this law provides for a term of imprisonment of no less than five years and a fine of no less than FRW 5 million for the killing of a protected animal.

was also some resentment of the policy of conservationism, but such sentiments were very much isolated.[32] In general, the approach was one of a pragmatic acceptance of conservation for the purposes of national development, but one frequently caveated by personal interest: a woman living in Kicukiro district, to the southwest of Kigali, commented, 'I respect the environment, but I do collect firewood from fallen branches. You cannot protect the environment and starve' [J9]. This pragmatic approach predominated. One or two respondents went further and articulated a personal enjoyment or emotional connection to their environment. A woman in Nyaruguru district spoke of 'the beautiful hills that ornate Rwanda like flowers', suggesting that she gains pleasure from looking at the landscape [C1]. In sum, though, Twa have largely absorbed the global conservationist message, as passed down by the Rwandan government, of nature as separated from culture (i.e. that the environment is there to be used and protected for human ends) and as commodifiable for the purposes of national development.

How does this approach relate to how Twa see themselves? While we did not record any stated desire to 'return' to a life in the forest, how did our respondents understand their past in relation to their present situation, in particular in the context of notions of indigeneity or distinctness from other groups?

There was certainly some recognition of a former connection to the forests among our respondents. For example, this statement by a woman from Muhanga district: 'The forest is very important. It attracts rain, as I said, and we like forests very much. We lived in forests for many years, breathing a cool air, hunting and eating' [J1]. This speaks to an emotional attachment to the forests that continues despite no longer living in the forests. Yet, the comment that Twa no longer live in the forest is given factually, and without resentment or the expression of a desire to return to that way of life. J1 is typical of our respondents. Others explicitly link Batwa to the forests, but also as a past connection and not one of longing for return. D2, a young mother in Nyaruguru district, stated:

> There are HMPs who used to live in forests. They were taken from there and settled in communal settlements and now they live just like other people. It looks like they have almost forgotten their sylvan lifestyle

[32] A man from Karongi district felt that wildlife was accorded greater importance than he and his family: 'Animals are older than us because they are even more important because you find in the park they are of more value than we are' [B3]. He went on to suggest that they were, in contrast, treated like dogs.

> because they live in the middle of others and interact with them and enjoy the same rights as others. *Now they are fearless.*

This statement suggests that the speaker is creating distance from those former forest-dwellers ('they' rather than 'we'). She further suggests that it was the promise and practice of inclusion, of living among others, that has caused them to forget their former lifestyle, but not entirely ('almost'); and her judgement on this change is clear ('now they are fearless'). Apparently, inclusion offers much more than the former life in the forests. This is not to say that the disconnection from the forests is not recalled as painful for some: a woman from Rusizi district, which is home to part of the Nyungwe National Park, told us that she did not know much about the connection of Twa to the forest but that her father did not like talking about it [A2]. This could suggest that recalling the old way of life was painful. However, while a handful seemed to express a fondness for forest life, the greater majority rejected that past or appeared to be estranged from it.

Moreover, the majority of our respondents appreciated the forest not as Twa but as Rwandans; that is, not for any special relationship that this particular group has with the forest but for the benefit that it brings to all within society. For example, a man living in Karongi district talked at length about the community's relationship to nature. In addition to telling us that the Twa of the past harmed the environment 'because they did not know the value of environmental species for the country. They did not know that wildlife is a source of foreign currency which is needed for the country's development', he demonstrates that he has accepted the government's reframing of conservation as national development, as opposed to the individual or local benefit that nature protection might bring. He also shows that he sees himself as part of the broader collective: it is not about what he can take from the forest but about sharing in its bounty for all Rwandans. This approach was echoed by a woman from Rusizi district, who told our interviewer, 'In the early days, forests were also particularly important for the HMPs, we called them Batwa, as they used to collect foods from the forest. That is the reason why we very much value the forests' [A1]. While this appears to suggest a special connection to the forests based on identity, her reflections quickly turned to the value of nature because it brings in foreign tourist money. The special connection that might once have been is thus turned towards the government line on conservation, with A1 concluding with the observation that Batwa are extra motivated to protect the forests now because they are valuable to everyone.[33] Similarly, government messaging on the environment that pushes the idea of national pride in the beauty of the country is also being heard and accepted, as suggested earlier by G10 describing Rwanda's wildlife as bringing 'good rank' internationally. What we see here is the government's use of conservationism to reinforce government policy on national unity, which, in the case of the Twa, is falling on fertile ground.[34]

3.4 'All I Need Is Land . . .'

If our Twa respondents do not seek a return to the forest and show little connection to the forests beyond the government's messaging of utility and national pride, what is it that they do want, and what does that tell us about how they envisage their place in Rwandan society?

The simple answer to this question is land. Our interviewees understood access to agricultural land as key both to a good life and to their ability to, in their words, 'make progress'. Not all our interviewees were without land.[35] However, even where there was access to land, we were frequently told that it was insufficient to provide subsistence living; that is, food for the family and a little extra to sell for other goods. The lack of land or of enough land was commonly given as the basis for their poverty. As Musahara and Huggins noted in their overview of land policy in Rwanda, land scarcity is particularly associated with poverty because there are few non-agricultural activities available in rural Rwanda (2005: 274). This finding is confirmed by a more recent study, which noted – perhaps not unsurprisingly – that the size of the plot is also correlated with poverty (Potel et al. 2020).

[33] An alternative version of this sentiment was expressed by a woman in Karongi district [B4], who noted that, while Twa used to hunt for food in Nyungwe Forest, the forests are now for firewood, timber for construction, and to bring rain. She wants the government to protect the animals in the forest and prevent hunting so that the money that tourism generates will trickle down to her. She thus feels sufficiently part of society to be likely to benefit from national tourism revenues.

[34] The 'nationalisation' of the forests also appears to be accepted by other Rwandans; for example, in the work of the well-known author, poet, and disgraced politician, Edouard Bamporiki, in which he describes Rwanda as 'a nation clothed in forest' (sfi.usc.edu/news/2014/06/voice-darkness).

[35] For example, 'I have some land and I am very grateful for what I have because I live off it and not only me but also there are also friends who live by it. I cannot eat alone, I share with others. But there are those who have nowhere to live or no land to farm. I usually tell them that when they get some work and secure, say 100,000 Frws, they should buy some land. Having a plot is very important because I get proposals in millions to sell my plot but I do not want to do it' [CD1, elderly man in Nyamagabe district].

The desire for land was frequently expressed in a desperate and despairing tone. For example, a woman in Ngoma district told us emphatically:[36] 'all I need is land and nothing else! Because when you get land, you have got a good life . . . Because you cannot lack food when you have got land. When you are strong, because the energy I am employing in people's farms, I can also employ it in my own land' [I1]. This sentiment was echoed throughout the districts that we visited. Moreover, a clear connection was drawn between land and the ability to raise livestock.[37] Land was at the core of Twa hopes for the future and the lack of it was at the centre of their socio-economic marginalisation. While our data is insufficient to conclude that access to land is a 'fertile functioning' – that is, a functioning that supports and facilitates good functioning in other categories – it is sufficient to conclude that Twa themselves view their lack of land as a 'corrosive disadvantage' (Wolff and de-Shalit 2007: 121–122). That is, the lack of access to their own plot of land creates knock-on disadvantages in other areas of life and causes, in the terminology of Wolff and de-Shalit, disadvantage to 'cluster' or accumulate horizontally within a life, and vertically across generations.

Moreover, our interviewees not only connected their lack of land to poverty but also viewed it as a barrier to their inclusion in society. This was visible in how a number of interviewees contrasted their lack of land with the position of others. For example, a gentleman from Nyaruguru district responded to the question of what a good life meant to him as follows: 'A good healthy life is a life in which I have a plot to farm, where I am able to harvest like others' [D3]. Where the 'others' are unspecified here, another gentleman was clearer: 'We should get some land to cultivate, otherwise we will always remain behind others as HMPs' [D4]. Access to land is thus not only connected to individual progress or development in a material sense; it also represents inclusion.[38]

Part of the reason for Twa to turn to agriculture is the difficulty of accessing and making a living from the 'dirt' with which Twa are most commonly associated in Rwanda: clay. Our interviewees were split between those who viewed clay as an important part of Twa culture and those who wished to move away from pot-making as a barrier to their progress. One woman in Gakenke district told us: 'Of course we

[36] The interviewer has recorded the emphatic tone in their fieldwork notes.

[37] 'I cannot empower myself or live a good life without a plot of land to cultivate or without any livestock' [D3].

[38] This does not entail that land is the totality of how Twa view inclusion, as will be discussed in the next chapter.

cultivate, but pottery is what helps us much more to live as HMPs' [G9]. This sentiment was shared by about a third of those we spoke with, against two-thirds who rejected clay as the basis of their livelihood in favour of cultivating land.[39] The most commonly stated reason for wanting to move away from pot-making was the poor return on the effort involved: many interviewees mentioned the low price that pots now bring in. Moreover, nearly all our interviewees told us that accessing clay has become much harder, although these observations were particularly prevalent in the east of the country; for example, a woman in Ngoma district complained that their usual source of clay was no longer accessible because the land had been switched to rice production. As a result, 'It gives the impression that we are stealing the clay' [I3]. These complaints accord with reviews of land policy development in Rwanda, under which previously 'unexploited' land resources have been turned to agricultural use (Pottier 2006).[40] The low price and the difficulties in, and risks of, accessing clay mean that pottery was widely viewed as a last resort. G9, quoted above as stressing the cultural connection of Twa to clay, went on to say that 'doing pottery is the last option. If you have some other work and want to use a hoe, you go for that job instead of wasting time travelling to other provinces looking for clay.' As such, attitudes to clay can be summed up in the words of an elderly woman in Gatsibo district: 'Traditional culture is all about pottery, but the clay is nowadays far away and a pot is only 200 Frws' [E2]. The unviability of pot-making as a livelihood sees Twa turn to the cultivation of land as the only way of overcoming poverty and progressing.

However, the choice for land is not simply a question of economics but also speaks to the cultural importance of land cultivation and cattle ownership within Rwandan culture. An educated man from Gatsibo district with a waged job [F2] told us that a job is a means for earning enough money in order to buy land and then to acquire a cow. Land is the route to acquiring a certain level of membership in the community rather than simply being a means of subsistence. Moreover, land provides the ability to support livestock and, more importantly, cows. Cows are a very

[39] For example, the following statement by a man in Kayonza district: 'The most important job for HMPs in this area was that of pottery but it is no longer our top job. Only a few people still do pottery. We also strive to work land much like other people because we found that pots or pottery in general is a tiresome job with limited reward' [K5].

[40] While Law N° 8/2005 provides for compensation for confiscated or expropriated land, because the Twa did not own the swampland from which they collected clay, they received nothing when those lands were seized and reallocated (Adekola et al. 2021).

important part of traditional Rwandan culture and continue to play an important role in marking societal status but also in the formation and maintenance of social relationships (Bettez Gravel 1967; Mukasonga 2018).[41] The desire for land is a desire for social inclusion within society and denotes an acceptance of these social norms; that is, Twa understand their relationships to others through mainstream traditional Rwanda norms.

Access to land has long been a socially pressing issue in Rwanda (Mamdani 2001; Vansina 2004; Pottier 2006; and Manji 2006 for a broader African context); indeed, land access played an important part in the build-up to the genocide.[42] This pressure has been compounded in the post-genocide period by a growing population as a result of high birth rates and of large numbers of exiles returning to Rwanda. In their study on land policy, Musahara and Huggins concluded that Rwanda is experiencing land scarcity in 'absolute terms' (2005: 298). This is as a result of both demand-scarcity (the degradation of the quantity and quality of resources) and structural factors, notably the unequal distribution of resources, with land accumulating in the hands of a minority. At the same time, the centrality of land to the Rwandan way of life is clearly recognised within Rwanda's land governance structures (Doughty 2016: 133; Law N° 04/2005).

Rwanda's land policy – developed by the Rwandan government together with the Food and Agricultural Organization (FAO) and the World Bank, and laid down in the 2004 National Land Policy and in Organic Land Law N° 8/ 2005 – is centred around three key pillars: land consolidation, security of land tenure, and productivity increases. As a land-locked country with few subterranean natural resources, Rwanda is dependent upon its agricultural sector to drive economic growth. Law N° 8/ 2005, while asserting that all land in Rwanda belongs to the state (Article 3),[43] provides for long emphyteutic leases of between three and ninety-nine years (McAuslan 2013). It recognises the title of customary landowners, those who purchased their land or were granted it by the government (Article 5), and makes the registration of title to

[41] The state's Girinka programme, started in 2006, which provides a cow free of charge to each poor household, reflects the importance of cattle in Rwanda's social relations.

[42] Pottier writes that where land disputes were rife, such as in the densely populated northwest of the country, the killings targeted not only Tutsi but also Hutus involved in land disputes (2006: 510). Ingelaere goes further and suggests that the battle over power and land was 'grafted' onto the Hutu–Tutsi bipolarity (2009: 508).

[43] This, in turn, is based on Article 30 of the Rwandan Constitution.

land compulsory with the aim of securing clear and enforceable land rights to landholders. Security of title, in turn, was intended to lead to more effective land management, notably in relation to measures to address soil erosion; an increase in agricultural yields, by encouraging landholders to invest in soil quality measures, such as the use of fertilisers; and the creation of a private land market (Pottier 2006; Harrison 2016; Ansoms 2020).

However, security of title is crucially limited by the demand to increase productivity. To achieve effective agricultural use, the law includes clauses allowing for the confiscation of land where the landholder fails to exploit it 'effectively and efficiently' (Articles 62–65), and its reallocation to those citizens who have been deprived of their land (Article 87); that is, returnees. Moreover, Article 20 of the Organic Land Law prevents the registration of title for plots under one hectare, which constitutes roughly 80 per cent of all landholdings in Rwanda (Takeuchi and Marara 2022: 147).[44] Instead, landowners of smaller plots are required to consolidate their land as a means of transitioning the agricultural section away from subsistence farming to commercial mono-cropping. The law also recognised equal rights to land ownership, notably for women.[45] Taken altogether, Rwanda's land tenure reforms have been described as state of the art for Africa (Ayalew Ali et al. 2014), with Rwanda also being the first country in the African Union to complete land titling, with almost 8.5 million plots given formal title in less than three years (Lawry et al. 2023).[46]

The 2005 Land Law, together with the 2004 National Land Policy, were to drive a new Green Revolution in Rwanda, a process set in motion in 2003 by the Africa Union's approval of the Comprehensive Africa Agriculture Development Programme (CAADP), which aimed to

[44] The authors note that this provision has not been implemented, although it is not clear whether this is deliberate on the part of local authorities or is due to a lack of administrative capacity to inspect every field (Takeuchi and Marara 2022: 142; also Ansoms 2020).

[45] This followed on from Law N° 22/1999 regarding Matrimonial Regimes, Liberalities and Successions, which abolished gender discrimination in land inheritance practices for all legitimate children. However, the implementation of this widely welcomed law has been, at best, problematic – as detailed by Pottier (2006) and Lawry et al. (2023). In addition, Andersson Djurfeldt describes the pressure placed on women not to exercise their inheritance rights to land because of the issue of fragmentation, despite their clear legal rights and the strong political will to see them enforced (2020: 8).

[46] According to the World Bank's Doing Business indicators from 2020, Rwanda was ranked third globally in registering property (Takeuchi and Marara 2022: 149). For a history of land access in Rwanda, see Pottier (2002: chapter 6).

increase agricultural productivity by a minimum of 6 per cent (Milz 2011). Rwanda was the first country to sign a CAADP 'compact' in 2007 under the banner of the 'green revolution'. What this revolution entailed concretely was the launch of a Crop Intensification Programme, which comprised, in addition to monoculture, regional specialisation, a turn to commercial seeds, imported chemical fertilisers, pesticides, co-operativisation,[47] and greater use of agronomic science. These dramatic changes to farming practices drastically reduced the autonomy of land-holders to exercise their property rights by choosing how to use their land and subjected everyone's access to food to market exchange mechanisms. Ultimately, as Ansoms details, localised resistance to food price inflation and the capture of profits of rising productivity by traders rather than growers led the government to backtrack on the implementation of the green revolution (2020).[48] Indeed, already at the beginning of the century, Musahara and Huggins noted that Rwanda's strong central state structure was nonetheless not translating into an ability to change land use and ownership (2005: 285).

Despite these setbacks to the state's plans, its vision of a modern agricultural sector driving economic growth has meant that there is little place left for traditional smallholders (Ansoms 2009). The creation of a land market has replaced customary land governance practices, and land scarcity in the face of increasing population density is leading to ever greater fragmentation of land plot size, despite the state's best efforts to force land consolidation. This is putting huge pressure on subsistence farming. Access to land for Twa must thus be viewed against this backdrop of scarcity, fragmentation, commodification, individualisation of land rights, degradation and erosion of soil, and climate change (Dawson 2018; Andersson Djurfeldt 2020; Nyenyezi Bisoka et al. 2020).

The government's current land policy is laid down in the 2019 revised National Land Policy. This policy has as its guiding principle that all Rwandans must enjoy the same rights of access to land without discrimination (Ministry of Environment 2019: 16). However, the Policy contains only one line on inclusive access to land, as opposed to equal access, and it is the last line. It states: 'the land policy proposes the mainstreaming of gender, youth and people with disabilities for a more inclusive land

[47] This programme, and the wider changes to land governance, were complemented by forced villagisation, so that the scattered inhabitants of Rwanda's many hills were required to destroy their homes and move to areas designated by the government. See Pottier (2002, 2006).

[48] Harrison (2016) has a more favourable take on the state's efforts at land reform.

use and management' (Ministry of Environment 2019: 35). However, what both plans – 2004 and 2019 – share is an absence of reference to access to land for those traditionally excluded from land for cultivation, such as the Twa.[49] As noted earlier, where Article 87 of Law N° 8/2005 provides for the redistribution of land that is not being utilised, the beneficiaries are to be returnees, not the Twa. Instead, the underlying premise of the government's drive for economic growth via land reform is, as clearly stated in the first Land Policy, 'not everyone will own a registered plot' (Ministry of Lands and Forestry 2004).[50] Access to land is to be equal, but not inclusive.

In this context of dramatic land scarcity, it is difficult to see how Twa will be able to fulfil their desire for land without targeted government intervention to secure land ownership, which, under the current regime, seems unlikely to be forthcoming. This represents a serious pressure point in the state's reframing of global conservationism and indigeneity through national unity efforts and in the context of the land-titling programme. The success of the reframing depends upon the belief that the government will make good on its promise of progress for all; and progress is framed by our interviewees almost exclusively as access to land.

3.5 A Different Kind of Dirt

The answer of the UN Independent Expert on Minority Issues to her conclusion that forced removal from their 'ancestral lands' has caused Batwa in Rwanda to suffer 'irreversible damage' is that the government must 'develop initiatives to reconnect them with their ancestral habitats and cultural practices, recognize their rights to the natural resources of the forests, and develop programmes that value and preserve the traditional practices of their forest livelihoods' (UN 2011: para. 93). Our findings contradict this assertion and suggest instead that Twa in today's Rwanda have little special affinity with the forest or with the 'traditional practices' of which the UN Independent Expert writes. Even where one

[49] Dawson notes, on the basis of his study, that 'more than half of Batwa households depended only on agricultural labor, transporting materials or collecting grasses, as opposed to only a very small minority of returnees and less than a fifth of long-term residents' (2018: 8).

[50] See the observation by Pottier, reported by Purdeková, that 'the ideal development subject is "the resource poor farmer" who "voluntarily" gives up his/her land in return for "the promise" of a better future' (Purdeková 2015: 389).

accepts that Twa have been forcefully stripped of their traditional way of life, our data suggests that Rwandan Twa have no desire to return to traditional practices.[51]

Our findings chime with a 2014 study on local conceptions of environmental justice in the communities surrounding the Nyungwe National Park (Martin et al. 2014). This study found that rather than resentment at the enforced abandonment of locally significant cultural practices, there was instead strong support for park management policies that excluded human activity from the protected space. Part of this finding includes a lack of social acceptance of reliance on the forest, with very negative sentiments for those who continue to draw on forest resources, and respect within the wider community for those who give up hunting in the forest. Martin et al. proffer several explanations for this, from the likely equation of researchers with authority and the need to perform the official narrative, to the interaction of national narratives of progress and the 'modern' with global narratives about biodiversity, eco-systems, future generations, and environmental justice. They note, 'there is a very powerful political discourse linking the success of the Rwandan state to cultural unity, in which the traditional is fragmented and the modern is unified' (2014: 173). Moreover, their respondents also noted that hunter-gathering activities were not economically viable, and they saw material substitutes as either as good as or better than traditional practices. While the authors of this study do not include ethnic identifiers in their paper, it is likely that many of those living around the Nyungwe Park who once practised hunter-gathering would identify as Twa.

I would offer a similar explanation for our findings. The adoption and dissemination of the language and framing of global conservation by a strong central government is arguably visible in the responses that we received, whereby nature is perceived as a finite resource that must be managed. This would tally with observations in other parts of the world that the language of conservation is changing local people's understanding of their relationship to their surroundings (Pfeffer et al. 2001). In a study based in Mexico, Haenn found that local communities adopted the language and tools of the dominant power (in her case, the central state) in order to be heard: 'Once conservation was thrust upon them, the

[51] It is important to stress here that Rwandan Twa are choosing to exercise their agency in a particular way. The representation organisation of the Twa of Uganda is choosing a different path and does advocate for a return to the Bwindi Impenetrable Forest. See the United Organisation for Batwa Development in Uganda: https://uobdu.wordpress.com. Also Kokunda et al. (2023).

people of Calakmul adopted the language of environmental protection', but, she notes, 'this process included slippages as well as people's creative reworking of environmental issues' (2005: 28). The Campesinos resisted vigorously these attempts to redefine their identities and relationships with nature. Similarly, Sylvain's description in the Kalahari Desert of southern Africa of the confluence of ethnotourism with international indigenous identity politics as a means of carving out space for indigenous identity – a common feature of indigenous politics – finds no echo in Rwanda (2005). This non-use of ethno-entrepreneurialism is undoubtedly connected to a national context in which positioning oneself as a forest-dweller has few positive gains or is even possible (although Sylvain's distressing account suggests that the San do not obviously benefit from this positioning).

As with Martin et al., we found little to no resistance to government messaging about the environment, which takes an instrumentalist line. Haenn's central thesis is that conservation projects, although drawing heavily on global narratives, form part of state formation and the reinforcement of state power (2005). Drawing on Escobar, she notes that state-building 'requires the cultural construction of nature as a way to control specific territories and as a way to bind people within those territories to regimes of power' (2005: 29; Escobar 1996). Similarly, in Rwanda, the construction of nature through the message of conservation reinforces the one-Rwandenness of the national reconciliation policy; for example, in how the beauty of the parks gives dignity to all Rwandans.

The powerfulness of government messaging is one clear explanation for our respondents' responses. However, there is arguably something more going on here than simple acquiescence in the face of the inevitability of exclusion from a forest way of life and of a strong central state. The Twa appear to have accepted government messaging on the environment because it goes along with the offer of inclusion and development in a modern Rwanda. In his study of the ethnogenesis of the Twa in Rwanda, Taylor describes how the Twa connection to nature lay at the root of their social exclusion (2011). Their association with earth, mud, and forest entailed dirt and uncleanliness, which in turn entailed savagery, buffoonery, and gluttony, in a clear link between nature and moral inferiority. According to Taylor, the earth was perceived as impure and therefore occupations that made the least contact with it, such as cow herding, were the most esteemed: 'Pottery making, because it involved direct contact with the earth, was the least esteemed profession' (2004: 367). This positioning of Twa in the social hierarchy was reinforced by the colonial civilising mission, which continues to have effects to this day.[52] So even those Twa that left the forests and adopted a sedentary lifestyle remained despised for their daily working of clay. In this context, it can be no surprise that Twa repudiate a connection to nature and seek instead the social status of land cultivation and animal husbandry.

Yet, this negative connection to nature as being backward or uncivilised – the contrast with civilisation or culture – is far from uncommon as an attitude towards hunter-gatherers or other indigenous groups, and it does not appear to lead to an abandonment of traditional practices or claims to distinctness in such cases. Twa in Uganda, for whom negative stereotyping followed the same pattern, have not abandoned their claim to a forest-dweller's way of life. They apparently do not shrink away from the association with dirt (Ampumuza et al. 2020; Kokunda et al. 2023). Thus, while this negative cultural explanation is undoubtedly important in situating our data, it overlooks the positive offer that the Rwandan state is making. While some do regret the loss of pottery as a cultural practice, and the loss of Twa cultural practices more broadly (as detailed in Chapter 5), our interviewees saw only the cultivation of land as offering the possibility to improve their lives. As such, they are buying into the promise of progress. Whereas traditional land is a key part of articulating indigenous identity in global discourse, for the Twa in Rwanda, the desire for land cultivation is non-traditional and instead symbolises the aspiration to inclusion and belonging in the mainstream.

The desires expressed by our respondents should be seen as an exercise of agency at the site of jurisdictional encounter between global conservationism, development, and the Rwandan state's project of national unity. The combination of discourses of conservation and development in the particular context of Rwanda's prohibition of ethnic distinctiveness, including indigeneity, risked marginalising and excluding the Twa. However, the state's heavy investment – both legally and at policy level – in the discourse of national unity has seen the global discourses of conservation and development co-opted or refracted by this encounter into a site of inclusion for Twa. And it is a convincing offer: despite the

[52] This correlation in Rwandan culture between nature and inferiority was reinforced by the so-called civilising mission of colonialism: colonialism was to bring order and hygiene into dirty and backward worlds (McClintock 1995: 31–36). According to McClintock, this point is made clear in nineteenth-century adverts for soap and other cleaning products, which strongly connect cleanliness to empire. Moreover, Radkau notes that the real impact of colonialism on the environment and local ecology emerged long after, precisely through the changes that it wrought on structures of power and daily habits (2008: 153).

fact that many do not have access to land and are unlikely to gain access to it, at the time of our fieldwork, they still believed in the possibility of it. For inclusion policies to work, the Twa need to believe that this is a realistic prospect for them and that they enjoy a government that cares about them; that is, that the offer of equal inclusion is genuine and the state is capable of making good on it. The discourses of conservation and indigeneity that attempt to produce the Twa either as poachers or as dispossessed thus underrate the power of the Rwandan state to produce an alternative reality, and the agency of the Twa – their adaptative capacities – in choosing to believe in it.

4

Progress, Mind-Set, and *Agaciro*

The Twa as Development Subjects

The indigenous identity politics that arose in the 1970s in part took the form of an attempt to formulate an alternative concept of development in opposition to Western models. Distinct from opposition rooted in African socialist ideologies, what came to be labelled 'ethnodevelopment' presented a version of development that saw indigenous people portrayed not as an obstruction to progress but instead rooted in traditional indigenous culture (Stavenhagen 1986; Engle 2010; Hodgson 2011). The growing recognition that Western development models had a disproportionately negative impact on the ability of indigenous peoples to maintain their way of life was bolstered by the rise of the transnational environmental movement and the notion of sustainable development. This vision of a development model, in which indigenous activists embraced capitalist principles insofar as they were used to further the continued existence of indigenous culture, now constitutes a core element of the global discourse of indigeneity (Engle 2010).[1] Further, it is now also well established within the human rights mainstream.[2] Indigenous peoples form not only a separate category as human rights subjects but indigenous activists assert a uniqueness as development subjects as well. Development through and for culture sees the aim of development as the maintenance of a separate identity.[3] Despite the success of the indigenous movement in embedding

[1] Engle, however, builds a powerful argument that the attempt by indigenous rights activists to co-opt capitalist models into their own cultural agenda has become less of a critique of Western development models and instead is a supplement to a 'chastened neoliberalism' (2010: 184, citing Kennedy).

[2] See, for example, the Sami case before the Human Rights Committee, which recognised that Article 27 encompasses the possibility of the adaptation of traditional practices using modern technology: *Länsman et al.* v. *Finland*, Communication No. 511/1992, U.N. Doc. CCPR/C/52/D/511/1992 (1994).

[3] This reverses earlier approaches that saw a failure to recognise indigenous peoples as an ontological harm that inevitably led to socio-economic harms by perpetuating discrimination and marginalisation and instead makes the focus of indigenous rights existential.

this version of development within a global indigenous narrative, it finds no space in contemporary Rwanda.

While national unity has been the core principle and goal of the rebuilding process in the aftermath of the genocide, it was not the only tenet to come out of the Urugwiro Process. Instead, the goal of reconciliation and rebuilding was to be the creation of 'a united, democratic and prosperous country' (NURC 2016: 49–50). As such, 'Rwanda recognises that [the] reconciliation process cannot be possible without focusing on poverty reduction strategies' (NURC 2016: 89). Reconciliation requires socio-economic development that is both fast (NURC 2016: 88) and based on shared goals. Similarly, good governance was identified as essential to achieving national stability. Good governance was equated very early on with decentralisation (NURC 2016: 67; Chemouni 2016), based on the idea that unity and reconciliation could only be achieved by both changing the relationship between the governed and those in power and by overcoming a subculture of passive obedience that made people vulnerable to sectarian manipulation (NURC 2016: 69; McDoom 2021). Development and unity therefore go hand in hand here.

As everywhere, therefore, development in Rwanda is a political project (Uvin 1988; Skouteris 2010). The state's agenda is explicitly to de-politicise poverty, turning ethnic groups into development subjects. This chapter explores the construction of Twa as development subjects within the Rwandan context and asks how they position themselves within that landscape formed by the intersection of the global development discourse and Rwanda's unity and reconciliation agenda. The previous chapter suggested that the Twa's acceptance of global conservationism as refracted through the state's nationalisation agenda was premised on their belief in the state's promise of progress. This chapter interrogates that promise of progress and examines the ability of the Rwandan state to offer a believable vision of a prosperous and self-reliant Rwanda capable of legitimising its unity project.

4.1 Locating the Global Development Subject

4.1.1 The Global Development Imperative

While there are an infinite number of ways to characterise development (it is frequently referred to as a 'plastic' concept, e.g. Rist 2021), global development is perhaps best understood as a discourse composed of a set of practices that are diverse, and often contradictory, but that are underpinned by a belief that development can and must be achieved. It is this belief in the imperative of progress that creates a more or less coherent narrative (Rist 2021; Unger 2023). The belief that societies should attempt to build a better future – that they should 'progress' – is a very old one (Rist 2021). In her novel *The Barefoot Woman* (2018), Scholastique Mukasonga memorialises her 1960s childhood in rural Rwanda. Amongst the fear and hardship of displacement, and under the shadow of the violence to come, the novel shows Mukasonga's mother – a wise woman, knowledgeable of the traditional ways and determined to preserve them – as nonetheless equally enthralled by the idea of 'progress', where progress is Christian values and white bread, or the white person's things. This desire for progress, in Mukasonga's telling, was widely shared in the community. Thus intertwined with colonialism, development is nonetheless constructed as a forward-looking narrative of progress;[4] that is, it is the West's answer to colonialism and therefore is unconcerned with accountability for or with rectifying past injustices.

The modern development narrative is a particular type of the progress imperative and is formed by the belief in linear progress through economic growth and modernisation of both the economy and society (Sen 1999; Adelman and Paliwala 2021). Moreover, it is a belief that is seductive and therefore widely shared; as White has noted, 'the secret of development's power lies in its capacity to enlist others to its own agenda' (2002: 410). Similarly, Escobar has assigned the success of the development narrative to its ability to 'colonise reality' (1995: 5). As well as a belief, development is also a key – perhaps the key – global organising concept of the post-1945 era (e.g. Pahuja 2011), one that is even more comprehensive than the preceding organising dichotomies of civilised–barbarian or colonising–colonised (Kothari 2019b), precisely because the desire for progress is shared. Indeed, this social production of space, or geopolitical imagination, is one of the most easily recognisable features of the development discourse.

In addition to being a key part of the global imagination, development is also the core demand made of and by states of the Global South, to the extent that being 'developing' is one of the main global characteristics of such states and the standard against which their performance is measured (Harrington 2023), both by global organisations and by states

[4] The term development in Kinyarwanda is *iterambere* or *amajyambere* – quite literally 'the stuff of the future' (Purdeková 2015: 373, citing De Lame 1996: 285).

themselves. Development gave newly independent states an organising mission. The imperative to develop, the forms that development takes, and the monitoring that ensures compliance bind the diverse set of practices into a recognisable global discourse of development. These practices flow from a structural consensus among and within global institutions about what development means and who is to be subject to its disciplinary force.

This is not to suggest that global development is not fiercely contested – for example, by Nyuerere's African socialism (*ujamaa*) or the idea of development as self-reliance or, more recently, as solidarity, or, indeed, as a form of indigenous self-determination (Engle 2010; Kothari et al. 2019; Rist 2021). Yet, these alternative visions have not been able to resist the juggernaut of the globalised narrative and its imaginary of modernisation – at least, not yet (Rojas and Kindornay 2014). For this reason, the notion that the development myth has died a quiet death, as suggested, for example, by Wolfgang Sachs in his foreword in a recent development dictionary, seems misplaced (2019). To note that the shift in language to 'sustainable development' reveals that no state is fully developed removes neither the development imperative nor the particular form of geopolitical organisation that it institutionalises. Moreover, his suggestion that the promise of development is 'long gone', replaced with concerns about daily survival, is clearly not true everywhere and not, our data suggests, in Rwanda.

Yet, of course, global development has not remained static across the decades; and it is, as Oliver de Sardan has so brilliantly exposed, riddled with 'incoherence, uncertainty and contradictions, which are nonetheless structurally inscribed in development institutions' (2005: 5). Rather, as Foucault noted, the success of a discourse arguably lays in its ability to adapt, absorb, and redefine itself from within, so that it appears to be changing while the power relations that underpin it remain the same (1980). The global development narrative has undergone such seemingly fundamental definitional shifts: for example, from Rostowian modernisation, driven by state-led industrialisation and large infrastructure projects, to economic growth driven by market-led, private-sector growth, to human development, with its focus on capabilities and well-being (Rostow 1960; UNDP 1990; Rodrik 2007). Development now also includes a requirement to meet the standards of the rule of law and good governance, to foster inclusive growth and inclusion more broadly, to achieve gender equality, to provide strong public services, to ensure participation at all levels of society, and, above all, to eradicate poverty.

Yet, the de-growth movement notwithstanding, the commitment to economic growth as the main driver of development and the power dynamics that underpin the development imperative remain essentially unchanged.

4.1.2 *The Perpetual Becoming of Development Subjecthood*

The development subject produced by this global development narrative is the object of intervention in order to realise development and about whom development knowledge is produced. Development subjects have traditionally been located in what Escobar has called a 'space for "subject peoples"' (1995: 9), otherwise labelled as the Third World, or developing countries, or, more recently, the Global South. The characterisation of the development subject has shifted as the discourse itself has shifted: from barbarians and the uncivilised to rights-bearers and digital entrepreneurs. Yet, the emergence of development from the entwinement of colonialism and capitalism entails that the development subject is primarily an economic actor (e.g. de Soto 2000), although a necessarily insufficiently realised one. The development subject is at the same time discursively homogenised and starkly differentiated along development's key lines, whereby s/he/they are constructed in different ways according to the development practice at stake; for example, the development subject can be a worker, a woman, or a community member, depending upon what the intervention requires. As such, the development subject is also a racialised, localised, and gendered subject, being frequently redrawn within the same intervention. In a project focused on the access of small-scale farmers to national and regional markets, it is likely that the same participants will be variously conceived at different moments as entrepreneurs; by their gender; by their ethnicity or location; as rights-bearers; or in relation to the impact of their activities on conservation efforts or on climate change goals, for example as water users or as polluters or as holders of local knowledge or as community members – all depending on the boxes that need ticking to meet the funder's requirements according to the facet of development to be emphasised and the determination of who should benefit from it.

Underpinning these fluid characterisations, a core character of the development subject is of being insufficiently realised. As laid out in Escobar's insightful analysis, the development subject is marked by 'lack' (1995): a lack of material things (mass-produced goods), a lack of good institutions (e.g. (intellectual) property rights), a lack of knowledge (such as on basic hygiene), or a lack of the right attitude or mind-set or priorities (e.g. Banerjee and Duflo 2012). It is because the development subject – in whatever incarnation (i.e. regardless of whether they are defined as *Homo economicus* or as the bearer of the Right to Development) – is always insufficiently realised or mature that they are to be subjected to interventions by development institutions, experts, and actors in order to bring the development subject and their lives up to the standards of modernity as characterised by the metaphorical 'North'.

To be a development subject is thus to have one's existence formed as a perpetual becoming. This demands of the development subject that they are simultaneously passive and active. The passive development subject is the recipient of outside knowledge, materials goods, rights, and moral improvement, as noted earlier. In contrast, the active subject is development's participatory subject. The required participation of development's subjects has become, in recent decades, a core part of the development narrative (Kothari 2001; Tan 2011). This is participation not merely as economic actors but also participation in development projects as stakeholders and as citizens in holding government to account, notably local government via the drive towards decentralisation.[5] This focus on participation is visible, for example, in the re-drawing of neo-liberal development as inclusive development or inclusive growth (Gupta et al. 2015). Similarly, participation is the beating heart of the human rights-based approach to development (HRBA), which is less concerned with the realisation of socio-economic and cultural rights than with the right to talk about the realisation of these rights and the right to do so in an inclusive, or non-discriminatory, manner (Alston and Robinson 2005). The formulation of development as participation allows development's subjects to be portrayed as active agents of their own development – as economic actors, as community participants, as citizens – and at the same time as requiring external intervention to support them in making demands of their local and national authorities (e.g. IOB 2018). Likewise, the demand for evidence-based policy-making in development, such as randomised trials, suggests that a development subject is to remain a studied subject, whose opinion on their own lives – important in holding state authorities to account – is not to be fully trusted by development experts (cf. Rodrik 2007; Banjeree and Duflo 2012).

[5] The imperative of participation is, it seems, a broader trend and a feature of global governance narratives more broadly. See Urueña (2012) and his analysis of global constitutionalism and global administrative law.

So pervasive now is the conceptualisation of the development subject as a participant in their own development that Kothari has described participation as 'a new grand narrative of development' (2001: 139). Development as or through participation necessitates a reconsideration of accountability and legitimacy within the state. As Tan notes, the state is problematised, and it is the domestic political structures that need reforming in order to facilitate inclusion and accountability (2011: 172). It is a model that confines politics to the domestic order and limits it to questions of how to achieve development goals rather than a broader discussion over either the means or ends of living together (cf. Ferguson 1990). Thus, while participation is now considered to be essential to the development enterprise, its role is not to localise development knowledge production about the lives of development's subjects or to challenge how the global development narrative is conceptualised and enforced, but it is instead a tool, Tan suggests, by which global institutions hold the developmental state to account – including cementing alliances between government and private actors.[6] In this way, then, the development subject as participant is necessary to legitimise the global development enterprise and is co-opted into global mechanisms for disciplining developing states.

However, participation is not only a means by which to discipline developmental or Third World states. It is, I suggest, also a means of disciplining the development subject. Article 2 of the Declaration on the Right to Development, in constructing the development subject as 'the active participant and beneficiary of the right to development',[7] does so as a moral imperative: the human person, as the central subject of development, *should* be an active participant. Development is a duty as well as a right. As Kothari's work on the tyranny of participation suggests, the performance of participation exerts a form of social discipline on the individual subject via a need to conform to established social norms (2001). Indeed, the drive to progress – itself the daily form of participation in development – also exercises a form of discipline at the individual level. To be a development subject, then, is to be both pulled and pushed

[6] As Lander notes, based on her empirical work in Mongolia, there is a subtle but important distinction between participatory governance and governance participation, whereby the latter leads to 'nominal participation [of communities] in pre-determined governance structures' (2021: 209). Such manoeuvres are made in order to ensure that local communities do not derail nationally based development plans – in Lander's case study, involving the extractive industries.

[7] Declaration on the Right to Development; G.A. Res. 41/128 (1986).

towards development through the moral imperative to develop individually and the demand to participate in the collective legitimising of the project of development.

4.2 Development Rwandan Style: 'Positive Values Supporting Societal Transformation'

The post-genocide Rwandan state has, until recently, been lauded as a development 'darling' (Crusafelli and Redmond 2012; McNamee 2021).[8] This is because of its acceptance of the macro-economic orthodoxies of development, its commitment to 'good governance', and, above all, its success in achieving the indicators of development, such as poverty reduction. On all these markers, Rwanda is the best student in the least-developed-country (LDC) class.[9]

The state's development approach was enshrined in Vision 2020, a plan that emerged out of the Urugwiro Consultations throughout 1998 and 1999 – a country-wide series of consultations on how to rebuild the country after the devastation of war and genocide. This plan was developed into two Economic Development and Poverty Reduction Strategies, running 2003–2012 and 2013–2018, respectively, which were implemented nationwide (EDPRS 1 and 2). The Vision 2020 strategy was updated to 'Vision 2050' in 2015, to be implemented via a National Strategy for Transformation (NST 1) and a new EDPRS, which was issued in 2022. Together, these documents are the key statements on the country's development plans. They lay out a vision of development based on modernisation theory that will achieve high economic growth, requiring 12 per cent in the period 2018–2035 and 10 per cent between 2035 and 2050, and ensure progress to middle-income status.[10] This growth is to be driven by private investment, international capital

[8] The quote in this section's heading is from Vision 2050 (MINECOFIN 2015: 14).

[9] For example, according to the 2024 World Intellectual Property Report (WIPO) innovation index, Rwanda ranks number 1 for innovation in the category of lower-income economies: www.wipo.int/web-publications/global-innovation-index-2024/en/gii-2024-at-a-glance.html.

[10] These ambitious targets, set before the COVID pandemic, obviously have not been met. The World Bank recorded an annual growth rate of just under 8 per cent for Rwanda in 2023: World Bank Press Release, 'Rwanda's Economic Performance Strengthened in 2023 Despite Continued Challenges', 28 February 2024: www.worldbank.org/en/news/press-release/2024/02/28/rwanda, with predictions of 7 per cent growth in 2024–2026. However, the first half of 2024 saw growth of 9.7 per cent (www.worldbank.org/en/country/rwanda).

inflows, and attracting green economy financing, as well as by expanding the Agaciro sovereign fund (Ministry of Finance 2013: xvi). In its first Poverty Reduction Strategy Paper (PRSP), the government described the ambition to 'leapfrog the stage of industrialisation and transform her [Rwanda's] subsistence economy into a service-sector driven, high value-added information and knowledge-based economy that can compete on the global market' (MINECOFIN 2002, quoted in Ansoms 2011: 245). The emphasis here is thus on market-led growth of a diversified, future-proofed economy, as suggested by sentences such as: 'The education system will be market-led to match Rwandans' skills with the modern industries and services that drive the economy' (Vision 2050, MINECOFIN 2015: 16). Indeed, President Kagame has stated clearly that the private sector is expected to 'take the driving seat' on both economic growth and poverty reduction (Ministry of Finance 2013: viii).[11]

While the vision of development is to be realised by private sector-led economic growth, the focus of Rwanda's development strategy is reducing poverty and a better quality of life for all Rwandans. Vision 2050 takes this goal further and speaks of the elimination of poverty altogether, echoing the first goal of the Sustainable Development Goals, SDG 1 (Vision 2050, MINECOFIN 2015: 7), and commits to ensuring that no-one is left behind. To achieve this, and as part of its development strategy, Vision 2020 created a range of social welfare programmes, most notably the Vision 2020 Umurenge Programme (VUP), which provides direct monthly financial support to households in which no member is able to work (VUP-DS), and includes a Public Works component (VUP-PW), providing short-term employment on community infrastructure projects or other local public works. Together, these schemes aim to provide a safety net to the poorest households. The Livelihood Enhancement programme offers financial services and skills training.

These social welfare programmes target the poorest for priority assistance via the categorisation of the population into *ubudehe* categories. *Ubudehe* categorisation is based on self-assessment, checked by local

[11] Despite this professed commitment to economic development being led by the private sector, the creation of a private land market is tightly controlled by the state. Indeed, the enfolding of development into the unity and reconciliation agenda entails that the envisaged transformation of the economy and of society is ultimately to be led by the state to achieve state-set goals (EDPRS 2013: viii). For this reason, Ansoms sees 'a profound mismatch between the Rwandan elite's ambitions and the rural realities on the ground' (2011: 248).

authorities, and is reviewed every three years (Havugimana 2023).[12] The UNDP report suggests that although the VUP programme has been successful in reaching the poorest households (e.g. the most recent data from 2016/2017 shows that Direct Support reached 36.2 per cent of the 40 per cent of the population categorised as most in need), where it has not achieved its goals is in 'graduating' households upwards; the 2018 Joint Sector Report found that only 17.4 per cent of households categorised in *Ubudehe 1* had moved out of that category since the programme began. However, there is evidence that, while beneficiaries have not progressed to category 2, the programme has had a significant impact in assisting people in moving away from a life of extreme precarity, for example begging, day-labouring, or roadside selling (UNDP 2020: 66).

In addition to the VUP, the implementation of Vision 2020 led to the creation of a community-based health insurance (CBHI), known as Mutuelle de santé, which seeks to provide universal access to healthcare at the local community level. Under the scheme, the state sets different premiums and fees according to the *umbudehe* categories, so that wealth is redistributed via cross-subsidisation. The state pays all premiums and fees for citizens in category 1 (now D and E). According to the UNDP, CBHI has a significant impact on household well-being, including nutritional intake and labour productivity; indeed, the UNDP found that it has a 'catalytical impact on standards of living' (2020: 71).[13]

While the clear focus of these programmes is poverty reduction, they also aim at reducing inequality and fostering feelings of inclusiveness (Goodwin 2022). Further elements of the social welfare programmes created under Vision 2020 include the now famous *umuganda* initiative, a community-based programme that requires everyone in the community to work together one day per month to achieve public goals. While most of the work is directed towards public infrastructure, such as maintaining roads and bridges, *umuganda* action also constructs backyard kitchen gardens for poorer households and improves or builds houses for the poorest members of the community (UNDP 2020). In

[12] See, however, Gaynor (2014), who suggests that, because the poorest two categories do not pay local tax, the local authorities were incentivised to 'correct' self-assessment to place most people in category 3. Our interviewees frequently complained of being incorrectly categorised.

[13] While it is undoubtedly having a big impact on those who benefit from it, the UNDP also noted that slightly less than 70 per cent of the poorest 40 per cent of the population were included in its coverage. There is thus some way to go in ensuring that all of Rwanda's poorest have access to free healthcare (UNDP 2020: 81).

addition, the Girinka programme, started in 2006, which builds on the deep cultural significance of the cow as a symbol of status, aims to provide a cow free of charge to each poor household, the offspring of which are then given to the next poor household on the list. The aim is to reduce poverty by providing an additional source of rich nutrition, notably for children, as well as fertiliser for crop production, and by creating an extra source of income through selling what is not consumed or used within the household (Nilsson et al. 2019). The gift of the first calf to another household also aims to increase community cohesion. At the national level, reducing the inequality gap is one of the key targets of the development strategy, improving the Gini co-efficient from the current level of 0.43 to 0.3 by 2050 (Vision 2050, MINECOFIN 2015: 17).[14]

Rwanda's commitment to poverty reduction via economic growth is not the only way in which the government speaks the twenty-first-century language of development. Another outcome of the Urugwiro Process was the commitment to good governance. Good governance in the Rwanda context – focused on the level of the district – has taken the form of a thorough-going decentralisation policy, the use of annual performance contracts (or *imihigo*), and a strong commitment to root out corruption, with the aim of achieving citizen-centred government (Gaynor 2014; MINECOFIN 2015; Chemouni 2016). The aim is to foster greater accountability both downward, through citizen participation, and upward to the central level, through the *imihigo* contracts (Chemouni 2016; Goodwin 2022). The focus of participation is on weekly meetings at the village level (*inteko z'abaturage*). These meetings serve as the main forum through which citizens receive information and through which they participate in government programmes (MINALOC 2018b: 58). This is also the forum in which villagers, in theory, take collective decisions about who is to benefit from resource delivery programmes, such as Girinka, and where they participate in national unity initiatives such as Itorero and Ndi Umunyarwanda (NURC 2007). Weekly citizen meetings are also held at the district level, in which citizens can make requests or bring complaints (MINALOC 2018b). Participation in the meetings at village level is required, although non-attendance does not appear to be punished and the extent to

14 The World Bank, however, notes that inequality has been rising because of the benefits of economic transformation, which are accruing mostly to the educated: www.worldbank.org/en/country/rwanda/overview. See also de Schutter (2025).

which these meetings are genuinely open to citizen input is disputed (Gaynor 2014).

The focus on good governance in Rwanda as target-based and data-driven is another way in which Rwanda is a poster child for development.[15] Rwanda strives to become a 'data-driven economy' (Vision 2050, MINECOFIN 2015: 10), with clear targets for all aspects of development. Huge amounts of data are collected across every area and level of government in order to monitor the success of welfare programmes, as well as the performance of individual administrators. The 2022 Local Administrative Entities Development Agency's (LODA's) report on the VUP programme, for example, is full of statistics and comparative rankings. A field example is the e-Girinka project, which electronically monitors every cow issued under the Girinka programme as well as their beneficiaries (LODA 2022).[16] Management language of target monitoring pervades Rwanda's development documents, such as the traffic light scheme to monitor progress in the 2022 EDPRS. Similarly, as discussed in Chapter 3, Rwanda has bought into the entwinning of development with environmentalism through the language of sustainable development, and its development plans include a transition to a green economy (e.g. Vision 2050, MINECOFIN 2015: 11).

In sum, Rwanda, in its own words, 'aspires to be a modern, innovative, equitable, accountable society' (Vision 2050, MINECOFIN 2015: 16). While this requires adherence to the macro-economic fundamentals, nothing short of a 'societal transformation' is required. Development is to be achieved in Rwanda through 'positive values' and 'home-grown solutions' rooted in Rwandan culture and through a national self-determination based on solidarity and *agaciro* (Vision 2050, MINECOFIN 2015: 14).[17] These values – reinforced by the Itorere programme designed to forge model

[15] See the World Bank's 2021 World Development Report, 'Data for Better Lives', for an insight into the belief in data as an unmissable part of the good governance agenda; wdr2021.worldbank.org; more recently, see the 2024 UN Pact for the Future's commitment to a data-driven future: www.un.org/sites/un2.un.org/files/sotf-pact_for_the_future_adopted.pdf.

[16] See www.ekaye.gisagara.gov.rw/girinka/about.php for an explanation of the system in Gisagara district.

[17] In a 2015 speech, Kagame repeated the goal of Rwanda's development vision: 'When the government mobilizes resources and shares them with its citizens ... if they have good ideas and a positive mindset, they do not wish to be on government's assistance. Instead, they help the government to lift others who are still lagging behind ... Technology and technical skills are universally known to be the key to development. We should not be queuing holding a basket waiting for people to drop aid into it. That's not how we will achieve self-reliance' (cited by Eramian 2017: 114).

citizens[18] – are to be at the heart of Rwanda's economic and social development and constitute the 'fundamental principles' of Rwanda's participation in an uncertain global economy.[19] Development is therefore not merely economic but requires social development at the state and community level, as well as the personal development of all its citizens. As clearly stated in an earlier development strategy, Rwandan development 'is about each Rwandan playing his or her part in the development of the country' (Ministry of Finance 2013: xiv). The Rwandan development subject is thus not a passive recipient of welfare but is expected to be an active contributor to their own improvement. In this way, development not only requires of individual citizens that they progress materially and immaterially – that is, through education, training, and skills – but also morally.

Development in Rwanda demands a positive mind-set – a word that came up repeatedly throughout our fieldwork and in conversations with NGOs, local officials, and government ministers. Mind-set is at the core of Rwanda's development plans. Eramian, in her insightful ethnographic study of post-genocide personhood in Rwanda, has characterised this focus on the mind-set of individuals as 'the positive thinking imperative' (2017: 112). By way of illustration of this phenomenon, she cites a speech by Kagame in February 2009 in which he encouraged Rwandans to smile more, particularly at foreign tourists. The obligations to 'work hard', develop the right mentality, and contribute to the 'New Rwanda' find a place in the Vision 2050 strategy, which repeatedly claims that Rwanda is setting itself a 'uniquely high level of ambition', and that, to achieve this, an 'unconventional mind-set' will be required (Purdeková 2012; Vision 2050, MINECOFIN 2015: 16; Eramian 2017).

The flipside of conditioning material progress on moral improvement is that poverty in Rwanda is linked to ignorance. The 2007 National Policy on Unity and Reconciliation emphasises the need to combat

18 According to Sundberg, in her ethnographic study of the Itorere programme, 'model citizens . . . are active, entrepreneurial individuals who earn their right to public services by taking care of their own welfare and by turning to the market rather than the state in search of livelihoods' (2016: 29). Graduates from the programme sign contracts that commit the individual to participate in unpaid services to the community and are designed to make citizens more results-orientated and committed to self-development. This has led to a 'fever' of development everywhere in Rwanda (Purdeková 2015: 371).

19 The vision of self-reliance articulated here is not the same as that espoused by Nyerere in the Arusha Declaration (Mazrui 1973). Whereas Nyerere's ideas aimed to create independence from the global order, Kagame's idea of self-reliance is easily nested within it. There are, though, some similarities in the methods to achieve self-reliance, such as forced villagisation, emphasis on self-reliance at village level, etc. (Ansoms 2009).

poverty and ignorance in order to achieve unity (NURC 2007: 12). This is further specified in the following way:

> (1) sensitizing parents on fighting poverty and ignorance by sending their children to school; (2) sensitizing Rwandans to join profit-making associations and cooperatives; (3) impressing upon Rwandans on promoting the culture of creating jobs rather than always looking for employment; (4) sensitizing the private sector and Rwandans in general to invest in rural areas; and (5) sensitizing the Rwandan Diaspora to actively participate in economic development of their country.

The replacement of the contemporary global development language of behavioural economics (e.g. incentives (see Banerjee and Duflo 2012)) with a moral language of 'sensitizing' is noteworthy. This emphasis on individual moral improvement is a refraction of good governance within global development discourse, shifting the focus from the creation of institutions that stimulate economic growth to individual responsibility. Here, we see development in Rwanda being folded into the overarching unity and reconciliation agenda (NURC 2016).

The positive thinking imperative is accompanied by what Ansoms has called an 'upgrading of rural life', whereby the government attempts to impose modernity by decree by prohibiting the outward appearance of poverty (2011: 247). Twizeyimana describes the requirement to wear shoes, be clean, use mosquito nets, adhere to the health insurance guidelines, wear school uniforms, construct toilets, make compost pits, and dry dishes on tables (instead of on the grass) (2006, cited by Ansoms 2011); and Ingelaere details the system of fines levied on Rwanda's poor for failing to follow the rules (2011: 73). Similarly, fashioning Kigali into a modern city has demanded that street vendors disappear.[20] The development subject is thus expected not only to work hard to achieve progress but also to perform development, both internally – by changing one's mind-set – and externally – by smiling more and using tables. The development narrative, as re-interpreted and implemented by the Rwandan state, is thus a thorough-going process of social reprogramming from each individual Rwandan outwards. Moreover, it is an explicitly future-orientated one (Benda 2018). The focus on the future is not surprising given the demographic changes in Rwanda since 1994; a more than doubling of the population to just

[20] The ban on street vendors is enforced by administrative regulation at district level. See panorama.rw/street-vendors-rights-must-be-realized-_research.

under 14 million has meant that 70 per cent of the population are now under thirty years of age.[21] However, it is also an essential element of re-imagining, of progress, which is itself future-orientated.

4.3 'All I Need Is a Way to Start . . .'

It is clear from our data that the Twa in our study understand the development imperative and what is required of them. Moreover, they are willing to perform their part as development actors. As a woman from Rusizi district told us: 'We can achieve development. It is not like we do not long for it' [A1]. Yet before elaborating on what being a development actor meant for our interviewees, it is important to be clear about the precarity of their existence revealed in their stories: the reliance on petty labour; on being paid in potatoes or firewood; on receiving goats that die or heifers that do not bear calves; on shelters that wash away in heavy rain. There is misery and desperation in these stories. As one individual told us, 'poverty may drive you mad' [H1].

However, there was also determination and a belief for many in the possibility of a better life. In talking about their lives, Twa had clearly bought into the idea of material progress. Moreover, our respondents viewed themselves as responsible for improving their own lot through hard work. The means of doing this was primarily through purchasing livestock or by beginning a small business. The desires of our interviewees, their hopes for themselves and their families, are well expressed by a woman from Rusizi district in response to the question of how she could empower herself:

> [Through *ubudehe*] I can start a small business that would help me to buy food, clothes and address other basic needs. It all depends on what business you are in; for instance, if you invest around 20,000 Frws, you may be able to provide for basic needs such as food. I would get that from *ubudehe*, for instance. I can work for thirty days and get paid that amount of money. My contribution would be to work, I can carry things to the market, things like aubergines or cabbages. If I get that assignment regularly and earn, say, 1,000 Frws (this is possible if the market is far), I can make savings; for that to happen though, I would need to work for a few days per week, at least three days where I would earn 3,000 Frws, or 2,500 Frws or even 7,000 Frws. Unfortunately, you never get that sum of money at once. I can save gradually.

[21] World Bank dataset: data.worldbank.org/country/rwanda.

> Then, I can start a business with small amounts and then build up progressively. In that way, I can access property but that is still aspirational. Even if I was to save a few thousand, I still will need to take some of the money to buy food. I would only hope that God will provide for other ways to earn some money, then I would reach 5,000 Frws. Then I would improve my business and get involved in something else more profitable . . . like bananas, then cooking bananas, etc. I could increase my earnings and savings the more I persevere and change the investment from lower to higher. I can improve my life in that way. [B2]

Similarly, a young man in Rutsiro district talked of his desire for a loan: 'I would take just around 200,000 Frws and try to pay it back within one year and I would work hard to move forward' [K9]. Such determination was also displayed by a middle-aged man in Karongi district, who told us: 'I have many projects in my head. I am simply not sure if I will manage to implement them in my lifetime' [A3]. When asked about his projects, he explained,

> The reason why I like to set a goal is because I started from very humble beginnings as a keeper of a chicken belonging to someone else. From that chicken produce, we bought a young goat and that goat is what eventually made 50,000 Frws. Of course, it took some time because the goat was very small when we got it. But I made a written goal of ensuring that the chicken would end up providing me a cow . . . I have also made plans to get money and buy two small pigs, because I believe that if I am fortunate in my plans, I can empower myself in a short while without having to steal anything.

As this quote suggests, the goal of most of our interviewees was self-reliance. This was emphasised by a man from Nyabihu district, who stated baldly, 'We should be responsible for solutions to our problems' [K5].

The dominant vision of development expressed by our interviewees was thus that of the development actor as entrepreneur. The main focus of younger and middle-aged Twa was being able to save money, not as security against risk but for investment in an entrepreneurial project. Older Twa understood progress as an imperative but were more likely to sketch a vision of development as a better domestic life, which consisted in small improvements to their lives culminating in buying land. An elderly man in Bugesera district explained the progress he wanted or what empowerment in his life meant to him:

> One of the good things I want to do is to improve this house so that it can be in a far better shape. I want to renovate it so that it can be a good place

> to welcome other people. There are many other things I would want to achieve. Empowerment includes having the pig I mentioned or obtaining the cow I requested or I intend to buy, God willing. [G1]

His vision of progress is modest and includes a social element that is not purely concerned with material betterment.

While material progress is the dominant vision of development expressed, it is not the only development messaging that has taken root. A man from Nyaruguru district, in the south of the country, explained:

> We discuss things like the importance of education for our children, hygiene for our children, but also for ladies. We sensitise people to abandon the habit of our ancestors of frequently using insulting words. We instil in people the sense of avoiding to harm others; of lending money to one another for various pressing needs. We discuss issues like children dropping out of school. The idea is to acknowledge every person's dignity. [C2]

This makes clear that our interviewees understand progress as more than material progress, or even social progress, but, crucially, also moral progress. Nearly all our interviewees spoke of the importance, as expressed by a widow from Rutsiro district, of 'striving for dignity' [K9]. Progress was intimately connected in our conversations with mind-set, a term repeatedly used – as, for example, by a woman from Kicukiro district: 'It [mind-set] is important in my striving to make progress and improve my living conditions' [J6]. This sense of moral progress also takes the form of gender equality, a key part of the global development narrative and one well embedded in Rwanda governance (Goodwin 2023). For example, a man from Karongi district talked about the plans that he and his wife make together: 'Without some gender balance in a household, there cannot be any progress' [A3].

Interviewees were keen to demonstrate that they had the right mind-set and that they were capable of being empowered, which was connected for them with being a good person as well as a good member of the community. K8, a middle-aged man from Nyarungenge district, spoke of others being behind him in mind-set. D3 told us: 'even if I never went to school . . . I have a good reputation as a hard-working person; that allows me to be self-confident'. Other interviewees noted that having livestock and managing them well gives them dignity, which in turn gives them status in the community, expressed as being able to go to and speak at village meetings. Progress is thus also behaving in the way that other Rwandans do, both in terms of livelihood – not day-labouring but self-employment – and in the sense of working hard and managing one's affairs well, such as caring appropriately for livestock. A woman in Gatsibo district, eastern province, said of herself: 'We work the land to empower ourselves. . . . owning a cow has empowered me and I am more confident in life, able to clean up and be in gatherings with others' [F1]. In this way, Twa see progress as conveying moral membership in society, which is achieved by complying with the dominant norms, and is both connected to and independent of material progress.

However, while the Twa clearly buy into the personal responsibility inherent in *agaciro*, they are not blind to the reality of their own situation. This is well captured by a woman from Rusizi district, who told us: 'I can only change my living conditions if I am able to empower myself. We have the physical ability to work hard in empowering ourselves but lack the necessary resources. . . . The core problem is that we have nothing to start with empowering ourselves. We have limited means to do anything for ourselves' [A2]. This sentiment was repeatedly put to us by our interviewees, not only in relation to access to financial resources but also in terms of access to training or employment. One man told us that he had been trained as a builder but was struggling to get the necessary work experience to be able to start his own business: 'The assistance I need is in finding a job. . . . All I need is a way to start. Then I can build columns or roofs of modern houses among other things. . . . In order to properly master a profession, you need practice. If I was to work with knowledgeable people, I would improve' [F2]. His goal, he stated, was to work hard, save, and buy a plot of land. But this is only possible with external assistance.

A woman in Nyaruguru district, while nonetheless repeating her belief in empowerment and in her ability to empower herself, demonstrated a clear-eyed view of her position. She told us, 'I do all I can through my work to empower myself and improve the living conditions of my family' but stated that hard work and mind-set alone were not enough. Asked if she could explain why, she stated,

> I can give you one example relating to the cultivation of potatoes. . . . We have a big plot of land, nearly one hectare. But we do not know when we will get the seeds. Looking at what they cost, we cannot get them by ourselves. We are therefore waiting for assistance from people at the Sector because we cannot afford the seeds and the fertiliser. [D1]

Similarly, a young man from Nyamagabe district told us:

> We need money. With money, we can even rent land. We would then use the harvest to further invest in renting other plots. But we are not there yet. We still depend on working for others. As my mother keeps telling me, we make other people rich by working for them and remain behind. What she says is accurate! Our energy is spent on working for others with little reward! [C2]

Another man forcefully told us: 'You cannot be responsible for your own life while you use your labour for others, you cannot attain a good life' [J2].

Thus, although our interviewees are keen to show that they are good development subjects, committed to progressing materially and morally, they do not accept that it is all on them. While they accept personal responsibility to have the right mind-set and to work hard, they know that they cannot progress without external assistance to get out of the poverty trap. Empowerment and progress are not things that can be willed into existence. Or as the gentleman from Nyamagabe district put it: 'What we need now is money.[22] HMPs are able to think for themselves. If we get money, we can be societal models' [C2].

In addition to refusing to accept that mind-set alone is sufficient to improve their lives, the Twa are far from being the passive development subject of some critical development accounts or the meekly compliant yet resisting subject of those focused on resistance. Indeed, they are active complainers. We were repeatedly told across interviews of unfairness in the distribution of material goods.[23] These complaints concerned the failure to receive benefits that others had enjoyed and were not limited to location. For example, 'The problem that we have is that other HMPs are provided with health insurance but that is not the case here in Kayonza district' [K5].

Despite often living in isolated rural areas, our interviewees were nonetheless well informed about what was happening in other places. A woman in Rusizi district, for example, was apparently in possession of the necessary information in order to be able to make the following complaint: 'Other

[22] He amended this later in the interview to land and money. While I have selected quotes here that highlight the entrepreneurial ethos that we encountered, nearly all interviewees also spoke about the importance of land as providing security and often the means to begin a business, i.e. the food to be sold at market.

[23] For detailed consideration of the unfairness alleged by our interviewees from the perspective of Rwanda's decentralisation plans and the space created for participation in development planning, see Goodwin (2022).

people were provided with housing. In Ruharambuga, people were given new shelters; in Nyakabuye, the same. Even closer to here, in Nyamagana, in Nyakarenzo, people benefited. But here in Gihundwe, nothing was done, especially in this village of ours of Kanombe' [B2]. While we were not able to verify this statement in its entirety, interviewees in Nyakarenzo did confirm that they had been given a plot of land and a house that included a kitchen and toilet, as well as forty-five iron sheets for the roof. This suggests not only that information about the distribution of public resources travels but also that our interviewees were generally well informed about the various government programmes. They knew what assistance such programmes offered and who had benefited from them in their local community, as well as further afield. Moreover, they were willing to complain loudly when they were not the ones benefiting.[24]

The complaints of unfavourable treatment were centred on the local authorities and continuing top-down practices of authority. Constituents are rarely spoken to as equals, something that we witnessed in interviews with local leaders at all levels in how they spoke of Twa but also in how they spoke to the Twa participants during our group feedback sessions.[25] As an elderly lady in Rwamagana district told us, 'you call a local leader, instead of providing you with a solution, he or she despises you as if he didn't understand you' [G6]. Similar complaints about the attitude of local officials have been recorded in other ethnographic studies – for example, Sundberg's work on a neighbourhood in Kigali (2016). However, the grievances are made so vehemently here because they concern not merely the distribution of material goods, or a patronising attitude, but are interpreted by our interviewees as a denial of equal care, and thus a broader denial of inclusion in the modern Rwanda.

This connection between progress and inclusion-as-equal-care was beautifully articulated by one interviewee in response to a comment by

[24] The complaints targeting local leaders were not simply related to the distribution of goods but also concerned a lack of voice and an unwillingness of the local authorities to engage with their ideas about the allocation of necessarily limited resources, i.e. it was not only about hand-outs but also about the ability to shape how development was implemented in their community. For example, a man from Nyarungenge district commented: 'I suggested that before giving us cows they should provide us grazing space. We have asked for those bushes around us to keep cows grazing but they refused. Instead of again wasting money by giving us cows that are beyond what we can manage, maybe they can exchange that cow into money and give us money to start some businesses' [K8].

[25] In an in-depth interview, one district leader did, however, recognise unprompted the problems that a lack of access to land causes HMPs, which he acknowledged was not their fault.

the interviewer that President Kagame had stated that no-one can give you your dignity but that you give it to yourself. This man in Rusizi district stated:

> That is right. But to give yourself dignity, you need to start somewhere. Your living conditions determine how able you are to claim your dignity. Poverty prevents you from even appearing where others are. And being able to meet others without any feelings of shame is what makes you claim back your dignity. When you live in similar conditions as others, you are liberated from your own doubts and are able to claim your dignity. If you feel like you are assisted just like someone else is assisted, you cannot hesitate to go where others are. But that is not possible when you do not have the same benefits as others, when you are not empowered like others, and your child cannot go to school, how can you improve your life? How can you have dignity in that case? If we were assisted like other Rwandans are assisted, we can also feel truly Rwanda, I would not care whether I am called Mutwa or HMP. But calling me now a HMP does not change anything as long as I am still HMP, as is the case. I have not seen any positive change yet. We live in houses which were built but not finished while others were completed. Others were provided doors and windows but not us HMPs. We were only provided limited assistance, not like others. Reclaiming your own dignity is linked to feeling treated equally. [B1]

While most of our interviewees did not attribute the unfairness they felt to being Twa, a significant minority, like B1, did. A woman that we spoke to in Nyaruguru district told us: 'Local leaders here do not take our problems seriously. They dismiss them as Batwa problems. They do not welcome us the same way they welcome non-Batwa. They do not render justice to us as they do to others' [D1]. This belief among some that they are being denied access to material resources, as well as to inclusion in programmes such as Girinka, VUP, and medical insurance, because they are Twa undermines the state's efforts to de-politicise development and, indeed, the reconciliation and unity agenda more generally.[26]

4.4 Progress as Imperative and Promise

4.4.1 Rwanda's Development Narrative

Discourses are formed by discursive structures, such as metaphors, images, and other discursive tools (Foucault 1980), and a positive mind-set is the

[26] Unfair treatment in their perception: we regularly put such claims to local leaders for their response and the claims were denied. We were not able, however, to investigate the truth of the claims by examining the actual distribution of resources or how decisions are taken.

central structure of the Rwandan development narrative. Progress is therefore not merely about material well-being but also about taking responsibility for oneself, of living *agaciro*, where dignity comes from within. In this way, progress becomes a moral imperative and a defining notion of what it is to be a (good) Rwandan.

Eramian finds a similar desire for progress aligned with self-reliance, self-sufficiency, and personal responsibility in her research on the middle classes in Butare. She suggests that the 'enterprise ethos' among the subjects of her research is a means of seeking inclusion in the modern global order. By aspiring to work for oneself and by expressing it in the language of entrepreneurial culture, Rwandans are aligning themselves with the 'language of power' that is 'valued in the global economic order' (2017: 108) – that is, they are aligning themselves with or laying claim to a particular form of development subjecthood. Yet while Eramian writes that the notion of the 'self-made man' is imported from Anglo-Saxon entrepreneurial thinking, at the same time she highlights how it finds traction within Rwanda because it connects with an important distinction in Rwandan culture (2017: 100). While diverse types of patronage have been key to social organisation in Rwanda (C. Newbury 1988a), a key criterion of the production of status in Rwanda has been and is the distinction between working for yourself and working for others (Sommers 2012). To be 'progressed' is to work for oneself, even in the simplest of ways, such as being an independent seller of vegetables at the market. Eramian suggests that this distinction draws on traditional patron–client relationships, or, at least, it is understood in the same way by her interview subjects, who compare being a domestic servant to servitude or being treated like a 'peasant' (2017: 104).

The individual subject suggested by this form of desire for progress also draws on a longstanding belief – identified by Taylor in his study on Rwandan traditions of healing – in individual responsibility, whereby misfortune is linked to earlier transgressions (1992). Similarly, Eramian suggests that the rise of Protestantism, particularly the Pentecostal churches, played a key role in reinforcing enterprise culture, of which the ethos of personal responsibility and individual progress are such strong elements (2017: 102; also Longman 2010).[27] The global tale of

[27] See, e.g., the Umenezero Family Choir, a gospel choir, singing 'Agaciro', illustrating how the messages of salvation and striving for dignity entwine and reinforce one another: www.youtube.com/watch?v=Iis6jBl99Ew. This relationship between Pentecostal religions and narratives of progress has been well documented in other African countries, too (Bornstein 2005).

the individualised development subject as entrepreneur thus finds fertile ground in the Rwandan context.

The ethos or spirit of entrepreneurialism within global development is often framed as the willingness of development subjects to take risks to succeed (e.g. de Soto 2000). In Rwanda, though, the strong emphasis on mind-set is rooted primarily in colonial distinctions between the civilised and the 'backward'. Eramian highlights that the verb *évoluer* (to develop or to progress) draws on the colonial distinction between elites and the ordinary colonial subject. She notes that the noun *évolué(e)* emerged as a term within Francophone colonial regimes to refer to those within the colonised populations who, through exposure to Western civilisation (styles of dress, education, religion, habits, etc.), became 'evolved' or civilised persons – albeit, we should add, of a lower order. Mukasonga's mother aspired to be considered *évoluée* in her desire for white bread and all things *Mzungu* (2018).

Somers suggests, in his study of Rwandan youth, that a lack of entrepreneurial spirit is seen as 'typical' of a Rwandan reluctance to take a risk, or even more strongly, of Rwandan 'backwardness and resistance to development' (2012: 200). This attitude is embedded in Rwanda's development narrative: we were repeatedly told by local officials that the problem with the Twa was their poor mind-set. As a non-Twa neighbour in Gasabo district put it, 'There is a problem which somehow is related to culture, their works, their conduct and beliefs. They [the Twa] need to be motivated and integrated in order that they feel free in society in mind-set' [K7]. This national narrative of mind-set draws on the classic stereotypes and ideologies of the development subject identified by Olivier de Sardan, particularly the stereotype of the 'traditional peasant'. Here, 'superstitions, customs, mentalities are repeatedly and routinely called upon to account for the "backwardness" of peasant populations' (de Sardan 2005: 77) – except, in this context, it is not a stereotype being asserted by development practitioners but by state actors, local authorities, and, to a certain extent, Twa themselves.

The language of *évolué(e)* makes visible the connection of the development subject to the colonial subject. Mbembe's analysis of coloniality identifies the native as a 'great child', 'incapable of autonomous thought' and unable to make a 'distinction between vice and virtue' (2001: 33). He continues: 'The apparent calm of native life resulted from indolence, laziness, and especially that lack of providence that drove him/her to immediate gratification without care for the morrow.' Moreover, and particularly pertinent to the Rwandan context, the native is 'quick to slip back into the most brutal excesses of the animal world, he/she was incapable of resisting violence', so that he/she 'could not, alone, succeed in the long and difficult ascent toward the good and the beautiful' (Mbembe 2001: 34). In this way, the colonial sovereign characterised itself as protective, as exercising a sort of familial guardianship over the native. The narrative of mind-set and the 'traditionalism of the peasant' were key to the colonial denial of the possibility of agency for the 'backward native'.

This colonial subject was thus necessarily subjected to the 'commandment' form of colonial governance, which 'constantly muddled the imperatives of morality, economics and politics' (Mbembe 2001: 31). The social policies of successive colonial regimes were designed not only to enrol colonial subjects into the structures of capitalist production but also to alter their moral behaviour. Where Foucault suggested that the modern state exercises pastoral power – that is, the power to ensure salvation in this world (1982) – Mbembe has taken it further and posited that a key legacy of colonialism is that post-colonial African states are constructed or imagined in such a way as to make the state the 'organizer of public happiness' (2001: 31). To this end, he suggests, the post-colonial state has arrogated the colonial prerogative to exercise an unlimited hold over every individual and to project on to them a civilising ethics for disciplinary purposes.

We can read the emphasis within Rwandan's development approach on home-based solutions as an attempt to overcome part of the colonial legacy of the disassociation of colonised societies from their own histories (Mudimbe 1988). Home-based solutions, as well as the emphasis on home-grown accountability (Ingelaere 2011), can be seen as disruptive of the homogenising force of global narratives and thus as a counter-hegemonic attempt to assert authority over global modes of development and the formation of the post-colonial self. Read in this way, home-based solutions are disruptive and a radical assertion of an authentic Rwandan self. Yet, these attempts remain located within the global model of development that is predicated upon economic growth and the demand for progress is not a challenge to it. Moreover, poverty remains associated with ignorance and laziness in today's Rwanda, as it was during colonialism. Rwanda's development model has thus assumed as a central task of government the need to civilise its citizens and uses the notion of progress, both moral and material, as a disciplinary tool to achieve that progress.

Mind-set, imbued with both explanatory force and salvatory imperative, is a feature of global development discourse, with its origins in the structuring categories of colonialism. It is a concept that combines fear of traditionalism with the entrepreneurial ethos to form a powerful regulatory tool, and it finds deep acceptance in post-colonial Rwanda. Thus, while Vision 2050 is very much a document of modernity – future-orientated, in which time is linear, and progress is both mandated and measurable – Rwandan development is nonetheless equally a model of global development and imbued with its colonial legacy.

4.4.2 *Twa as Development Subjects*

How, then, should we interpret the engagement of Rwanda's Twa with the progress imperative? Eramian notes that Rwandan officials confine their mind-set criticisms to the rural poor, whereas the middle-class Butare residents of her study use the positive thinking imperative as an everyday means of judging everyone in their social orbit. Positive thinking (or the lack of it) is thus a tool for rationalising a slow pace of material improvement, as well as a means of social positioning and of claiming equal status or inclusion in Rwandan society. Yet, while those of lower social status did not feel able to claim a positive mind-set in Eramian's study, the Twa in our study had no such hesitations. The majority of our interviewees not only accept the framing of themselves as modern development subjects but, by asserting their positive mind-set and desire to progress, they are also actively claiming it. In doing so, they are, I suggest, also laying claim to equal worth or an equal status within society. By drawing on the development rhetoric of positive thinking, ambition, and progress to place themselves in relation to others, the subjects of our research are thus seeking inclusion via the subjecthood of development. This inclusion is not as citizens of a global economic order (at least not directly) but as equal citizens of the New Rwanda.

Interestingly, Eramian notes that the desire to work for oneself is almost more important than actually achieving it, 'since the expression of the wish does the crucial work of setting the person apart as someone with the "will to improve"' (2017: 108, citing Li 2007). Here, positive thinking is understood to unleash creativity and entrepreneurial ambition; and while a will to succeed is not quite akin to succeeding for her subjects, it is not far off. In their struggles to succeed, Eramian notes that 'positive thinking is a crucial form of agency available to Butare residents ... who have fallen short of realizing modern, autonomous selfhood in their work lives and livelihoods' (2017: 121). Yet she goes on to note that this constitutes a 'sad irony' because the emphasis on a form of agency rooted in self-help entails that failure to become self-reliant or to remain positive must be attributed to one's own personal failings rather than to structural barriers to prosperity and well-being.[28] In this way, a positive mind-set conditions the agency accorded to development subjects.

However, while our interviewees accepted both the imperative of progress and the centrality of individual mind-set in the definition of what it is to progress, they nonetheless challenged this framing's limitations that suggest that they are either 'backward' or solely responsible for their own struggles. They desire *agaciro* and buy into the idea that empowerment must essentially come from within. Yet they are not fools: positive thinking alone, our interviewees repeatedly asserted, cannot lead to the self-reliance demanded of them. The Twa instead attempted to reposition the global narrative, powerfully magnified by the state, that individualises their struggles, instead locating their development subjecthood in a broader socio-historical context – a context, for example, that has determined that many Twa do not have access to even a small parcel of land. Our interviewees understood the barriers that kept them poor as being structural, notably their lack of access to land. Moreover, they have no hesitation in blaming local authorities for the present unfairness they perceive in the distribution of resources, and they are willing to use the tools at their disposal to push their claims, notably assertions of ethnic-based discrimination – a powerful rhetorical strategy in contemporary Rwanda.[29] This laying claim to equal treatment through the performance of a positive mind-set translates into a demand for equal treatment in practice. Behind the complaints about their unfair treatment by the local authorities is a belief that they should be treated equally.

4.4.3 *Progress as an Exercise of Agency?*

In his analysis of the concept of progress within international law, Skouteris has suggested that narratives of progress are 'powerful rhetorical strategies of (de)legitimation' (2010: vii). However, according to Skouteris, this requires a 'capacity to claim decisive use of the vocabulary [of progress]' in the specific context (2010: 223). Whether or not this capacity exists is determined by the extent to which an actor can make its narrative authoritative; and this is determined by the extent to which it is

28 Similarly, Purdeková has claimed that the clear effect of Rwanda's development efforts is disempowerment (2015: 389).

29 We return to the rhetorical or linguistic strategies used by our interviewees in Chapter 6.

persuasive. For progress to be a legitimising force for a political project, it must be believable to those who are asked to legitimise it. Yet, Kothari sees the possibility of agency as strictly limited within development. Contemporary development narratives of participation are tyrannical, she claims, because of how the process of participation too often reifies 'local knowledge' and thereby solidifies existing power structures. She writes, 'participatory approaches simplify highly complicated social relations. . . . What counts as "local knowledge" is very often the effect of specific kinds of techniques of power, of regulation and of normalization' (2001: 152). Menzel, in her field study of victims of sexual violence in Sierra Leone, identified empirically very similar problems with notions of 'local agency'. However, Menzel has suggested that we do not abandon a focus on agency but reformulate it, seeing it not as something that one has or does not have but rather as 'a quality that actors' doings may have in a specific context' (2020: 587). This notion of 'situational agency' focuses on how 'enabling experiences' lead to motivation or a belief in the possibility of being an actor and/or having agency (Menzel 2020: 592). This is similar to Whyte's notion of situated concern, expressed as the subjunctive form of subjectivity as a form of practical wisdom, an attempt by interdependent people to manage uncertainty and steer a course, and an acknowledgement of their inability to assert control under conditions of doubt, hope, will, and potential (2012: 186).

The Twa in our study broadly accept the model of development presented to them because they want something out of it: a better life materially and because performing a positive mind-set is a means of asserting their inclusion in the modern Rwanda as full Rwandan citizens. At the same time that they experience progress as an imperative, and accept it as such, it is also a promise. Rist notes that social beliefs, such as development, are 'performative' (2021: 22). That performance can be little more than acting – a playing to the gallery of local leaders, government authorities, and foreign researchers. However, while our interviewees were performing the correct mind-set in their conversations with us, they also appeared to genuinely believe in the possibility of progress. That progress is tangible or believable to them is largely a result of the state's emphasis on pro-poor programming, their inclusion in these programmes, and the state's success in improving both access to and the quality of education and healthcare. As a gentleman in Gatsibo district told us: 'These [state] programmes give me hope of a better tomorrow' [F2].

There are many reasons why we could interpret our interviewees' desire for progress as a denial of agency. We could highlight the lack of real choice in the face of the combined disciplinary force of development and the good Rwandan narratives, suggesting perhaps that the Twa are forced to want 'progress' because they have been denied the possibility to claim indigeneity. Alternatively, one could read the acceptance of the progress imperative as agency not as a promise of inclusion but as a form of resistance. Thomson has suggested, following Scott, that everyday resistance in Rwanda is hidden in routine compliance (Scott 1985: 278–279; Thomson 2013). In this context, this would entail that Twa are identifying as development subjects as a subtle form of resistance, again because they have no other options.

Yet, we should be cautious about such explanations. To accept them completely would be to accept that dissatisfaction with one's life has no material or internal causes; that is, it is purely a question of misrecognition, by which one is ascribed a position of being under-developed. As Nanda notes in her work on hybridity, 'under-development thus becomes akin to a state of mind, resembling low esteem, rather than the hard objective facts of brutal exploitation and low indices of well-being' (2001: 182), and thus mirrors the colonial notion of mind-set. Seen in this way, inclusion in development or progress is to take up the chance to transform one's life conditions.[30] As Ferguson highlights, the yearning for material improvement – for a life like that lived in the West – is not simply a question of mental colonialism or the inability to imagine an alternative, 'but an aspiration to overcome categorical subordination', where reference to a traditional way of life is often a polite name for extreme poverty (2006: 20–21). Instead, a large part of the success of the Rwandan development narrative is because its subjects believe it has the possibility to offer them a better life.

Likewise, viewing agency solely as resistance is, I think, too simplistic a way of understanding the jurisdictional encounter between global development and the state's unity and reconciliation policies. Our interviewees are in one sense complying with the framing of them as de-ethnicised development subjects; yet they complain loudly about unfairness at every turn.[31] The complaint of unfairness is an open challenge to the local authorities. It is true that the vast majority of Twa in our study are not

[30] See Ferguson (2006: 18–19) for a description of a similar finding in his fieldwork in Lesotho in the early 1980s. As Ferguson notes, 'the question of cultural difference itself is (everywhere, no doubt, but perhaps especially in contemporary Africa) tightly bound up with questions of inequality, aspiration, and rank in an imagined "world"' (19).

[31] Their complaints were not only articulated in the privacy of our interviews but were also repeated in the meetings that we held to present our research findings, at which both

blaming the government in Kigali or the president himself; even less are they challenging national unity as the overarching value or the framing of 'the good Rwandan'. Instead, I suggest that rather than resisting the state's narrative on development, they are using the space that is available to them to articulate their demands for material and moral inclusion. The choice to view the interaction between (local) authorities and the Twa as (everyday) resistance characterises the relationship as one in which the authorities exercise domination over the Twa because they are vulnerable through their socio-economic need. But this overlooks the fact that both need something from each other. The Twa need material resources and want recognition of their Rwandanness; in turn, the local authorities need their participation in state programmes in order to meet their contractual targets. That is, local leaders need the Twa to perform as good development subjects. This dynamic opens up space for Twa to assert themselves at the local level and in their daily lives. The intersection of these powerful narratives of development and of unity – the jurisdictional encounter between them – has formed the space of action for Twa and entails that they need to tell a story of themselves as poor rather than historically marginalised. That they choose to engage with this framing is because of what they gain by doing so.

4.5 The Promise of Progress as Inclusion

The values of the global economic order come, for Rwanda's poor, in the form of New Rwanda Inc. (Crisafulli and Redmond 2012). However, this is more than just packaging. Development in Rwanda is refracted by the overarching goal of unity and reconciliation. The regulatory power of the global development discourse is made tangible in the everyday imperative of people to progress, in the gossip about who works hard and who does not, in who has benefited from the state's largesse and who has not. This power to shape the development subject is remoulded through the aims of this post-colonial state: the Rwandan state uses the promise of progress to legitimise its political project of turning ethnic subjects into development subjects.

Our interviewees experienced the world as one in which they are behind – a word they repeatedly used to describe their situation – and the state is there to assist them in catching up. They do not wish to be

members of the Twa community and local leaders, from ministry and district level downwards, were present.

apart but want the same access to resources and opportunities as other Rwandans. That development subjecthood – formed here by the interaction between global development and the Rwandan state's attempts to create good Rwandans – sets the frame for how Twa can view themselves as development subjects is obvious. However, what characterisation of this as tyranny or resistance can miss is the willingness of a group like the Twa to participate in the promise of progress, as well as their ability to navigate within the confines of development subjecthood to assert their demands. While the modern world is happy to grant equality in terms of an imagined membership – for example, a prohibition on racialised hierarchies – the Twa are demanding inclusion in modernity through access to the material goods that they hope will enable them to live a better life. The promise of progress is a powerful and seductive narrative; but for that to be so, the promise must be believable. Moreover, this subjecthood is, for our interviewees, not a de-contextualised one; that is, it must, they assert, take account of their historical marginalisation and address it. By accusing local authorities of failing to deliver or of discriminating against them on grounds of ethnicity, they are willing to employ powerful language in order to force their inclusion as equals in Rwanda's development process. Progress is not something that they are willing to wait for.

Menzel's definition of situational agency does not solely focus on the will to act but also encompasses the actual effects of that will; that is, to speak of agency, actors must have the ability to realise part or all of their desired outcomes (2020: 592). The sheer poverty of our interviewees, and the desperation that many expressed alongside their hope, suggest that they are not yet able to realise their desires. Yet, they believe in the possibility of a better future for themselves as Rwandans. The Twa in our study demonstrate a thorough understanding of their own situation grounded in their lived reality of it. They are not deluded or in denial about their situation or frightened of apportioning blame. They push back against the de-politicising effect of development and its processes, whereby the emphasis is placed on the individual and their mentality. However, they do so not to emphasise their ethnic apartness but to demand recognition of structural dynamics and their right to the attributes of Rwandanness, notably land. Their answer is thus not to refuse to participate in the modern Rwanda but actively to seek it. Although the notion of mind-set and its centrality to the definition of progress is indeed a 'technique of power', borrowing Kothari's phrasing, this does not eliminate the possibility of agency. Our interviewees experience development subjecthood not as tyranny but as a frustrating push for inclusion and access to a fair share of material resources. Laying claim to development subjecthood is a means of enabling them to assert their inclusion as Rwandan citizens of equal worth.

5

Becoming Rwandan

While Twa seek inclusion, what does becoming Rwandan entail? Benedict Anderson famously described the nation as an imagined community (1983). Homi K. Bhabha wrote of the centrality of narration to the nation (1990). This conceptual language of imagination and storytelling suggests that for individuals and groups to be able to imagine a future together, they need to accept some elements of an embedded or innate identity based on a shared past;[1] and they need to be able to conceive of the realisation of their 'self' project – their identity, goals, and interests – within the mooted identity. This shared act of imagination is brought into being by narrative.

At the core of the 're-making' (Strauss and Waldorf 2011b) or 're-imagining' (Pottier 2002) of Rwanda in the post-genocide period has been the attempt to create a strong civic nationalism or Rwandan identity divorced from ethnic groups. Indeed, in the wake of the genocide, removing the categorisation of the population into ethnic categories (*Ubwoko bw'abantu*) from public life has been a key government mission. In place of membership in sub-groups, the government has made major efforts to replace ethnic identification with a single superordinate identity: Rwandanness (Gaertner and Dovidio 2012; Moss 2014). Rather than focusing on improving relations between groups, therefore, it has chosen to dissolve those sub-group identities in a process known in social psychological terms as social recategorisation (Moss and Vollhardt 2016).[2] Alternative narratives of identity are dismissed, de-legitimised, and, ultimately, criminalised. This has led to fierce criticism and, empirical evidence suggests, resistance from within (e.g. Thomson 2013; Purdeková

1 While most primordialists argue that this sense of 'natural' identity can only be based on ethnicity, constructivist and situational approaches suggest that it can be created by shared presence on a given territory over time (Brown 2000).

2 It is worth highlighting that in Rwanda, as in Burundi but unlike many other African states, ethnic difference is not horizontal but is vertical; that is, difference is hierarchical, giving one group rank over the other(s). See Lemarchand (1993: 159).

2015; Reyntjens 2024). There is little doubt that focusing on a core national identity reinforces the political legitimacy of the ruling elite. As Makhunga notes, 'In an ethnicised context where the political mobilisation of the Hutu majority would numerically defeat the Tutsi minority, the de-ethnicisation of identity in postgenocide Rwanda and the construction of a non-ethnic nation-state is absolutely crucial in maintaining power for the ruling political party' (2019: 384). This lays at the heart of many of the strong criticisms of Rwanda's unity narrative, as does the manner in which the government goes about enforcing it. However, it is not only a matter of demographics: the post-genocide government has, it is claimed, 'staked its moral claim to legitimacy' on the success of its policy of national unity and reconciliation (Thomson 2011: 439).

Yet shared identity-building was arguably necessary for a country devastated by genocide and civil war and the related large migration flows both into and out of the country, as well as within it. From a population of fewer than 7 million, the genocide killed some 800,000, internally displaced between 500,000 to 1.5 million, and saw 2–3 million people flee to neighbouring countries (Prunier 2009: 4). Around 2 million returned in 1996–1997, known as 'new caseload' returnees, mostly Hutu, to add to the approximately 700,000 'old caseload' diaspora who returned when the Rwandan Patriotic Front (RPF) took power, mostly Tutsi. This diaspora and their descendants were estimated to be 25–40 per cent of the population by 2006 (Purdeková 2015: 38). These major demographic upheavals – the killed, the imprisoned, the exile, the returnee – meant that a new society had to be built and an identity created that was capable of bridging these experiences and their associated traumas (Sentama 2022). The violence destroyed not only the physical and institutional infrastructure of the country but also the intangible basis of society: that sense of solidarity or trust that makes everyday living together possible (Ingelaere and Verpoorten 2020). The government's response, in contrast to a revolutionary break (Anderson 1983: 193), has been to interpret the genocide as fratricidal violence and embed it in the new regime as a warning of a potential future.[3] This gives an urgency to the need for unity.[4]

[3] I was struck while travelling in Rwanda by the contrast between the 'glorious dead' of European nation-building and the nature of genocide memorials in Rwanda, in which corpses and skeletons are frequently on gruesome display to drive home the terror and horror.

[4] Purdeková, however, draws attention to the fact that the nationwide grassroots consultations in 1996/7 on the causes of disunity found that ethnicity was not mentioned; rather, participants ascribed the violence to greed, exclusion, and ignorance (2015: 132).

Despite the full resources of the state being invested in engineering a dominant Rwandan identity, Twa report that they continue to face regular discrimination, primarily from fellow Rwandans. Moreover, the suspicion that local authority decisions on the distribution of resources discriminate against them based on their Twa identity is never far from their minds. As detailed in the previous chapter, continuing poverty and a corresponding inability to achieve their self-realisation goals – to progress – can quickly lead to complaints of ethnic-based discrimination. Yet our Twa interviewees are identifying as Rwandan. They are rejecting a vision of themselves as indigenous and at least some of our interviewees are finding hope in a national narrative of belonging. This chapter explores the processes and form of the imagined community in contemporary Rwanda in the light of global discourses of difference, focusing on the space of identity that the state narrative of unity allows for Twa to realise their self-projects. As such, it examines how Twa are navigating their subjectivisation as Rwandans.

5.1 Rwanda's Unity Project

As described in Chapter 1, unity is at the core of Rwanda's national reconciliation efforts. The goal of reconciliation, therefore, is unity (Sentama 2022).[5] In this grounding principle of unity, a strong national identity – 'Rwandanness' – is central. According to a National Unity and Reconciliation Commission policy document, 'Key to any strategy [of national reconciliation and unity] was the redefinition and promotion of a shared National Identity – *Rwandanness* – in which every citizen of Rwanda considers him/herself as Rwandan first, beyond anything else' (NURC 2016: 53). This message is reinforced by the legal framework, which criminalises references to ethnic identity through the crime of divisionism. Individuals are thus forced to comply with the government narrative on identity, in which ethnic identity or group-based membership

[5] As opposed to, for example, healing or justice – as is commonly understood within transitional justice (Williamson Sinalo 2018). Sundberg notes that the words 'reconciliation' and 'unity' in Kinyarwanda are very similar, and their political meanings are not defined in government policy. She concludes from her research that 'unity is occasionally recognized as a complicated and incomplete process and the target of continuing efforts' (2016: 118). In contrast, reconciliation is understood as a concrete task and, moreover, one that has been completed. For consideration of the problematic intertwining of reconciliation and unity, see Sentama (2022).

is not seen as a layer or aspect of Rwandan identity but a form of opposition to it, maybe even an indication of genocidal ideology.

Law N° 47/ 2001 on the Prevention, Suppression and Punishment of the Crime of Discrimination and Sectarianism introduced sectarianism as a crime, with Article 1 defining it as 'the use of any speech, written statement or action that divides people, that is likely to spark conflicts among people, or that causes an uprising which might degenerate into strife among people based on discrimination'. Since 2003, the focus has shifted to prohibiting divisionism and genocidal ideology, with the new 2003 Constitution criminalising the 'revisionism, negationism and trivialisation' of genocide. This was given more specific form in 2008 in Law N° 18/2008 related to the Punishment of the Crime of Genocide Ideology, which explicitly criminalises expressions and acts of genocide ideology with penalties of up to twenty-five years in prison and a 1 million FRW fine. For those who have previously been convicted of genocide and who are then convicted of genocide ideology under this law, the penalty is life imprisonment (Article 5). Current or former leaders convicted under this law, in addition to facing twenty-five years' imprisonment, can be subjected to a higher fine of 2 million FRW. Moreover, children are also subject to this law, with special provisions for charging under-twelves with genocidal ideology (Articles 9–11).[6]

In addition to severe penalties and broad application, the law also casts a wide conceptual net, defining genocide ideology as including 'aggregate acts' of dehumanising a person by 'marginalising, laughing at one's misfortune, defaming, mocking, boasting, despising', and so on (Article 3(2)). Uncertainty about how to implement this provision led to a revision in 2013 to better specify the crimes the law aims to punish (Law N° 84/2013; Purdeková 2015: 127). The focus was then laid more explicitly on genocide denial, minimisation, and justification, although concerns continue to be raised about how broadly such terms are interpreted by the courts and about the law's compatibility with international human rights standards (Parmar 2017).

These laws are implemented. According to official government statistics, quoted by Amnesty International and further cited by Reyntjens, during the period 2007–2009, prosecutors brought 1,845 cases to court on charges of either divisionism (Law N° 47/2001) or genocide ideology (Law N° 18/2008) (Reyntjens 2024: 164). A Rwandan newspaper article in

[6] Purdeková cites a local news source as reporting that two primary school girls have been jailed for genocidal ideology (2015: 126), i.e. these provisions are enforced.

2020 reported statistics from the Rwanda Investigations Bureau (RIB) showing that 2,300 cases had been filed in court under Law N° 18/2008, but that, since 2019, there had been a 39 per cent drop in the number of prosecutions.[7] This was attributed by the RIB, according to the article, to a 'growing enlightenment' among citizens. Sundberg's ethnographic study in the 2010s certainly suggests a widespread awareness of these laws and their implications for individuals. Rather than 'enlightenment', Sundberg reports that nearly all her interlocutors believed that it was not safe to utter ethnic identifiers in public and one of her interviewees insisted that he knew several people who had been sent to prison for it (2016: 171–173). Our interviewees were also not only aware of the laws; many were also familiar with the potential penalties. These laws, together with the various legal mechanisms created in the aftermath of the genocide, have placed, according to Doughty, law-based or punitive harmony at the centre of Rwandan life (2016) and have led, according to others, to 'narrative closure' (Hintjens 2008; Purdeková 2015: 48).

In addition to criminal penalties, the message of Rwandanness is inculcated through mandatory sensitisation programmes – above all Ingando,[8] Itorero, and Ndi Umunyarwanda – as well as the many hundreds of unity and reconciliation organisations established at the local level to amplify the message; indeed, according to Purdeková, the unity imperative is mainstreamed throughout every area of Rwandan life (2015).

5.1.1 *The Model Citizen*

The previous chapter, focused on the Rwandan development subject, suggested that the global development subject resonated strongly with the form of model citizenship that is at the heart of the Rwandan state's governance practices. The core of these practices is the Itorero programme, which is government-run and mandatory for all citizens (NURC 2009a). Itorero is the main vehicle through which the government sensitises the population to its vision of the new Rwanda.

[7] Kerry Jabo, '2,300 People Prosecuted for Genocide Ideology in Five Years – RIB', *The Chronicles*, 15 June 2020: www.chronicles.rw/2020/06/2300-people-prosecuted-for-genocide-ideology-in-five-years-rib.

[8] Ingando was a forerunner of the Itorere programme, but still exists for special targets of sensitisation, such as soldiers and teachers, or those considered dangerous to the state (Mgbako 2005; Purdeková 2015; Sundberg 2016).

For most citizens, participation in the programme takes place in their village or neighbourhood and consists in attending training sessions for a few hours a week. While the official aim of the programme is to create independent-minded and self-reliant citizens, the programme is a space in which the government seeks to forge the model Rwandan citizen (Sundberg 2016). The oft-repeated slogan of Itorero is 'One people, one vision, one nation, one team' (Sundberg 2016: 123), and the model citizen to be produced by the Itorero programme – the *intore* – has self-discipline, the right mind-set, and is future-orientated. In the language of the NURC, participation in the programme is to lead to sweeping mind-set change and a break with the recent past (NURC 2009a). Itorero prescribes 'how Rwandans should relate to themselves *normatively* … and what can and cannot publicly be said about this identity, *practically*' (Sundberg 2016: 142, emphasis hers). This notion of unity or *ubumwe*, Purdeková has suggested, goes further than nationhood and simple de-ethnicisation and is better understood as the production of 'togetherness' (2015: 39).

According to Sundberg, *intore* was the name of the king's personal soldiers in the pre-colonial era, and the contemporary use of the term to denote the state's citizenisation programme is part of the broader neo-traditionalisation of Rwanda's nation-building (Sundberg 2016: 27; also Purdeková 2015: 377). *Intore* identity, participants are taught, is about both duties and rights, combining the idea of self-sacrifice for the good of the king/state with individual responsibility (Sundberg 2016: 28). The return to a pure history is brought to life by reviving traditional 'home-grown' practices and readopting traditional values.[9] The kings of the past are portrayed as transcending ethnic identities. Likewise, the new Rwandan society is to be based upon allegiance to a shared nationhood, an allegiance that is built on the rejection of the sub-ethnic identities of Hutu, Tutsi, and Twa. In this way, a specifically Rwandan morality is connected to ethnic neutrality. Or, in Sundberg's words, 'the new Rwandan autochthon' is created in opposition to those who do not accept the removal of ethnic identifiers (2016: 101).

This nation-building initiative has led commentators to view the programme as little more than 'mobilization around government policy and ideology' (Sundberg 2016: 17) – a 'strategic rite' (Purdeková 2015: 357) in

[9] These values are reflected in the following community practices: *ubudehe* (poverty reduction); *urugerero* (national service); *umuganda* (community work); *imihigo* (public service contracts); *gacaca* (local justice), and *abunzi* (local dispute resolution).

which citizens are '"trained" to better perform as governable subjects' (Strauss and Waldorf 2011b; Sundberg 2016: 22). The result of the Itorere programme, according to Sundberg, is not the desired change of mind-set or the related internalisation of the government's narrative but rather 'the conviction of one's unavoidable subjection to the practical enforcement of that ideology' (2016: 40). If, following Foucault, the modern state's powers work through technologies of administration to ensure self-discipline among its citizens, in Rwanda, the state reaches into the most intimate spaces of life, notably one's self-conceptualisation and relations to others. Sundberg's conclusion of the reach of the state's interventions is that they engender individuals to see themselves not as citizens or autonomous individuals but as subjects of state rule, 'vulnerable to the dangers that this rule embodies' (2016: 43). Her interlocutors were not cynical about the government's efforts but were conscious of their exposure to state power.

5.1.2 'I Am Rwandan'

The second pillar of the unity agenda, and the main form of messaging on Rwandanness, is the Ndi Umunyarwanda (I am Rwandan or Rwandanness) programme.

The Ndi Umunyarwanda programme was launched in November 2013 and is a national programme targeting all Rwandan citizens. According to the 2015 amended National Policy on Unity and Reconciliation, Ndi Umunyarwanda requires 'a normative shift' (NURC 2015). This shift entails overcoming the ethnic divisions imposed upon Rwandans by outsiders to understand themselves – and their fellow citizens – as first and foremost Rwandans. To achieve that, it 'provides a forum or space for Rwandans in various social groups to discuss issues related to national unity, reconciliation and development. … By focusing on a shared citizenship – citizenship as a shared fate – the program restores the bond and solidarity between Rwandans' (NURC 2015: 112). Details of the programme are, beyond this statement by the NURC, scarce. The concept document links the programme to *agaciro*, giving it the sub-title 'the right path to regaining the dignity lost by Rwandans' (NURC 2013).[10] The document goes on to state that Ndi Umunyarwanda is not

[10] This document exists in Kinyarwanda and has not been officially translated. I have read it using ChatGPT. *Ndi Umunyarwanda* appears to be the only programme about which official information is only available in Kinyarwanda.

'a mere programme' but, uniquely amongst government programmes, it is, instead, 'a way of life' (NURC 2013).[11]

How the programme works in practice is equally unclear. Requests for information on what the programme consists of and how it is implemented from contacts within Rwanda, who should be well placed to know how it works, have resulted in a blank. What seems apparent from the description by our interviewees is that Ndi Umunyarwanda is made concrete as a series of messages drawn up by the NURC and communicated in the context of other programmes, such as Itorere or Ingando, but also within the compulsory public meetings that take place at village level, such as Umuganda. The state's unity efforts are further reinforced by organised religion, primarily the Catholic and Protestant Churches. According to Cantrell, for example, the Anglican Church in Rwanda uses its pulpits to preach the government assertion that there are no separate ethnicities in Rwanda, only Rwandans (Cantrell 2022: 327). More than a dozen of our interviewees told us that they know that they are equal because all are equal in the eyes of God; for these believers, they felt a sense of belonging within their local community most strongly when in church or involved in church-based activities. The space of equal belonging created by churches thus plays an important role in reinforcing the government's message of national unity (Ingelaere 2011; Cantrell 2022).

Ndi Umunyarwanda arguably finds its origins in the experiences of Rwandan exiles in post-independence Uganda. According to Mamdani, there the question of indigeneity in relation to post-colonial subjecthood had become central: where colonialism had privileged the non-indigenous, independence was to see this reversed (2001: 166). For Rwandans in Uganda, this question became acute with the spread of guerrilla war in 1984. The guerrillas – largely made up of Banyarwanda refugees – had to deal with the challenge of being labelled non-indigenous by the Ugandan regime. They did so by attempting to overcome the politics of autochthony. In place of an autochthone/non-autochthone dichotomy, the rebels reframed belonging as a question of residence. In Mamdani's words: 'The effect was to distinguish the political community from the cultural community and the future from the past. . . . If a cultural community was an outcome of historical processes, the political community was defined more with an eye on the future' (2001: 170). He goes on,

[11] According to my ChatGPT translation, the programme 'defines how we live, coexist, experience joy and pain, and form our beliefs and disagreements' (NURC 2013).

'By redefining the political subject as the resident, and by considering the historical fact of migration as politically superfluous, the reform moved away from the inherited world of the settler and the native in one single stroke' (171). The refusal to tolerate claims of indigeneity[12] and the focus on a unity open to all within the country is an answer to the question of the post-colonial Rwandan subject, by way of Uganda.

While there are few scholarly studies on Ndi Umunyarwanda or on the impact of the programme, it has already faced substantial criticism for emerging out of the movement calling on Hutus to issue public apologies (The Rwandan 2013; Blackie and Hitchcott 2018). The programme was born out of a Youth Connect conference in the summer of 2013 in Kigali.[13] At the end of the conference, President Kagame invited all Hutu to apologise publicly on behalf of their parents and relatives for crimes committed during the genocide against the Tutsi in 1994; in other words, he asked those who had not yet been born or who had been very young children to atone for the sins of their family members. This call for public apologies by Hutu individuals on behalf of others intensified over the subsequent months and crystallised in policy as the Ndi Umunyarwanda programme (Blackie and Hitchcott 2018: 28). This genealogy is the basis for a key criticism of the programme: that it is contradictory. By placing ethnic identity at the heart of a programme designed to overcome it, the programme identifies Hutus, and especially their children, as a distinct group within the programme at the same time as proclaiming 'We are Rwandans' (Ssuuna 2013; Doughty 2016; Blackie and Hitchcott 2018). Moreover, Hutus are identified as the cause of the genocide and must accept and atone for a collective, group-based responsibility for it, irrespective of whether they themselves participated in it.

The framing of Rwandan identity on offer thus appears to be predetermined; and it is one in which roles and status have already been assigned: some are victims and others are perpetrators. Doughty has described this framing of Rwandan identity as 'genocide citizenship', whereby access to the benefits of citizenship is determined by one's position in the official account of the violence of the 1990s (2016: 58–59). This

[12] Fear of the Hamitic Hypothesis is another reason to disavow the concept of indigeneity within Rwandan; see Chapter 2.

[13] Youth Connect (also known as Youth Connect Dialogue or YCD) is a programme designed to help the youth in Rwanda talk openly about their history, repent, forgive, and heal in the post-genocide period; i.e., it aims to achieve unity and reconciliation among Rwanda's youth. See, esp., Benda (2019).

suggests that, contradictory to the NURC's claim of a shared Rwandan identity, the form of belonging on offer is not shared but is instead divided. In a 2013 interview, the Rwandan poet, film-maker, author, and one-time MP Edouard Bamporiki said: 'I know that some are not happy to be Hutu because what was done by Hutu during the genocide brings shame to their relatives and friends. *If you could change your identity*, you would see that more people would want to be like a survivor, a Tutsi' (Blackie and Hitchcott 2018: 34, emphasis mine). De-ethnicisation thus labels some Rwandans – primarily Hutus or those who resist the unity narrative – as wicked (or, making use of a biopolitical frame, as 'bad life' (Turner 2014: 428)), and thus in need of being uprooted and made good. A central part of this critique is thus that Rwanda's unity narrative is deliberately not accessible to everyone; that is, either through the genocide narrative or through the model citizenship espoused, the policy privileges Tutsi and Tutsi cultural identity (Reyntjens 2011; Sundberg 2016; Purdeková and Mwambari 2021; Cantrell 2022). Baldwin has termed this 'survivor nationalism' (2019). Others have highlighted that it is morally wrong to attach guilt to individuals based solely on their membership of a group (Turner 2014; Wama Marobe 2015). The programme's origins in the positioning of Hutu identity as shameful would therefore appear to undermine its goals of bringing about unity through a common identity: Bamporiki did not wish to change his identity to Rwandan, but to Tutsi.[14]

However, it is not only Hutus who are forcefully positioned within the programme. As Blackie and Hitchcott have noted, Ndi Umunyarwanda places on all Rwandans the moral duty to identify as Rwandan for the good of the country (2018: 25). The extent of this moral duty is on clear display in the NURC Barometers, in which interviewees are asked whether they would rather die than commit genocide or sow ethnic discord (e.g. NURC 2015). Such an extreme test of citizenship leaves little room for disagreement or other forms of self-identification. Blackie and Hitchcott conclude that 'an ordinary Rwandan citizen is denied the agency and power to disagree with the government in public and therefore is afforded only the identity of an obedient and law-abiding citizen' (2018: 25). Thus, even where an individual falls within a

[14] It seems, however, more complex than this. In YCD, the children of perpetrators are also explicitly seen as victims of the genocide. According to Benda, 'YCD was primarily a platform for the restoration of CPs [children of perpetrators] to their rightful place as blameless Rwandan citizens' (2018: 130).

privileged category of Rwandan citizenship, they are also trapped in a pre-determined notion of Rwandanness.[15]

In addition to concerns about the origin of the programme and its forced positioning of individuals within a 'genocide citizenship', two further critiques are made. The first is, as already noted in the introduction to this chapter, that the emphasis on national unity has been used as a tool by the RPF-based elite for entrenching their power. This, then, has allowed the silencing of opposition voices in the name of national unity (e.g. Buckley-Zistel 2006; Purdeková 2015; Reyntjens 2024). I do not engage in this debate because it is not the question that I am asking here.[16]

The second thread of criticism does not concern the use to which such policies are put but instead challenges them on their own terms as to whether they are successful in overcoming the ethnic divide by forging a shared identity based on 'Rwandanness'. Indeed, there appears to be a scholarly consensus, largely based on ethnographic studies, that the policies of national unity and reconciliation, while perhaps understandable and even laudable, have failed;[17] worse, they have been counterproductive. That is, instead of removing ethnicity from everyday life in Rwanda, the effort to impose unity and the draconian methods of enforcing it have instead, it is suggested, made ethnicity more salient at the same time as driving it underground (McLean Hilker 2009; Ingelaere 2010a; Thomson 2011). A study of identity and ethnicity considerations among Rwandan youth in 2004/2005 concluded that ethnicity retained its relevance and was hyper-present in how young people navigated their social worlds. In the words of McLean Hilker, 'it [the promotion of a unified Rwandan identity] has created an atmosphere in which public discussions about ethnicity are taboo yet continue in private. The result has been to emphasize rather than de-emphasize ethnicity and reproduce the "ethnic" logic that underpinned the genocide'. She concludes simply that the policy 'is not working' (2009: 96; see also Mgbako 2005; Sundberg 2016). Buckley-Zistel reaches a similar conclusion, that 'the Rwandan government is trying to fabricate a unity without reconciliation' (2006:

[15] See also Williamson Sinalo (2018) for reflections on the obligation placed upon genocide survivors to forgive as part of unity and reconciliation.

[16] I discuss this decision in a little more detail in Chapter 1.

[17] Reference is often made to the fact that from 1976 to 1987 in Burundi, ethnicity was also prohibited, which, critics argue, did nothing for long-term stability – an example that they point to as demonstrating the inherent instability of prohibiting ethnic identification 'by fiat' (e.g. Cantrell 2022).

112). Similarly, Ingelaere's study of the experience of 400 'ordinary peasants' of Rwanda's political transition led him to conclude that 'the instrumental stance on ethnic identity adopted by the post-genocide regime is not only erroneous but counterproductive' (2010b: 273; also Longman 2017). The conclusion of much of this scholarship is that the emphasis on national unity and the means of enforcing it have not only not succeeded but are dangerous because they fail to address underlying group tensions. On this understanding, Rwandan identity cannot create a shared identity because it is ultimately rooted in difference that it refuses to address.

While Tutsis and Hutus have been assigned their respective roles in the official narrative of the genocide, the Twa are mostly invisible in the reconciliation process, as the state sees them as irrelevant to its account of how the genocide occurred (Thomson 2009). Moreover, the prohibition on divisionism means that they are also not able to give an account of their experiences as Twa in the reconciliation forums. However, while being excluded from the reconciliation narrative is a form of continuing marginalisation, it arguably also offers Twa a freedom to negotiate their place within Rwandan society that is not available to others.

5.2 A Global Politics of Difference

Attempts by state institutions to forge unity out of diverse and often divided societies have been a recurrent feature of both Rwandan history and African history more generally (Mamdani 1996; Purdeková 2015). However, contemporary Rwanda is fashioning its own path on identity and unity – a path that diverges from global approaches to the management of group-based difference, particularly ethnic difference.

5.2.1 *The Protection and Management of Difference*

The management of diversity within states, particularly ethnic and national identity, is a key part of the contemporary international legal order. This is so despite the fact that minorities do not fit easily into the dominant theoretical conceptions of the state, whether, in line with Hobbes, as a formation of self-interested individuals keen on the protection of private property or as a coalition of actors formed by class-based interests (Hannum 2007). Under the post-Second World War regime, international law has developed treaties that prohibit the extermination of groups based on their difference;[18] that prohibit the forcible removal of groups from an area of territory due to their ethnic identification;[19] that grant (limited) rights to self-determination;[20] and that promote the enjoyment of one's own cultural, language, or religion.[21] While the definition of a minority has not been comprehensively settled, the Permanent Court of International Justice, ruling in the interval between the two world wars, determined that although a state cannot be required to recognise a minority group,[22] the question of whether a minority community exists is one of fact rather than law and thus cannot be settled by reference to national law alone.[23] These rights and protections are supplemented by legal guarantees of non-discrimination, which contain the understanding that – in relation to discrimination on racial and ethnic grounds – there can never be a justification for direct or intentional discrimination.[24] At the regional level, the African (Banjul) Charter of Human and Peoples' Rights, in addition to repeating protections against destruction and discrimination, also contains a duty upon individuals to maintain respectful relations with others.[25]

This package of rights and protections stops far short of offering the right to autonomy or independent statehood to minority groups; nor

[18] For example, the 1948 Convention on the Prevention and Punishment of the Crime of Genocide, 78 UNTS 277, which prohibits the destruction, whole or in part, of any national, ethnical, racial, or religious group. The definition includes the forcible removal of children, and thus the destruction of a group's future by preventing the transmission of culture, language, and identity.

[19] Ethnic cleansing, although not a separate crime under international law, is included as a crime against humanity under Article 7(1)(d) of the Rome Statute; 2187 UNTS 90, 589 and 595.

[20] For example, Article 1 of the twin International Covenants on Civil and Political Rights, 999 UNTS 171, and on Economic, Social and Cultural Rights, 993 UNTS 3. The right to self-determination is notably limited by the principle of *Uti possidetis juris*; see the Declaration on Principles of International Law concerning Friendly Relations and Cooperation among States in accordance with the Charter of the United Nations (1970), A/RES/2625(XXV).

[21] Notably, Article 27 of the International Covenant on Civil and Political Rights; 999 UNTS 171.

[22] That a state cannot be required to recognise a minority was concluded by the League of Nations rapporteur on minority issues, 'Remarks of Mr. de Mello Franco of Brazil', quoted in Hannum (2007: 54).

[23] *Greco-Bulgarian 'Communities'* case, PCIJ, Ad. Op. of 31 July 1930, 22.

[24] For example, the International Convention on the Elimination of All Forms of Racial Discrimination; 660 UNTS 195. At the EU level, see Council Directive 2000/43/EC of 29 June 2000 implementing the principle of equal treatment between persons irrespective of racial or ethnic origin.

[25] Article 27 of the Banjul Charter; 1520 UNTS 363.

does it necessarily place upon states the obligation to ensure that minority groups flourish.[26] However, taken together, these rights and protections not only presuppose the right of minority groups to continue to exist[27] but also demonstrate the importance accorded at the global level to the recognition of difference.[28] This approach or the general trend is encapsulated in the Human Rights Committee's statement of the purpose of Article 27 (the minority rights protection provision). The Committee stated: 'The protection of these rights [Article 27] is directed to ensure the survival and continued development of the cultural, religious and social identity of the minorities concerned, thus enriching the fabric of society as a whole.' In a nutshell, the global human rights regime is premised on the belief that diversity is both a fact and a good thing in all societies, and that difference should therefore be respected, protected, and managed.

As the international and constitutional law scholar Muna Ndulo notes, however, 'two of the major challenges that continue to plague African states are national integration and the management of diversity in the governance of states' (2022: 153). He suggests that the only way to control the tendency of African politics towards the violent politicisation of ethnicity is to manage ethnic differences. He contrasts a management approach with the elimination of ethnic differences, which includes internationally illegal methods – such as genocide, forced population transfer, and forced assimilation – as well as secession and integration. This entails that only a managed approach to ethnic diversity that preserves that difference can comply, Ndulo suggests, with human rights standards (see also McGarry and O'Leary 1993).[29] This conclusion is the basis for the trend towards a 'global ethic' in citizenship education that

[26] The Human Rights Committee left the question of positive obligations under Art. 27 to protect a minority's identity and the practice of culture, language, and religion open in General Comment 23, stating only that they may be necessary. CCPR General Comment No. 23: Article 27 (Rights of Minorities); adopted at the Fiftieth Session of the Human Rights Committee, 8 April 1994, CCPR/C/21/Rev.1/Add.5.

[27] The right to group existence as a people is explicitly recognised in Article 20 of the African Charter on Human and Peoples' Rights.

[28] States can, however, refuse to see minorities on their territory (although not, of course, physically exterminate them), e.g. France. The Human Rights Committee has repeatedly pushed back against this approach, e.g. General Comment No. 23, para. 4, 186. This, then, is better understood as an exception to the general frame.

[29] See McGarry and O'Leary (1993) for a typology of managed approaches to ethnic conflict. It is perhaps worth noting that they were not particularly optimistic about any of the models achieving durable peace.

incorporates multi-culturalism into a basic understanding of human rights, according to Russell (2018: 387).[30]

This fundamental premise of difference finds its contemporary moment in the central role now accorded within global discourses of difference to indigenous peoples, to the extent that the key contemporary model of alterity is indigeneity.[31] This is made manifest, for example, in the creation of the 2007 United Nations Declaration on the Rights of Indigenous Peoples (UNDRIP);[32] on the emphasis given to protecting indigenous groups by the World Bank in its lending policies;[33] and by the inclusion in the revised draft convention on the Right to Development of an article dedicated separately to indigenous (ethno)development.[34]

As the acceptable pole of alterity, indigenous peoples are to be included by being set apart in order to maintain their distinct ways of life. Although the basis of the claims to institutionalised difference within the global movement is cultural rights (Engle 2010), the demands made under the protection of culture are significantly broader, encompassing rights to property, autonomy, and political representation.[35] As Escobar develops in his study of Black communities of the Pacific in Colombia, these claims are better understood as encompassing the right to an identity, the right to territory or space of being, the right to one's own vision of the future, and the right to be part of a global movement (2008: 243). Escobar, one of the leading theorists of counter-hegemonic cosmopolitanism, has detailed how the articulation of separate identity is a means of using the tools of modernity (rights, non-discrimination norms, communication tools, etc.) to 'redraw the existing hierarchy of power and privilege' and that by distancing themselves from the dominant norms, it is possible to produce 'differentiated voices' or 'alternative modernities' (2008: 227). Counter-hegemonic or insurgent globalisation

30 According to Russell, 'The Rwandan state draws on key elements of global models around citizenship and human rights in its national education documents; local actors then interpret these national models in their local context in ways that often undermine the original intention of the models' (2018: 386).

31 This is, in part, driven by the arrival of the Anthropocene and the search for alternative modes of human living/survival. The danger of this for indigenous peoples is well articulated in Chandler and Reid (2019).

32 A/RES/61/295; published on 13 September 2007.

33 For example, WB Operation Manual: OP 4.10 – Indigenous Peoples, July 2005, revised 2013.

34 Article 17, A/HRC/WG.2/23/2, 6 April 2022. The 1986 original Declaration on the Right to Development spoke simply to 'all human beings' (A/RES/41/128).

35 See note 32 of this chapter.

studies thus articulate a right to alterity, so that difference becomes the key means of resisting modernity, whether framed as neo-liberal economic hegemony, the legacies of colonialism, or state power more generally (de Sousa Santos 2007; Escobar 2008; Blaser 2010). To that end, Rodríguez-Garavito and Arenas have asserted that 'global social movements are as much about difference as they are about equality' (2005: 242). Where difference is the key quality to be encouraged and managed, integration, as opposed to separation or distinctness, is viewed as assimilation – a process that is now widely seen as a form of cultural genocide. Relatedly, a failure to resist integration on the part of a minority group is taken as evidence of domination or of false consciousness.

5.2.2 Claims to Twa Indigeneity within Rwanda

The socio-political organisation of Twa began in the 1960s. Early organisations, such as the Association pour le Relèvement Démocratique des Twa (AREDETWA), which was formed during the transition years to independence, focused on inclusion and improving socio-economic conditions. In the 1980s, Hutu officials within the Catholic Church in Rwanda took an interest in the state of the souls of the 'backward' Twa, which led to the formation of two organisations: the Association for the Social Progress of the Twa and the Association for the Integrated Development of Marginalized Groups in Rwanda. The common feature of these efforts to address the marginalisation of the Twa was that they did not involve the participation of the intended beneficiaries, and they were concerned primarily with the integration of Twa rather than the assertion of a distinct identity (UNPO 1994: 13; Ndahinda 2011: 236).

The first organisation established by Twa themselves, the Association pour la Promotion Batwa (APB), was formed in 1991 in the space created by the political liberalisation laid down in the 1990 Arusha Accords. It was, according to Lewis and Knight, the first autonomous association for Batwa in Africa (1995: 99). The aim of this organisation, according to the same source, was to create a forum for discussion and an information hub about Twa lives so that attention could be brought to their terrible living conditions and social exclusion. The ABP quickly began establishing contacts with regional 'Pygmy' organisations and began advocating on the international stage via its membership in the International Alliance of Indigenous-Tribal Peoples of the Tropical Forests. The ABP leadership made contact with the World Bank and the UN, and, in 1993, joined the Unrepresented Nations and Peoples Organization (UNPO).

However, in the same year, the ABP suffered a split, with some Twa choosing to form a splinter group, the Association pour le Développement Global des Batwa du Rwanda (ADBR), with the latter finding favour with Habyarimana's regime at the expense of the former. National legal recognition of the ADBR followed in 1994.

The rivalry between the two organisations was rendered moot by the genocide. A series of meetings in Kigali in 1995 of surviving members of the organisations led to the formation of an umbrella association: Communauté des Autochtones Rwandais, or the Rwandese Community of Indigenous Peoples (CAURWA). CAURWA represented the first clear use of the language of indigeneity as an advocacy tool for Batwa. Shortly after forming in 1995, members of CAURWA attended the UN Working Group on Indigenous Populations. By 2001, CAURWA had achieved widespread international recognition as the representative organisation for Twa in Rwanda and were active participants in the international indigenous movement (Lewis 2000: 7). However, claims of indigenousness were becoming increasingly unacceptable under Rwanda's unity narrative and, in 2002, CAURWA was drawn into a political tussle with the government over its name and purpose. Survival in the new landscape required CAURWA to drop the language of indigeneity to become COPORWA, the Community of Rwandese Potters,[36] with the mission of fostering the full integration of Twa into Rwandan society (Ndahinda 2011: 239). The re-named organisation continued to advocate for better living standards for the Batwa and to keep the discrimination and marginalisation of the community on the national agenda. Ndahinda has suggested that, through its social programmes of support, COPORWA initiated a process of 'socio-political self-acceptance' (2011: 239) – that is, that members of the community begin to accept themselves as Twa, and as having a place in Rwandan society, rather than Twa being simply a term of abuse. The extent to which COPORWA is still active today is, however, unclear.[37]

The indigenous discourse is an existential one. It is important not to downplay this or to suggest that the discourse and the rights that it promotes are not vital to the continued existence of many communities, who struggle to survive in the face of the rapaciousness of capitalism and all that it entails in terms of environmental destruction, dispossession,

[36] COPORWA was a partner in the project that created the data used in this book.

[37] The organisation's main website has disappeared and been replaced with a much thinner WordPress version that is not being updated. As of June 2025, the main phone numbers were not working, with their office in Gikondo apparently having been vacated.

displacement, and cultural annihilation. To suggest that identity is constructed rather than essentialised, and to see that construction occur through local struggles, does not entail that a community is not deserving of recognition, protection, and respect. Indeed, counter-hegemonic cosmopolitan and Third World studies, many of which focus on indigenous groups, have made clear the dangers of de-politicising resistance; of being deaf to alternative voices and knowledge and to the legal forms that they draw upon (inter alia, Rajagopal 2003; de Sousa Santos and Rodríguez-Garavito 2005). What I wish to highlight here is simply how central the maintenance of identity difference has become to how we understand not only resistance to hegemony but, crucially, inter-group interaction between majorities and minorities. How we understand engagement with modernity is an important part of how we (outsiders, scholars) view the Twa in Rwanda.

5.3 A Turn to Rwandanness: Pragmatism and Empowerment

So how are Twa faring within the strict unity storyline? Asking about identity is fraught with difficulty in Rwanda and so we largely allowed our interviewees to raise the subject themselves. When they did so, we asked follow-up questions about how they felt about what they had just told us – such as an example of discrimination, a positive statement about inclusion, or an observation of how they live – and about what it meant to them.

That all of our interviewees chose to speak openly about their identity as Twa tells us that group-based identity remains highly salient in how they think about and understand their lives. However, to note that Twa identity remains relevant does not tell us how they think about that identity. What became clear from our interviews is that while a small group rejected all group-based names and identified solely as Rwandan, the vast majority of those that we spoke to described themselves as Twa. A statement by an elderly gentleman from Kayonza district was typical: 'Instead of calling us indigenous or HMPs, we would prefer to be called Twas because that was historically our name' [K5]. Yet, while this seemingly unambiguous statement appears to be a claiming of Twa identity, our data suggests that such an interpretation is misleading. Rather, our interviewees frequently viewed being Twa as a barrier to progress in their lives. Thus, while most self-identified as Twa, it was not a happy association and was, instead, often a description of what was wrong with their lives.

In addition, Twa identity was not understood as indigenous by the vast majority of our interviewees. In all the talk on identity that we recorded, only a handful of those we spoke with self-described as indigenous, with one gentleman suggesting that the name indigenous had been imposed on them by outsiders.[38] Thus, in place of seeking to reclaim the Twa label from its negative associations and using global indigenous discourse as a resource to assert demands for inclusion as Twa, our interviews indicate instead a turn towards Rwandanness.

5.3.1 *Overcoming Twa Identity*

Twa culture was viewed by many of our interviewees as something to be overcome, with Twa identity being a barrier to their progress. This is particularly the case in relation to what are widely viewed as traditional Twa economic practices. Twa culture in this broad economic sense – the way of life, the socio-economic markers of Twa identity – was portrayed not simply as a thing of the past[39] but as something that still needed to be fully left behind or overcome. For a small number of interviewees, this was a cause of regret but not for most, who not only took a pragmatic approach to the decline of traditional economic practices but also welcomed it. One gentleman in Nyamesheke district, in the north of the country, told us: 'The negative things about traditional culture are that we used to live in bad living conditions. We had to struggle a lot to get clay and earn a living. We would also carry loads like traditional beer and be paid for that. There was no dignity in that' [G1]. In southern Rwanda, a Twa woman confirmed that traditional Twa identity was something to be left behind: 'Wherever they [Twa of the past] were, there were some issues, including trading insults. Even now there are still places where this still happens. There was also a culture of begging. There are those who do not understand yet the times they live in and adapt accordingly. They are still stuck in traditional culture' [B2].

Our interviewees thus associated these behaviours – just as our non-Twa interviewees did – with Twa identity. The extent of this negative stereotyping for some was put forcefully into words by one interviewee: 'Personally, I hate the name Batwa, even if I am one .... To say Batwa in public, I hate it. It is not written on my forehead. I hate it' [L2]. If being

38 G1: a middle-aged man from Nyamasheke district. These findings effectively replicate those by Ndahinda from his doctoral study (2011: 249).

39 This was drawn out in more detail in Chapter 3.

Twa is to be poor and socially outcast, it is not surprising that most people wish to be something else. Moreover, the strong moral fervour of the good Rwandan narrative of self-achieved *agaciro* means that to engage in these practices – to be understood in the terms of our interviewees *as Twa* – is to fall short morally as well as economically. This process is given further impetus by the dominance in the country of Christianity and the importance of religion to individuals. One woman from Ngoma district told us: 'There are so many things we are no longer practising from traditional culture, like those habits of worshipping the dead, witchcraft. We are saved. We are born-again Christians. We no longer do that' [J12]. In short, as portrayed in our data, to be Twa is to be the antithesis of (a good) Rwandan.

This negative approach to Twa identity – particularly as it relates to economic practices and hence to being poorer on average than other Rwandans – connects to the strong desire for progress and, relatedly, to self-empowerment discussed in the previous chapter. What we found was that moving away from Twa traditional practices was understood by our interviewees to be key to improving their lives; put more robustly, there was a very strong connection in the minds of our interviewees between the possibility of socio-economic progress for them and jettisoning what they understood as being Twa.[40]

Where we encountered misery and hopelessness, this despair was frequently coupled with Twa identity. The following statement from a gentleman in Rusizi district was typical: 'In general, nothing goes well. We are not making steps forward like others. We keep staying behind. We live indeed like HMPs' [B1]. Likewise, adopting the correct, entrepreneurial attitude was associated with moving beyond Twa identity. A young man in Nyaruguru district explained: 'We cannot stick to being just Batwa and wait for some assistance to come because of this' [D3]. Instead, this man told us, Twa had to take responsibility for themselves.[41] The majority of our interviewees thus appeared to accept the government's connection between anti-divisionism, or unity as Rwandans, and socio-economic development; that is, co-operation towards development was not only good for them as individuals and

[40] For example, 'discrimination towards us is traditional culture' [G11]. Similar findings were reported by Adamczyk in her earlier study (2011).

[41] One interviewee in Ngoma district, however, viewed the focus on identity not as a means of overcoming socio-economic disadvantages but as a way of avoiding addressing them: 'They just circumvent things [the material disadvantage]. Why can't they leave us alone and we keep the name of Twas?' [J12].

for their families but also necessary for society as a whole. Standing in the way of achieving *agaciro*, in the minds of our interviewees, Twa identity thus precludes development subjecthood and undermines their duty as good Rwandans.

It is thus also not surprising that few Twa welcomed the alternative designation by the government as historically marginalised peoples (HMPs). This label caused confusion, was subject to frequent ridicule by our interviewees, and was widely viewed as insufficient to address their marginalisation:

> Even the name itself HMP is problematic, even if it reflects how we currently are. Others make progress but when they see you, they say, look at that HMP. Should we always be captured under that label? The name is like a bad omen to us. Perhaps the state cannot do anything for us if we remain labelled as HMPs. [B2]

As this statement makes clear, the main reason for rejecting the HMP label is the way in which the designation of being historically marginalised appears to trap Twa in an ongoing marginalisation.

Thus, although we found a clear self-identification as Twa among our interviewees,[42] this was not evidence of a desire to retain the label as Twa, and was not only a rejection of the name HMPs but was instead a description of what was wrong with their lives.[43] I3 captured this ambiguity well: although she informed us that she preferred the label 'Twa' to those of indigenous and HMP, stating emphatically 'I am Twa!', she went on to tell us: 'the authorities should prohibit that thing of saying that I am a Twa'.

5.3.2 *The Promise of Rwandanness*

In contrast to the negative perception of Twa identity, our data suggests a largely positive association with Rwandanness. Being Rwandan offered our interviewees the potential of a better life, both economically and

[42] 'Instead of calling us indigenous or HMPs, we would prefer to be called Twas because that was historically our name' [K5]. 'I am a Twa' [K2]. 'We are most happy with Twas' [G2]. 'I am a Twa and I cannot deny it' [G3]. These statements cohere with earlier, non-Twa-specific studies that ethnic markers retain their salience in daily social life (e.g. Buckley-Zistel 2009).

[43] Our findings, then, contrast with those in a 2017 study by Ntakirutimana and Collins on the implementation of the HMP label in Rwanda. They interpreted high levels of self-identification as Twa as evidence of both a rejection of the HMP label and a strong desire to retain their Twa identity.

socially. It also offered the possibility of greater inclusion in society. As a man from Rulindo district put it, 'Though they call us HMPs, I personally think we should be called Rwandans like others, because we are Rwandan much like others are' [K12]. Others, when asked what gave them joy in their lives, told us that being Rwandan together with others made them happy. The clear connection to the promise of progress was made explicit by a woman from Karongi district: 'People are not supporting traditional culture. We should forget all that and live as Rwandans. Then we should benefit in all development programmes like all other Rwandans' [B4].

One of the main reasons for our interviewees to view Rwandan identity so positively is arguably the association with declining discrimination against them, something they attributed to the government narrative on a single shared identity. One man in Nyaruguru district told us in response to the questions concerning what the good life means to him:

> Another thing that makes me happy and I would like to share is that he [the president of the republic] addressed the problem of our marginalisation as we now are able to interact and share with others. We used to be discriminated against. We could not drink from the same cups as others. Now, we are no longer treated differently from other people. [D3]

Similarly, a man from Kayonza district spoke of the improvements that the government policy on national unity has brought to their lives. Ndi Umunyarwanda is, as reported by our interviewees, beginning to change people's behaviour, at least outwardly:

> You used to go by in the past and people would whisper, 'look at them, they never improve'. The Ndi Umunyarwanda programme is therefore important because it has abolished that. . . . We are more confident with Ndi Umunyarwanda. I even heard that the government is about to abolish this thing of calling us HMPs so that we may be like all other Rwandans. [K5]

This man clearly felt that the message on Rwandanness was open to him; that is, he was not excluded from ideas of Rwandan identity because he was Twa.

An analogous confidence in the possibility of inclusion as Rwandan was suggested by a middle-aged woman in Gatsibo district who had a small business selling vegetables at the market. She told us: 'We are able to sit and talk without discrimination based on who you are. Those who insist on ethnic identifies have problems of their own and I do not pay attention to what they have to say' [F1]. Similarly, a woman describing a dispute with the cell leadership told us that she had responded to being dismissed as just an HMP in the following way: 'I said that we are all Rwandans. We follow the laws, so we should apply and use the laws of the nation ... I am also a Rwandan' [C4]. The confidence that these women displayed in their Rwandan identity allowed them to dismiss the prejudice of others, suggesting that unity narratives are able to provide an ontological security that being Twa cannot. This is starkly in evidence in the statement by a different woman: 'To be Rwandan is better. Yes, I forgot all about Batwa' [L4]. The turn to Rwandanness is thus not simply about the promise of economic progress.

Yet, this is clearly not the whole story: a sizeable number of mainly male interviewees stated that daily acts of prejudice continue, such as name-calling or the refusal to accept or offer hospitality to or from Twa. This is reflected in a statement by a woman in Kicukiro district: 'They still, here in this area we live in [Kigali], call us Twa but they say at our church that you can only be marginalised by history when you do not know God ... they cannot stop calling us Twa' [J9]. This comment highlights the mismatch between official messages – one can only be marginalised by the past – and the daily reality for many Batwa. However, even where prejudice continues as part of daily life, what is clear is that the situation is much better than it was (whenever that was[44]). An elderly woman from Gatsibo district, who contrasted the bad past with the present, told us: 'We are allowed to share our views without someone saying that is a Twa lady and she should not be allowed to speak ... They bleed the same blood as we do. This is why Kagame has put an end to it [discrimination]' [F1].

The one-Rwanda narrative is not only giving marginalised individuals confidence in their place in society; it is also empowering Twa to actively assert their equal place in society. Even where interviewees reported continuing prejudice, they told us that they used the government's unity narrative to challenge it, defending themselves and disciplining others. A man from Nyamesheke district explained:

> We live peacefully with other villagers but they are not always friendly to us. They never stop calling us by that name. They call us names, children but also adults call us names. They still call us Batwas and other names that I cannot repeat here. ... People still use what is in their hearts. For instance, recently I went to a bar and we drank banana beer. Then someone bought a beer but refused to share with others. I asked him

[44] It was not clear when our interviewees were talking about the past how past the past was.

> why he refused to share his drink with us while we are all Rwandans. Isn't that discriminatory behaviour and divisionism? He took off and ran away. So, even if we say that we are all Rwandans, people have not yet fully grasped the value of that. [G1][45]

While this quote shows that prejudice continues, more importantly here it indicates both an internalisation and an instrumentalisation of the narrative contained in Rwanda's unity laws. Some Twa are thus using the message of unity to demand directly their inclusion in society in relation to others and to local authorities, and to practise their inclusion internally by viewing prejudice as a problem of others. Our interviews therefore suggest that the unity narrative is empowering Twa individuals to challenge prejudice against them and has created feelings of societal inclusion, despite continuing acts of prejudice.

5.3.3 *Twa as Cultural Identity*

Most of our interviewees have accepted Rwandanness as a single, superordinate identity, as demanded by the state's unity narrative.[46] The broad acceptance of the promise of Rwandanness that our data indicates does not entail, however, that our interviewees have bought wholesale into it. In particular, there was a reluctance among a small but not insignificant group to relinquish entirely certain Twa cultural practices and thus their cultural identity as Twa. A distinction is thus made between certain economic practices – such as begging and day-labouring that are indicative of the 'wrong mind-set' – and those cultural practices for which the Twa were historically admired and which brought them joy – such as dancing and singing. As with a woman from Kirehe district, there was deep regret at the decline of Twa cultural performances; she told us: 'You should advocate for the restoration of the culture of forming cultural performance groups, which should involve us' [J6]. Others saw traditional Twa culture as something to share with other Rwandans and thus as a positive contribution to a broader Rwandan culture. An elderly man from Nyamagabe district in the west of the country told us: 'Sometimes when we are able to secure a drink [of traditional beer], we

[45] Similarly, a man from Karongi district: 'I do not like people who call me a Mutwa. When they do, I tell them that I am not a Mutwa but a human being. I do not get angry but I correct the person politely, with a smile' [A3].

[46] J4, a man in Nyagatare district, when prompted to say more about the various labels of HMPs, indigenous people, or Twa, responded: 'I do not own those names'. Which name do you prefer? 'I am Rwandan.'

sit around and decide to have some fun, including dancing. When we dance, we do it as our forefathers did. In such cases, other people join us and we have fun together' [CD1]. These sentiments chime with those recorded by Adamczyk in her fieldwork a decade earlier. She found communities that were very proud of their Twa culture, notably dancing, singing, and pot-making, and individuals who articulated a layered approach to identity. Our data, though, suggests that this pride is fading out as the cultural practices are lost.

Others, all male, understood their culture – their songs, dances, and performances – as (also) a commodity and resented what they saw as the appropriation of it by non-Twa without financial compensation.[47] This is related to the common complaint that dancing at ceremonies is no longer paid, presumably because it is seen as a part of shared Rwandan culture and as something that everyone does rather than a special cultural practice of one group that should be rewarded.[48] Several men, however, spoke proudly of being an *intore* dancer, training others in traditional dances, suggesting that it has been possible to find a place for Twa culture within the modern Rwanda. A similar desire to commodify Twa culture was expressed by a young man from Nyaruguru district, who wanted help in adapting traditional pottery to the tourist market.

Other sentiments of loss reflected on traditional practices of solidarity and sharing within Twa communities: for example, 'Traditional culture refers to that culture of the past that brought people together to share' [H4]. Another characterised traditional culture as 'generosity, love, and solidarity' [G14], although this was presumably limited to within the Twa community. Other, particularly elderly, interviewees clearly missed the security of a clear role as Twa within society, in contrast to the uncertainty of individual progress, with several explicitly blaming 'development' for negatively affecting Twa culture.

However, while we found that some individuals, notably older members of the community and more commonly men, were reluctant to let go of certain traditional practices, primarily dancing, for the majority of

[47] For example, 'Traditional culture is important because it can feed you if you use it as a commodity' [H1]. 'Our elders had their special way of dancing, which was called *intwatwa*. But the problem is now that other people try to imitate our culture and make money from it. Can you imagine that!' [K4]. Also, 'people who are dancing our traditional songs earn a lot of money and some travel overseas to present those traditional dances' [J8].

[48] This was, however, seen as unproblematic by at least one of our interviewees: 'now we live with all Rwandans. A Tutsi lady may start a song and we all dance to it; the same for a Hutu lady' [F1].

interviewees, and above all for the younger generation, these traditional practices are either losing their relevance or have already lost it. For example, when asked about Twa culture and the role that it played in his life, one interviewee in his twenties told us: 'By traditional culture, I understand culture of the past ... You will bear with me because I do not know much about it' [K9]. The extent of cultural loss already experienced is expressed by a woman from Burera: 'I think it [traditional cultural practices] was good though I did not witness it. But I hear older people talking about it' [F3]. Others had no sense of a separate Twa culture and instead talked of traditional culture as shared Rwandan practices, in line with messages from the Itorere programme; or simply contrasted traditional culture with being Rwandan. Even where the sentiment was one of loss, traditional culture was almost entirely discussed in the past tense, as something already lost.

What should we make of the sentiments of loss? Our interviewees largely accept the message of Rwanda's unity. They see Rwandanness as a vehicle for their inclusion, and they are making use of it to assert themselves in social situations and to remonstrate with those who seek to exclude or denigrate them based on their ethnic identity. While Rwandanness has not extinguished their identification as Twa in the present, it is a future promise that can only be fully realised together with the economic progress that they desire. Yet, at the same time, while older Twa are willing to accept Rwandanness as a superordinate political identity, they articulate a wish for layered identity; that is, being able to retain their cultural identity as Twa while being fully integrated in society and the economy as other Rwandans.[49] For most, however, they did not see their identity as layered. They saw their choice as between being Twa – associated with the desperate circumstances of their current lives: poverty, lack of land, and social marginalisation – and being Rwandan, and the future-orientated possibilities of progress and belonging.

5.4 The Offer of Rwandanness: Belonging and Progress

The simplest way to understand our interviewees' articulations of their identity is that they are parroting back the government line on identity, whether because of indoctrination or because of fear of criminal or social sanction. National unity policies police the space within which Twa can

[49] One woman in Adamczyk's study proclaimed that she was 'a Rwandan Twa woman' (2011: 187).

negotiate their identity. It is clear that our interviewees understand the government narrative and what is expected of them. However, it is equally clear that they do not accept that narrative wholesale: they reject the state-approved label of 'HMP', and – contradictory to the demand to view themselves as only Rwandan – they continuously assert their identity as Twa, albeit often unhappily. Instead, Twa are finding the space to negotiate their place within Rwandan society. Moreover, this appears to be not in spite of the strict boundaries of Rwanda's unity policies but because of them.

There are two elements to Twa acceptance of Rwandanness. The first concerns the fact that the unity narrative, and in particular the Ndi Umunyarwanda programme, is working to decrease discrimination and stigmatisation of Twa. That is, in the simplest terms, they benefit from others not being able to marginalise them – at least, not in an outright manner. In her 2008 study, Christiane Adamczyk had already found that the once strict division between Twa and 'other Rwandans' was, as she put it, 'softening' (2011: 181). While many still felt stigmatised, Adamczyk reported that the traditional practice of *kunena*, in which Twa were served food and drink separately to protect others from their impurity, is no longer widely practised. Our findings, based on fieldwork conducted seven to nine years later than Adamczyk's study, suggest that this softening has continued; stigmatisation remains present in daily life – reported to us primarily by young men – but a large number of our interviewees told us that incidents of discrimination were rare or a thing of the past.[50] This means that Twa have a reason to believe in the promise of unity. The unity narrative is improving their lives in decreasing their societal exclusion, albeit not perfectly – as the continued reports of discrimination showed.

That Twa feel a greater sense of belonging and are more accepted as such by the rest of society would also appear to be confirmed by official government findings. The desire to be Rwandan is widely spread throughout the Rwandan population, at least according to the Reconciliation Barometer survey data, collected at five-yearly intervals by the NURC.[51] In 2010, more than 90 per cent of the population,

[50] According to Gaertner and Dovidio, a common ingroup identity model can decrease negative attitudes to sub-groups as the ingroup encompasses previously distinct or rival identities (2012).

[51] The 2020 Barometer is the latest and was published in April 2025. Questions on discrimination and on Rwanda first were either not reported in the 2020 Barometer report or were asked/presented differently. For example, the question on feeling Rwandan above all

according to the survey, agreed that they are proud to be citizens of Rwanda and share common values; an even higher percentage reported that they want their children to think of themselves as Rwandans above other identities (NURC 2010: 55). The 2015 Barometer reported a slight increase in the number who are proud to be Rwandan – 95.6 per cent as opposed to 90.2 per cent – with the 2020 figures of those reporting themselves to be proud or very proud hitting 99.4 per cent of the population (NURC 2020: 51); 87.7 per cent reported feeling Rwandan above all other identities in 2015, which represents a major increase since 2010. These figures accord with a recent study by Beloff, who found that ethnicity simply was not relevant at all to the younger generation (under thirty-five). His participants saw ethnicity as something that was important to their parents but not to them (2025).

Moreover, 93 per cent either strongly or fairly agree that there is no discrimination 'whatsoever' in social spaces and 93 per cent also strongly or fairly agree with the statement that 'Now, Rwandans trust each other without discrimination' (NURC 2015: 97). This shows a significant improvement since 2010, when only 72.8 per cent felt that there was no discrimination in social spaces (NURC 2015: 99).[52] In addition to significantly lower levels of discrimination, there is evidence from a number of psychological studies that the emphasis on Rwandan identity is offering succour to the vulnerable more broadly, not simply to the Twa. In her study of post-traumatic growth in Rwanda among genocide survivors, Grayson found that the Ndi Umunyarwanda programme has played an important role in enabling Rwandans to think more positively about their own lives within the nation's future. She notes, 'There is personal hope (for self) and interpersonal hope (for others), sub-group hope (for minority group), and superordinate hope (for the Rwandan nation), and all of these are interlinked' (2017: 116). One interviewee also commented that the emphasis on unity, and the discussions about their lives in groups, resulted in 'those with little strength' having their strength

other identities has morphed into 'individual pride in a shared identity' (98.2 per cent). The Executive Summary appears to view this as the same question as placing Rwandan identity first (NURC 2020: xiv).

52 It should be noted that doubts have been raised with the author by Rwandan scholars about the trustworthiness of the Barometer's methodology and about the government's influence over the findings, a concern that the then-Executive Secretary of the NURC apparently also shared (Purdeková 2015: 282). On discrimination, however, the trends recorded in the Barometer are confirmed by ethnographic studies.

increased (Grayson 2017: 118).[53] This empowering potential of Rwandanness as a superordinate identity is visible in our interviewees' responses as well.

Williamson Sinalo, in a similar study, sees what she calls 'Rwandicity' as an ideology of Rwandan identity that provides space for post-colonial, post-traumatic growth (2018: 61). Her data suggests that Rwandicity is providing Rwandans with a narrative that helps them root their sense of self, community, and belonging (2018: 80). This idea that Rwandanness is creating space for individual and group belonging within the superordinate again tallies with our findings. The unity policy is thus more than the top-down negative of de-ethnicisation through criminalisation. Rwandanness is offering something positive, an ontological security, that is not fully replacing ethnicities but is providing strength and security to some.[54] What this suggests is that Ndi Umunyarwanda has moved the narrative beyond de-ethnicisation (Benda 2019) to inclusion. For example, one of our non-Twa interviewees told us that Twa were in leadership positions in their village and that this represented good governance. Another non-Twa interviewee concurred that good governance means everyone's voice being heard and that HMPs should be given power in the government. While Sundberg notes that in private discourse, among one's own kind, ethnic identities continue to be discussed and to play a big part in people's lives, what her participants did buy into was the rejection of Rwanda's group identities as hierarchical (2016: 174, 186).

The unity narrative, its strict enforcement, and its removal of hierarchical ethnic identification appear to be giving Twa, and others, the space to imagine themselves as members of the national community. In contrast to the earlier quote by Edouard Bamporiki, in a work entitled *Sin to Them, Shame on Me*, Bamporiki describes himself as stuck in the murderous past actions of his forebears and of other fellow Hutus. Yet, he is

[53] These benefits accrued to both perpetrators – who benefited from forgiveness and reintegration – and to victims – who felt that it gave them a safe space in which their pain could be heard and which lessened as a result. Victims also reported feeling empowered by telling their stories, of being heard, and of the wrong done to them being acknowledged by perpetrators (Blackie and Hitchcott 2018: 32). Blackie and Hitchcott's findings are supported by other studies, such as that by Mukashema and Mullet, which found that a positive attitude towards the reconciliation programmes had mental health benefits (2010).

[54] While the unity narrative is offering hope and empowerment to some members of society, it is worth noting that this should not be confused with reconciliation (Clark 2014b; Sundberg 2016).

able to be redeemed, to be born again, by the offer of survivors to embody a shared Rwandanness.[55] Gallimore suggests that the process Bamporiki describes is a shift from a collective ethnic 'we' – of being identified by one's membership in an ethnic group – to an individual 'I' within a broader and more open national community (2015: 84). Bamporiki himself notes that he is the one who gets to decide who he is, as opposed to being determined by his ethnicity. This belief chimes with the moral individualism of Ndi Umunyarwanda: I am Rwandan. What we see is that this belonging as full Rwandans is also opening up to Twa.

Twa are undoubtedly largely excluded from 'genocide citizenship' (Doughty 2016); this affects them materially, where returnees and genocide survivors are at the front of the queue in terms of the redistribution of land and in government programmes. Yet, this exclusion allows them to sidestep categorisation in relation to the genocide and thus they are able to navigate their identity more easily outside of the fixed positions of either survivor or perpetrator (cf. Paradis 2020: 10). Where Thomson has suggested that not being seen as Twa is harmful (2009), our data suggests that it provides space for Twa to negotiate their inclusion; for example, as we saw in the previous chapter, by demanding of local authorities that they be treated equally in the distribution of resources. That they do this suggests faith in their inclusion as Rwandans. Moreover, ontologically, the Twa feel secure in accepting the offer of Rwandanness, and they can rely on it precisely because it is top-down and enforced.[56]

The second part of the story of why Twa accept – sometimes fully endorse – being Rwandan is because of the promise of a better material future that is a central part of Rwandanness. Twa are not only able to imagine their place in Rwandan society but, as we saw in Chapter 4, they also buy into the promise of development. As a result of both their historical marginalisation and the Rwandan state's magnification of the development narrative, progress and Rwandanness have become entwined for the Twa.[57] Development subjecthood is only possible in interviewees' minds as Rwandan; at the same time, being Rwandan is

[55] Based on Gallimore's translation and analysis (2015: 76–77).

[56] Broche-Due has, in her work, highlighted that a total environment provides a pillar of stability among the complexities of modernity (2004).

[57] For Purdeková, this fusing of the development and unity narratives is deliberate; moreover, she notes that this is combined with the security narrative that portrays the state as the only means of maintaining peace (2015: 219). While this fusing is experienced by all Rwandans, as persuasively argued by Purdeková, I would conjecture that it has particular resonance for Twa.

a sign of being a development subject, which itself symbolises dignity and the 'right mind-set'. This willingness of Twa to embrace the entwinned narrative of unity and development is encapsulated by a quote from a young man in Adamczyk's research: 'Today, I am no Mutwa anymore. I am a Munyarwanda and I want to develop myself' (2011: 186).

However, while the unity narrative idolises the pre-colonial past and attempts to root national identity in Rwandan traditional values, this mooted harmonious past has almost no resonance with our interviewees. While other studies show that interviews repeat verbatim the new historical consensus on ethnic categories as a creation of colonialism, our interviewees do not do this. They do not treat ethnic categories as having no public meaning, presumably because they regularly experience its meaning in a negative way. The imaginary of a happily shared past does not accord with their own experiences of marginalisation or with the stories passed down by their forebears – which is why it is important to focus on the future. The promise of progress embedded in Rwandanness speaks to this hope for a better future.

That our interviewees have accepted this promise suggests that many Twa are taking a practical or pragmatic approach to their identity.[58] Describing attitudes towards identity as pragmatic can easily sound cynical or can be interpreted as a 'forced' reaction to top-down external pressures. In his work on acculturation from a cross-cultural psychological approach, J. W. Berry has studied social and cultural change in individuals and communities in the context of coming into contact with the Western world, primarily through immigration. He provides a useful frame for understanding our findings. Acculturation in this field of cross-cultural psychology is defined as the mutual influence of two autonomous cultural systems, usually in an unbalanced manner in which change is stronger in one direction than the other. However, acculturation should not be understood as a passive process; while it may be stimulated from outside, he suggests, it is driven by internal dynamics (1980: 217). Acculturation, then, differs from the usual framing of assimilation by minority rights scholars by necessarily allowing a number of alternative goals and processes (Berry 2005: 701). As Berry notes, acculturation can result in a rejection of the dominant culture and a reaffirmation of traditional values; that is, it does not necessarily result in absorption

[58] For earlier empirical accounts of pragmatic approaches to Rwandan identity, see Moss and Vollhardt (2016); Adamczyk (2011); and Blackie and Hitchcott (2018).

into the majority.[59] Where individuals opt for assimilation, they 'prefer to shed their heritage culture, and become absorbed into the dominant society' (Berry 2005: 705).

Assimilation is thus not always involuntary; it can be sought and desired by the non-dominant group.[60] This does not mean that as individuals they do not experience some form of loss, as some of our interviewees articulated, but their preference for becoming fully part of the broader society is stronger. Berry's work suggests that simply because change occurs in response to a dominant majority, it does not necessarily mean that it is also unwelcome. Indeed, while theories suggest that individuals prefer dual or layered identities, Moss found in her study on identity in Rwanda that people held complex views about the recategorisation of their identity and were certainly not all opposed to the imposition of a single, superordinate identity (2014). Of course, one could argue that Twa have little choice but to leave behind their former identity as Twa: those social practices that gave them a privileged role – as entertainers, as legitimisers – have gone; so, too, has the connection to the forests and a hunter-gatherer lifestyle. Moreover, a claim to indigeneity would certainly fall foul of laws prohibiting divisionism. Yet, while pragmatism is always a response to one's surroundings, our interviewees viewed the offer of Rwandanness – ontological security, belonging, and economic progress – as more attractive, with expressions of loss being confined in age and scope. That is, our interviewees appear to be actively choosing Rwandanness.

Moreover, identity is always negotiated – even in a carefully constructed and strongly enforced narrative (Taylor 1991). Although Sundberg suggests in her study of a neighbourhood of Kigali that her interlocutors experienced the Rwandan state as 'transgressing boundaries between the public and private' (2016: 23), they nonetheless included in their understanding of this transgression the ability of an individual to choose to appropriate the state's narrative as a means of self-empowerment and/or protection. Similarly, Moss and Vollhardt found that the vast majority of participants in their study neither fully endorsed nor fully rejected the state's single recategorisation approach. Instead,

[59] What makes Berry's framing particularly helpful is that it is drawn from his observations – and those of others – of the range of choices that non-dominant cultures make when confronted with Western culture rather than a list of ideal-type interactions.

[60] Particularly so where individuals feel that they have little to lose, e.g. I7: 'People hate themselves. We have been rejected for so long a time . . . people don't care much about their lives since no-one else cared for them before.'

they discussed 'a range of nuanced arguments discussing pros and cons of the policy, as well as ideas for modifying the approach' (2016: 349). Despite being broadly in favour of the unity narrative, they were creative in reshaping the top-down categories of belonging (see also Akpome 2014). Likewise, our interviewees claim their own naming authority; that is, they do not accept the label of HMPs. In insisting on being Twa, they are refusing to cede full discursive authority.

In a similar vein, Clark has suggested that Rwanda's reconciliation process, as represented by the *gacaca* processes, is best characterised as 'negotiated reconciliation', which he contrasts with the transactional account given by the Rwandan government and its various critics (2014b: 304). Individuals thus found their own way within and around the official narrative of reconciliation and unity, adapting it to fit the rebuilding of their lives.[61] In reflecting on why young Tutsi survivors and children of survivors accept a future-orientated perspective, Benda suggests that they gradually and pragmatically re-evaluate the socio-political dividends. This makes it likely that they will 'cast in their lot with [their] fellow future-oriented people' (2018: 132). This negotiation with or resituating of state narratives, no matter how firmly they are espoused and enforced, is not surprising: in *Afriques indociles*, Mbembe noted that Africans do not docilely accept Christianity but adapt it to their own needs (1988; cited in Van Hoyweghen 1996). Unity is thus negotiable and negotiated.

Moreover, this negotiation, or indeed appropriation for one's own purposes, does not necessarily need to be viewed as an act of resistance. Instead, what our participants suggested was a negotiated acceptance of Rwandanness. In their research in Uganda, Ampumuza et al. explored the various mechanisms that enact 'Batwa-ness' for their interviewees (2020: 2). They found a strong desire among Ugandan Twa to move beyond the dichotomy of oppressor–oppressed in order to reframe Batwa agency through 'counter-narratives'. In place of tales of victimhood and marginalisation, their interviewees put forward stories of themselves as active and engaged – for example, as forest ecology experts, political activists, community developers, and so on. What we found in our interviews was a conscious attempt to move beyond a Twa identity altogether that framed individuals as marginalised, behind, and separate, and instead an attempt to assert themselves as entrepreneurial, having the right mind-set, and Rwandan. In place of a counter-narrative, our

[61] From his interviews, Eltringham saw people neither embracing ethnicity nor dismissing it as a colonial fabrication; instead, he suggests, they re-situated it (2011: 271).

interviewees are, socially and politically, choosing the ontological and economic security of Rwandanness in place of identifying as Twa, and are thus reframing themselves in line with the prevailing narrative. As such, they are, *pace* Mahmood, 'inhabiting' the moral discourse of Rwandanness (2011: 42): making demands of local authorities and correcting others for their discriminatory talk. While this picture needs to be nuanced – some of our interviewees are choosing to enact their 'Twa-ness' culturally; or, rather, they express their desire to be able to do so – the content of the negotiation is arguably less important than the fact that it is an exercise of situated agency. The closing off of the possibility of claiming indigenous identity within the unity narrative does not therefore entail a denial of agency; nor does it mean that there is no other option but Rwandanness, although the price for defying the law may be high. Instead, identifying as Rwandan is an act of both hope and desperation. Critics highlight that the unity narrative regulates people into either model citizens or divisionist enemies, creating exclusion of the citizen 'who is either undesirable or not (yet) desirable' (Purdeková 2015: 362). While there is undoubtedly a pressure to perform the part of a model Rwandan citizen, seen through the eyes of our interviewees, Rwandanness is providing a tool for asserting their inclusion.[62]

5.5 Post-colonial Subjects?

In focusing on notions of citizenship, and particularly on Rwandanness as the singularly important mode of belonging, one could argue that the state-driven unity narrative is repeating the colonial emphasis on statehood.[63] Yet, there is more to Rwandan nation-building than simply outlawing ethnicity and the creation of a superordinate national identity, despite the seemingly simple dichotomy of unity or divisionism espoused in the legal framework. There is the promise of development and of security. There is also the focus on gender equality as a core part of Rwandan identity, which came back regularly in our interviews, in which participants spoke of the importance of equality of decision-making

[62] In Moss and Vollhardt's earlier study of the *Ndi Umunyarwanda* programme, their interviewees supported the unity narrative because they understand it to be necessary for the stability and development of their country (2016). Similarly, part of the reason that our interviewees supported the programme is likely to be a sense of duty: acknowledging that this duty also applies to you is to assert yourself as a full member of the community.

[63] Purdeková and Mwambari argue that Rwandan nation-building and identity politics are shot through with colonial durabilities (2021).

within a marriage, of the importance of reproductive rights, and of the lack of tolerance for domestic violence.[64] Unity allows for a plurality of identities within Rwandanness, although not multiple ethnic identities – at least, legally.[65]

Mamdani describes the modern colonial logic as one of segregation via the essentialisation of tribe and custom and the politicisation of cultural difference. This was institutionalised via customary law, whereby private norms – essentialised and enforced by the colonisers – were transformed into colonial tools that framed the subjectivity of the colonial subject (Mamdani 1996; also, in the Afghan context, Manchanda 2018). He suggests that the path of decolonialisation for Africa is to find a balance. By removing the 'tribal logic' (in Mamdani's terms), by seeking to govern the country for a single community of Rwandans, the Rwandan state is trying to find its own post-colonial path following the destruction of the social fabric. It is doing so by appealing to what it has identified as home-grown values, which accords with pan-African principles of self-reliance. Moreover, its approach challenges the global politics of difference by focusing on an individual narrative of finding place within Rwandan society: *ndi umunyarwanda* means 'I am Rwandan', not 'we are'. It is this emphasis on the individual – and on individualised moral responsibility – that fits so well with the entrepreneurial ethos of development discourse.

None of this negates the argument that the narrative of unity – and the focus on unity above democracy – works to legitimise those currently in power; nor does it deny the chilling effect of unity laws and the disciplinary force of the unity discourse, including widespread societal surveillance (Purdeková 2015; Reyntjens 2024). Many scholars and commentators suggest that the unity on offer is fixed and forced, and thus dangerous. Moreover, indigeneity as framed by the global narrative is not a discourse that is a plausible option for Rwanda's Twa at present. A yet more powerful critique is that the focus on unity is leading to the neglect of other potential causes of conflict or division within Rwanda, such as access to resources like land. However, for now, for the Twa, Rwandanness offers the pursuit of progress and thus is a rational choice for the realisation of self-interest; at the same time, Rwandanness is

[64] In this regard, Makhunga has noted the emphasis on other identities in Rwanda, such as age and gender, claiming that women are 'seen to "stand above" the particularities of ethnicity' (2019: 391).

[65] The Rwandan unity project is thus not well captured by Scott's notion of the high modernist state, in which homogenisation is contrasted with diversity (1998; Purdeková 2015: 37).

constructed as an ideology that offers the security of belonging through a simply constructed, and therefore accessible, identity. It is these twin promises that underpin Rwandanness that makes it so attractive to a marginalised group; our data does not suggest that Rwandanness is a second choice. Moreover, the very rigidity of the unity on offer – created by the legal framework – is what provides the possibility of ontological security, both by requiring others to treat Twa as equal and by making the offer of inclusion believable. Yet within this rigid frame, Twa acceptance of Rwandanness is partial, carefully chosen, negotiated. The Twa that we spoke to are seeking membership in a modern Rwanda rather than performing modernity as an act of resistance (cf. Bhabha 1990; Ferguson 2006).

6

Acted upon, Acting On

In contrast to previous chapters, which have focused on what our interviewees told us, the first part of this chapter explores the linguistic means by which Twa tell their story. In interviews, individuals would repeatedly assert that they had received nothing from the authorities and were frequently overlooked to the point of abandonment. Yet, the same individuals would often show off to the interviewer a cow or new roof, which they admit that they had received from government distribution programmes. This pattern is considered here as a distinct language practice. Is this a form of emancipatory language practice that protects the 'life within' (Lehman 1998); that is, is it a speech practice that resists intrusive questioning by outsiders? Is it a pragmatic attempt to extract maximum benefit by playing up the extent of their suffering and poverty? Or should we instead read the exchange as a practised form of subordination based on generations of marginalisation; that is, the Twa are expected to be desperate and marginalised by those around them, and it is safer to conform to these expectations?

Despite posing the questions in this way, I am not reading the speech patterns identified as a consciously manipulative practice to extract more resources; nor am I suggesting that the statements of despair and struggle are not genuinely felt. Our interview transcripts are saturated in deeply felt suffering. Instead, by exploring the context as well as the intent – in Austin's terms, the illocutionary nature (1962) – of the contradictory statements, I wish to understand better how Twa are mobilising their resources – in this case, linguistic resources – to assert their place in Rwandan society.

6.1 Illocution, Contradiction, and Negotiation: Navigating the Social

6.1.1 The Phenomenon

A middle-aged woman [I5] in Kamonyi district repeatedly tells the interviewer that she lives in misery, stating, 'I don't have a house or even land. I have nothing.' Moreover, she states that her husband and her children – the key, she says, to what a good life means to her – are all dead. What she needs, therefore, is sponsorship to provide her with money. As the interview progresses, she is asked about the house in which the interview is taking place. The interaction goes as follows: 'Are you the owner of this house?' 'Yes, it is mine!' 'Do you have the legal documents of ownership?' 'I have them!' She goes on to describe receiving land upon her return from Tanzania, part of which she cultivates and part of which she rents out. She talks of her happiness at going to her plot and harvesting vegetables to share with her daughter and grandchildren; she ended the interview because her grandson had arrived. This woman is therefore neither entirely alone, nor does she have nothing. Indeed, the state, as she indirectly acknowledges, is actively supporting her.

I5 was not alone in apparently contradicting herself. This language practice was a common feature of our interviews. Interviewees would state their desperation and abandonment, often dramatically, but then – without a sense of contradicting themselves (i.e. without apology or in any way acknowledging that what they had previously said was not quite accurate) – would openly acknowledge the assistance that they receive from the state, whether land, financial support, free access to healthcare, support with educational expenses, and so on. Indeed, the deeds to a house or the ownership of a cow or goat were often proclaimed with great pride and excitement, whereby the tone of their speech was equally contrasting. These statements of a total lack of assistance or of having nothing are almost always made in the early phases of the interview and are then contradicted as the interview progresses. This could suggest that the statements of desolation and abandonment are a default or starting position that reflects a victimhood born of a lifetime of socio-economic marginalisation. Such an interpretation sees these statements of abandonment as a genuine reflection of how our interviewees felt, despite the material benefits that they acknowledge receiving; that is, the support they receive does not mitigate their suffering. Yet, the contradiction is sometimes immediate,[1] suggesting that there is more going on than simply despair. Moreover, the acknowledgement of assistance was not done in a grudging tone or with an air of despondency – a sort of 'yes,

1 For example, when an elderly male [G14] living in Rwamagana district, Eastern Province, was asked, 'Can you afford to have your own house, pay school fees for your child, or even start a small shop?', he responded: 'Honestly, I cannot afford any of that, my dear!' 'Do you own this house?' 'It is mine!'

I have received this, but my life is still terrible' attitude – but in an excited or celebratory tone.[2]

This contradictory language practice manifests itself not only in relation to access to services and material goods, such as land or housing or healthcare, but also in relation to questions of voice. A woman from Kicukiro district, Kigali Province [I8], told us: 'We don't have anywhere to express our ideas and problems.' Yet she states later in the interview: 'I take our opinions to the sector, district, or even here in our village.' When asked a follow-up question about whether she experiences challenges in expressing her views: 'No challenges. I express what I feel I want to say if we have a village meeting.' Does the statement that she and her neighbours have nowhere to express their views simply reflect her sense that nothing happens as a result of expressing those views? Can the contradiction be explained by the distinction between expressing one's views and being heard?

A similar example comes from G14, an elderly male living in Rwamagana district, Eastern Province. His first statement was, 'Our life is miserable! Imagine a life without land.' When asked if he voices his problems and ideas anywhere, he responded, 'To whom do you think we should express our ideas? The one who was supposed to help us is the one who oppresses us the most. No-one cares about us.' This appears to be a statement of utter despondency and despair. Yet G14 is not helpless. Later in the interview, he describes understanding how the system of authority works in Rwanda because he travels regularly to Kigali for his work. He states openly that he knows where the ministries are and that he could make life difficult for village leaders by bringing his complaints directly to the top. How should we make sense of these statements by a man who proclaims his helplessness but also demonstrates his political astuteness and understanding of the system?

6.1.2 Ubwenge*: A Culture of Dissimulation*

The most obvious way to make sense of our interviews is to place the practice we encountered in the broader Rwandan linguistic context. A number of authors have highlighted the Rwandan linguistic practice of *ubwenge*, which refers to a traditional ethics of communication or

[2] Although the presence of a cow was sometimes not celebrated but lamented because of the lack of ability to feed it properly. Similarly, where livestock had been gifted but had died from disease or hunger, the tone was one of woe.

intelligent public speaking. Ingelaere writes that *ubwenge* 'refers to intelligence resulting in self-controlled public acts' but also 'to elements of wisdom and trickery, caution, cleverness, prudence' (2009: 520). As depicted by Ingelaere, speech acts in Rwanda are not an attempt to depict reality but instead 'serve the status connection between the interlocutors or the broader relationship with the socio-political environment surrounding them' (2009: 518). Communication is therefore esoteric, he claims, noting, crucially, that 'statements at the same time reveal and conceal' (2009: 518). This is aided by a language riddled with proverbs, metaphors, and poetry.[3] What cannot be said openly can be communicated as proverb – many of which highlight duplicity, such as 'the mouth does not always say what lies in the heart' (Purdeková 2015: 91). The success of this form of communication – as with all communication – thus depends not merely on the speaker's skill but also on the receiver's ability to decode the message.

This system of verbal exchange arose in the context of a deeply hierarchical structure, in which only the powerful had access to the 'truth' and ambiguity allowed individuals to speak without confronting the powerful. According to Thomson, this system entrenches the gap between the elites – those 'in the know' – and ordinary people who require guidance; she writes, 'the responsibility of knowing is something reserved for elites' (2018: 232). How one speaks, therefore, reveals the status and social position of the speaker, and *ubwenge* allows one to navigate these hierarchical relations.

6.1.3 Speech Acts

Language is never simply words. Speech, when directed as part of a conversation, is communication intended to have an effect on the audience. The simplest way to explain the language practice or speech act in our transcripts is to view it as an expression of genuine feeling: our interviewees feel despair at their living conditions, and, for some, that leads to feelings of abandonment and despondency, irrespective of whether they do in fact receive assistance from the state. This is to understand the statements as locutionary actions (Austin 1962). Yet, if speech is always a form of social action, we need to ask, with Wittgenstein,

[3] Thomson reports that linguists have identified some 2,500 proverbs in Kinyarwanda (2018: 232).

what the language game is that the speaker is playing (1963). Put in Austin's terms, what is the illocutionary effect sought by the speaker from the locutionary statements of despair and neglect, particularly when contrasted with the open acknowledgement of support?

Boyd White asks the question of how a particular language represents or constitutes the social world (2007). His focus is on discourses, such as the legal language, rather than on language practices, but his questions can, I suggest, help us in unpacking the contradictory language pattern observable in our interviews. Boyd White asks, 'who are the actors, what expectations govern their roles, what relations are assumed to exist between them?' (2007: 10). Boyd White goes further, suggesting that we also need to ask about the relationship between the language and the mind using it. Put differently, he instructs us to ask: what does the language do to me, and what do I do to the language? By this, he is asking how language limits our understanding of others and the world and our ability to engage with them, and how we use the framing power of language in our relations with others – for example, to dominate or resist.

From a different angle, discourse analysis within the field of sociolinguistics seeks to examine language as communication in context. One part of discourse analysis examines how individuals or narrators assign themselves agency through their linguistic choices (de Fina 2006). Another part of this sub-field focuses on narrative in order to unpack identity. Baynham, in his work, seeks to understand how individuals exploit 'narrative resources' (2006: 377) to perform their identity in the context of roles that are assigned to them, for example migrant or Moroccan. As with speech, then, identity is a performance. But it is also a meaning-making process. Schiff and Noy suggest that individuals make sense of their identity and their place in society through the filter of shared constructs – shared social knowledge and meanings – that they use to locate their place and to communicate it to others. 'Tellers borrow many aspects of the social knowledge and incorporate them into their life stories … thus they reconfigure social knowledge in their own terms. At the same time, the process of communicating their interpretation of reality entails negotiations with others, and therefore a renewed sharing of personal meanings' (2006: 348–349; Boyd White 1985). The quote from Schiff and Noy highlights the fact that the contradictory language practice used by our interviewees strikes me as odd precisely because we do not share social constructs. It is not merely that the practice challenges my assumptions about the social world, pushing me to rethink accepted notions or relationships, but it is unreadable to me.

Drawing on these two disciplinary perspectives on language practices helps us to pose the following questions of the Twa language practice: who the audience of the practice is; what shared constructs it speaks to; how the practice attempts to re-negotiate those shared constructs; and how place within society – that is, social identity – is being constructed and asserted.

6.1.4 *Articulating Agency, Negotiating Inclusion*

One way to understand the contradictory language practice is, as previously noted, as a genuine statement of despair – a reflection of the very real poverty in which many Twa live their lives – and, above all, as an appeal to outsiders for assistance.[4] This appeal to outsiders – whether directly to COPORWA or to the foreigners understood to be financing the research – was a constant across the interviews. Thus, in the main response to questions about what they need in order to live a good life, Twa stated that they need more support. This interpretation situates the language practice in the context of a foreign-funded research project, in which the audience is understood by the interviewee (erroneously) to have influence over the distribution of material resources, both state resources and non-state goods.[5] We were repeatedly told that we needed to inform the ministries in Kigali about the problems our interviewees face.

This seeming passivity could be interpreted as a form of resistance, whether to nosy outsiders (e.g. Lehman 1998) or to the power structures that determine Twa poverty. In her work on Rwanda, Thomson draws on Scott's thesis on the 'arts of resistance' to characterise ordinary Rwandan peasants as engaging in tactical resistance against the state's intense intrusion into their everyday lives. Thomson's study focused on national unity and reconciliation. In it, Thomson characterises those who speak truth to power as 'ordinary people who have "nothing left to lose"' (2011: 4). She suggests that being vulnerable entails that the participants in her study lack the personal resources and autonomy necessary to shape

4 For example: 'We think you have the potential to voice our concerns. You should make advocacy for us over there just for our problems to be heard because maybe you can be heard' [K11].

5 Interviewees also named a variety of civil society organisations that should support them, including the Catholic Church.

their lives. She goes on, 'They lack sufficient emotional and physical protection from the government, which in turn makes it difficult for them to anticipate, adapt to, resist, and recover from state-led interventions in their daily lives' (2011: 7). It is this, according to Thomson, that necessitates individual forms of micro-resistance. Thomson identifies three types of everyday resistance: staying on the sidelines, irreverent compliance, and withdrawn muteness. Statements of abandonment in the face of obvious inclusion in at least some government programmes could be read similarly as a form of resistance – a refusal to accept the government's claim to care for them or of failure to achieve its stated development goals. Asserting that they have received nothing from the state and are not heard could be seen as akin to the foot-dragging, quiet sabotage, careless labour, and so on that Scott characterises as forms of Malay peasant resistance (1990: 188).

However, the seemingly passive focus of Twa on simply being given what they need – what would be framed by those within the country as a 'mind-set' problem – is counteracted by the way in which they formulate their need for help.[6] As detailed in Chapter 4, our interviewees were adamant in endorsing the idea that dignity comes from supporting oneself, and they state a clear desire to be productive and to provide for themselves and their family. That might be through being given land that they can work or through being given the means to start a small business, for example selling agricultural produce. The statements of the need for external assistance were therefore made as a necessary first step towards progress, self-sufficiency, and a better life. For example, a woman from Rusizi district told us:

> I need assistance to solve my immediate problems. I need assistance in terms of money that I would use to solve daily problems as others do. Moreover, if I was to get livestock so that I would be able to have something to sell when I have problems, that would make life easier because I would have ways to solve my problems by myself. [B2]

The assistance, then, is as a means to a better life that is characterised by self-sufficiency rather than one of perpetual hand-outs.

The request for assistance is thus one grounded in the reality of their daily lives. In answer to the question of what she needs to enable her to

[6] For more on the framing of Twa as having 'mind-set issues', see Chapter 4. See also Ruhara and Kayitana (2017) for an examination of the entrepreneurial mind-set debate in Rwanda.

lead a good life, an elderly woman from Nyanza district responded: 'I should just get that cattle to make some progress like others. Such a cow or goat can bear many others, but what can I build on when every progress must have a foundation' [H5]. This statement is echoed by that of a woman in Kayonza district, who noted about a life of poverty, 'you cannot build on day-labouring and make progress. I cannot apply for a loan because I have no security' [K11]. These statements indicate that Twa are neither lazy nor ignorant: they understand that poverty is a trap from the practical experience of living it. The statements of need are made in the context of their awareness that they cannot get out of the trap on their own. In order to progress, to empower themselves, they need a helping hand. A woman in Rusizi district told us: 'If I had means, I could certainly engage in something to empower myself' [A1]. A1 went on to speak of her desire to start a small business selling aubergines, dried fish, cooking bananas, and sweet potatoes at the market. This is not a declaration of passivity – whether as an act of micro-resistance or not – but an active statement of self-empowerment. While our interviewees may lack some of the material resources that they need to shape their lives, they do not appear to lack autonomy.

This desire for self-empowerment goes together with gratitude for what they have already received. In such a reading, the contradiction between the acknowledgement of what they have received and their assertions of receiving nothing is a consequence of the confrontation between the reality of their lives and their desire to be 'good Rwandans', with dignified lives that contribute to the community. In the words of a woman from Nyaruguru district,

> Once I received the cow [from the Girinka programme], I have to struggle to find a spot where I can grow it grass and I get that from other villagers. I also farm and now I am planning on growing vegetables. I have harvested sweet potatoes. I do not have to buy them. I have made some progress because I used to buy everything with no resources but now I produce some of the things we need. State programmes have therefore allowed me to be a little self-reliant and I am grateful for that. [D1]

Likewise, a woman from Rutsiro district vowed: 'If I had capital, I would do everything possible to make progress even if it would come from assistance. . . . I would just take around 200,000 Frws and try to pay it back within one year and I would work so hard to move forward' [K9]. Again, what one sees here, in addition to acknowledgement of support, is an aspiration towards self-reliance and the dignity that comes with that.

How should we understand this assertion of dignity further? While I do not read Twa's contradictory language practice as resistance to the state, it could reasonably be conceived as resistance to the characterisation by authorities at all levels of Twa as having 'mind-set' problems (cf. Scott 1985: 236).[7] The societal trope of 'mind-set' is intended to be both a diagnosis and a motivational tool. Yet, it is frequently used instead to characterise the poor as passive and lazy and hence as at least partly responsible for their own situation. In her study on individual post-traumatic growth in the wake of the genocide, Williamson Sinalo notes that there is pressure on survivors to adopt a narrative of progress – both in terms of reconciliation and in relation to economic development. She quotes one Kigali banker who told her that poverty is a state of mind (2018: 41). Those with mind-set problems are thus seen as a barrier to national progress, and it is a label that is most commonly applied to Twa.[8] To have a mind-set problem is to be the antithesis of a 'good Rwandan', who strives for self-reliance and dignity (NURC 2007).

Scott frames everyday resistance – what he has famously termed in the context of Malay peasant life as 'the weapons of the weak' (1985) – as being set against those who seek to extract labour, taxes, rent, and so on from the peasantry. He suggests that these everyday forms of resistance require little to no co-ordination and make use of implicit understandings. These weapons include 'the war of words' or 'argument as resistance' (Scott 1985: 233). Here Scott reads the contest for symbolic authority that plays out in how wealthy villagers describe their poorer neighbours, and vice versa. Whereas the wealthy peasants seek to account for the poverty of their neighbours by describing them as lazy, unreliable, dishonest, and grasping, the poor hit back with malicious gossip and unflattering nicknames, and blame the landholders' greed and grasping nature for their economic woes (Scott 1985: 240). One can perhaps see the claims of unfairness that play out in the relationship of Twa with local authorities in Rwanda as something similar: yet, rather than insulting them, the Twa are reminding local leaders of their duties to provide them with the means to improve their lives. Similarly, by emphasising their

[7] An alternative reading would take a socio-psychological approach and perhaps view the statement of despair as a desire for community recognition of suffering, with the assertion of strength being a reminder of one's agency or empowerment: see, e.g., Klouzal (2003).

[8] See the statement of the minister of local government to the Senate in 2019 to the question of why the problems of Historically Marginalised Peoples had not yet been solved, cited in Chapter 2. Assertions of mind-set problems were also common in our interviews with civil society organisations working at grassroot levels.

poverty while simultaneously asserting their desire to progress, they are pushing back against the belief that they are beset by mind-set problems.

On this reading, *ubwenge* can help to explain the use of contradiction as a linguistic tool or resource; that is, by focusing on the position of the speaker (Baynham 2006). In his work on Ba Yaka Pygmy communication, Lewis highlights the use of mimicry to navigate through societal space. Lewis writes, 'Bayaka communicative strategies serve to maintain multi-species and multicultural relationships that reinforce the Bayaka view of themselves not as subjects in a society outside nature, but rather as a society of nature' (2014: 86). Mimicry is therefore a key part of communication with other sentient beings within the forest. But it is used not just with non-human species. The Mbendjele – a Ba Yaka community – explained that they mimic farmers' language and play into the stereotypes of them in order to get things from them safely. This research is helpful in two ways in understanding Twa language practices. Firstly, our interviewees are arguably playing into stereotypes of mind-set issues before asserting that they are 'good Rwandans' who want to live lives of self-reliance and dignity. As such, they are performing the idea of backwardness or of being left behind (cf. Bauman 2000). The technique of contradiction softens the critique of the local authorities in the context of being in a subordinate position; that is, agency is asserted in a safer manner, similarly to how claims of unfairness are made but usually stop short of accusations of group-based discrimination. Yet, despite 'pulling their punches', the meaning would remain easily comprehensible to the target audience – just as within *ubwenge*.

Secondly, the context in which the language practice occurs involves a form of mimicry. The Twa are mimicking not only their subordinate position but also the state's message of dignity through self-empowerment (NURC 2007). The Twa are repeating it back, and, in doing so, are reminding the local authorities of their obligation to them. In the context of his research in the Malay countryside, Scott writes of the 'logic of the accusation' (1985: 168). With this, he is drawing attention to the way in which the poor villagers blamed fellow villagers for their plight rather than the outsiders who came in to take advantage of land for rent. It is only in the context of membership in a shared community that members have obligations towards each other that go beyond material gain. Blaming local authorities rather than the past or the unfair global structure is a smart strategy in that it targets those within their realm of social action without challenging government policy or the basis of their inclusion in society, which they desire.

Where Thomson suggests in her work that the forms of obedience within ordinary Rwandans' resistance practices are tactical because they seek to limit their interaction with the authorities (2011: 15), I also read the contradictory language practices as strategic communication – but not as a means to limit interaction with the authorities. Instead, it is an assertion of their right to be included and to be treated with equal concern. The language of abandonment only makes sense if there is an obligation for them to be included that they expect the authorities to recognise. Similarly, an appeal to fairness assumes that one's audience accepts the speaker's inclusion in a collective and thus as someone to whom fairness is owed. Statements of abandonment are less an attempt, therefore, to subvert the state narrative of *agaciro* than a demand that it is fully realised. Where Scott writes of the 'resistant subcultures of dignity' through which 'vengeful dreams are created and nurtured' (1990: 200), the Twa are instead demanding that the promise of inclusion be fulfilled.

Moreover, these are not vengeful dreams. The contradictory language practice is not an exclusionary practice; that is, it is not about pushing Twa forward at the expense of other Rwandans. It is about catching up. This suggests a key difference between Scott's characterisation of the Malay countryside and Rwanda: whereas Scott frames his case study as a struggle over the definition of justice, there is no such struggle with the Twa. They are not presenting a different vision of Rwanda or of their place in it. Instead, their main complaint concerns the speed of their inclusion, not how that inclusion is being conceptualised.[9] The demand for more, the assertion of a desire to work hard and progress, is, in the words that Scott uses to describe Malay peasant life, 'a decisive assertion of their citizenship rights' (1985: 236). In this way, the contradictory language practice can be read as loudly[10] demonstrating their place in Rwandan society: they believe that they have a claim to a fair share of material resources and that their claim should be heard. The indirect audience of this speech practice – as filtered first through the community-based interviewers, then the foreigner researchers, then the ministry in Kigali – is thus the local authorities who determine resource allocation. Included in their locution is, therefore, an expectation or a hope of the illocutionary effect that their speech will have.[11]

[9] This should be nuanced: as we saw in Chapter 5, a group of Twa do complain about the lack of recognition of Twa cultural practices.

[10] Loud because of the abrupt or jarring character of contradiction.

[11] Hope perhaps more than expectation, given – as Chapter 4 suggests – the continued stress by local leaders on the mind-set problems of Twa.

This interpretation of the language practice as a claim for inclusion is supported by the meaning that our interviewees gave to the notion of fairness. Fairness was expressed as being with others in the community, not above them. This is reflected in an explanation by an elderly lady in Gakenke district of what the good life means. She told us: 'For me to have a better life it is when I have support that can raise me from where I am to an improved level. I don't want very high but at least in the middle' [G9]. This is a desire to catch up, to be equal – not to gain more at the expense of others. This reflects a strong accent on the importance of community in our interviews. We were repeatedly told by Twa that they are happiest when they have good relations with their neighbours and when they are sharing what little they have with others. The language practice suggests that this fellow-feeling is extended beyond neighbours to all Rwandans, not only members of the Twa community. G9's comment can thus be read as an assertion of her community of belonging. In this way, we can read the language practice as an active choice for inclusion as Rwandan, and to be co-creators of Rwanda through their membership of communities and in the governance thereof. Thus, while this strategic communication could be interpreted as individualised desires and/or demands, it is important to contextualise it within the importance our interviewees accorded to community, which is conceptualised broadly as everyone in Rwanda.

6.1.5 In Sum

This first part of the chapter has suggested that it is possible to read the contradictory language practice identified here as a form of resistance. However, if we wish to use the language of resistance, what the Twa are resisting is not the state or their neighbours but poverty and the labelling of them as having mind-set problems. Where there is a tendency in resistance studies to perceive the state as a bad actor, our data does not support such an interpretation. Instead, I have framed the widespread use of contradiction – of abandonment followed by acknowledgement of support – as an assertion by Twa of their full membership in society. In place of resistance to an overweening state, they are demanding that the local authorities live up to the state's promise of inclusion. This is a claim to equal concern, of access to full citizenship rights along with all other Rwandans. As part of this demand for equal concern, they challenge the label of poor mind-set by demonstrating their adoption of the narrative of *agaciro* and their willingness to work hard towards self-reliance.

Moreover, while the language practice of contradiction softens the message, the intended audience (the local authorities and, indirectly, central government and fellow citizens) is nonetheless expected to hear the illocutionary intent – and there appears to be little fear of retaliation. This is, then, rather different to the descriptions of everyday resistance that Thomson and Scott detail.

Thus, in place of the language of resistance, I am suggesting – as I have been doing throughout this work – that agency, understood as necessarily situational, is a more appropriate term to characterise the Twa's language practice and navigation more generally. By beginning with saying that they have nothing and are not heard, our interviewees are able to magnify their agency when they go on to assert their dignity. Seen as agency, the use of contradiction as a form of strategic communication can be characterised as an attempt to re-negotiate the social constructs that govern the position of Batwa in society. As such, they are attempting to mobilise linguistic resources – within the overarching pattern of *ubwenge* – to challenge their continued exclusion under the charge of 'mind-set' problems and to assert a positive place in society. Archer suggests that to be an agent and an actor, we need first to have a sense of self (2000). My suggestion here is that the security of the sense of self offered to Twa by being Rwandan is what anchors the agency reflected in these language patterns.

6.2 Subjectivity and Agency within and across Global Jurisdictional Ordering

This book set out with the intention of illuminating daily practices of global jurisdiction ordering in Rwanda and within Twa daily life. What have we learned from how the Twa experience and engage with their transformation into global subjects?

6.2.1 Varied Topographies of Global Law: Acted Upon?

In his classic work *The Idea of Africa*, Mudimbe describes how the Belgians and the Catholic Church colonised and Christianised the Congo. In doing so, they invented a new colonial memory that sought to replace the African memory and convert the colonised 'to a new order' – one that was predicated upon 'the erasure of tradition and the production of the convert within "modernity"' (Mudimbe 1994: 133). Mudimbe writes: 'The metamorphosis of a memory, such as that found in an African colonial territory, is not simply a symbolic occurrence. It takes place during a process of neutralization, re-creation and rearrangement of a site, of its geography, and of the values by which a tradition distinguished it' (1994: 134). The practices of global law equally entail the metamorphosis of a memory, transforming the geography, interactions, and self-understanding of individuals and communities. Local relationships are reframed and superseded by the demands and promises of global subjectivity; and by the possibility and imposition of new rights and obligations – such as the obligation to protect nature or the right to enjoy one's culture or to inherit land as an individual.

This reframing occurs through what Eslava has described in his study of global life in Bogotá as the 'intense escalation of legal production' (2015: 255).[12] Where the border of legal/illegal space does the heavy work of reconstituting the city of Bogotá as global, in Rwanda, legislation and administrative decrees are used to reorder both the physical and moral space of Rwanda, from the laws that form the parks and protect wildlife and those that mandate 'development' through administrative fines, to the laws that create a liberalised land market, overriding customary practices on land use and inheritance, to criminal law that de-ethnicises political and social life.[13] Law is the means of the state asserting authority over space and people, but also over imaginations of the future. Law is mobilised to achieve the state's moral purpose: to unify the country and to mould model citizens, to transform Rwanda's past as well as its future. Through these national legal reforms, the model of the good development subject is thus institutionalised, along with the right form of political economy and the correct attitude to nature protection. In this way, as Eslava astutely observes, local actors become 'performers of the international in disguise' (2015: 251).

Yet the effects of global law are both varied and mediated. An essential contribution of ethnographic studies within global law is to elucidate the unique ways in which global law transforms daily life in different places at a particular moment in time. This study has shown how the fragmented subjectivities (Urueña 2012) formed by various global discourses or

[12] As Eslava notes, 'the turn to law arises . . . from an assumption . . . that it possesses an infinite capacity to coordinate the social and physical world' (2015: 241). See also Boyd White (1985) for the modernist understanding of law as a technology of public management.

[13] In reaching for the law as the means of achieving unity and reconciliation, Rwanda is a model of the 'liberal legalism' famously decried by Trubek and Galanter as representing the hallmark of the first wave of law and development (1974).

jurisdictional claims play out unevenly in Rwanda's ministries, agencies, and local administrations, and in its villages and neighbourhoods – with some narratives gaining greater traction than others. Although global jurisdictional encounters are asymmetrical in terms of knowledge production and disciplinary power, local agency constantly threatens to destabilise established narratives. Moreover, these encounters are not static, and the friction created in the encounter sees discourses, and the narratives within them, alter over time through the changing engagement at the local level: accepting, reframing, mobilising, or resisting. It is the friction inherent to these encounters that creates the space for agency. For example, the friction between Rwanda's enduring colonial legacy and the development narrative helps to create the space for Twa to demand inclusion in the vision of a modern Rwanda.

In addition to further highlighting the variable topography of global ordering, this study makes two contributions to reflections on global jurisdictional encounters. The first is in relation to how jurisdictional encounters are mediated. The second concerns the importance of an understanding of agency that goes beyond resistance.

6.2.2 *Mediation of the Global*

An important aspect of the study of global legal ordering is how localities are brought into a relationship with the global; in other words, how the jurisdictional encounters take place. The centrality of law to global life requires institutions capable of translating global ordering narratives into daily life, whether city authorities, local authorities, courts, civil society, or national regulators. Recent studies have sought to de-centre the state, seeing the international as reborn through the local (e.g. Eslava 2015). This study, however, suggests the need for a broader consideration of the nature of mediated global administration. In Rwanda, the mediator is the state. In place of local authorities enacting regulation dictated by global demands, a strong central state – one that has deliberately crowded out other potential mediators – is instead engaging with global narratives, refracting them in the service of a clear national goal of unity.[14] Where states have elsewhere been characterised as mere

[14] I am not at all suggesting that we should be re-centring the state in our studies but am instead highlighting that the state retains a key role in certain contexts in how global or transnational law is mediated; see, further, the discussion in Zumbansen (2020).

extensions of the global order, the situation here suggests that the function of mediation is more complex. For example, Rwanda harnesses the global discourse of development to make its vision of citizenship meaningful; and the individualised duty to develop resonates at the local level in Rwanda in part because of the colonial mind-set debates that the post-colonial state has adopted. Similarly, the state has embraced the narrative of global conservationism, enacting its core principles through legal reforms and education programmes, actively implementing the model of capitalist-conservationism within its economic agenda. Simultaneously, the Rwandan state refuses to engage with the global discourse of indigeneity, and works hard – through government messaging on unity and development and through pro-poor programming and the stick of criminalisation – to ensure that indigenous or minority rights do not gain traction among its population. Rwanda thus mobilises its moral and material resources in order to navigate the dense and interacting demands of the global. While a mediator cannot dictate the content or form of global narratives, some are able to magnify or negate them, playing a key role in determining how the global is received by other actors.

Although Rwanda has adopted the neo-liberal idea of the entrepreneurial individual who is self-motivated and hard-working, this is not combined with moves towards a small state. The state is omnipresent. While governmentality in Rwanda is a little neo-liberal, it is a lot nationalist (cf. Ferguson and Gupta 2002). In contrast to Hodgson's thesis that the disenfranchisement within states brought about by the imposition of neo-liberal imperatives has led to the rise of civil society actors and to efforts to seek justice at the international level (2011), this is not something that we see in Rwanda. Instead, market-based technologies of control and the depoliticisation of knowledge are hitched to old-fashioned nationalist politics.

The dominance of the Rwandan state in mediating the reception of global ordering does not entail, however, that there are no other mediators. Civil society actors in the form of activists softly repeat Twa claims to indigeneity at local meetings, including a return to the forest. Regional civil society networks and family ties that snake across state borders ensure that people are cognisant of claims by Ugandan Twa to indigenous status and their expressed desire to return to the Bwindi Impenetrable Forest (Ampumuza et al. 2020; Kokunda et al. 2023). However, the dominance of the Rwandan state – its ability to mobilise its material and moral resources, including the discourses of development and conservation, together with the clarity of its narrative of national unity – fills the space and ensures, at least for now, that the ground is not fertile for an alternative ordering claim. Instead, the Rwandan state makes use of global development, refracting it through the prism of national unity, to offer Twa a plausible, accessible vision of a non-fragmented modern Rwandan subject. Thus, while Rwanda projects a tale of home-grown solutions for problems that were created by colonialism to its domestic audience, its approach is intimately entwined with its colonial past and with contemporary global jurisdictional assemblages.

6.2.3 *Situated Agency, Not Just Resistance*

The second contribution of this study to the field of global law is to suggest the need for a broadening out of how we study and understand the encounter with global jurisdictional claims. A Foucauldian analysis has been extremely useful in highlighting the exercise of power, subjecthood, and the formation of law-like institutional practices through his development of discourse as a frame of analysis. However, the dominance within the scholarly literature of Foucault's insistence on resistance, and to a lesser extent Gramsci's work on hegemony, as key to understanding power dynamics has led to the side-lining of other vocabularies and to a dominant focus on opposition or confrontation. This approach has combined with the rise of work examining social movements in the Third World (Rajagopal 2003): in place of understanding such movements through the lens of class-based interests or of national politics, attention was turned to identity as the basis of mobilisation, organisation, and attempted renewal. For example, in his reflections on the emergence of Black identity in the Pacific, Escobar notes that one of the 'ultimate' questions for identity is 'whether a strategy of opposition can lead to a strategy of construction of a new order and to a positive reorganization of the social' (2008: 207). That is, the central question for Escobar here is whether formulating identity as difference is able to bring about the social change desired.

Yet, this study suggests that resistance is not the only – or, I would argue, most appropriate – lens through which to understand Twa engagement with global narratives and thus with the state. What we see here is that the patterns of authority enacted by global discourses and mediated by the state do not call up resistance. Nor can the Twa response be characterised as a resigned or bitter compliance. Instead, we see a form of navigated acceptance. While the Twa push back against attempts to make them responsible for their poor living conditions by playing up to the right mind-set, this is situated within the broad acceptance of global development subjecthood as reframed by the state. As such, they are not contesting their subjectivity but pushing for more of it.

As I have argued throughout the book, there is a need to expand how we understand global jurisdictional encounters to focus on agency more broadly – an agency that is situated and, following Mahmood, that is open to how individuals and communities inhabit norms (2011). This involves stepping back from an understanding that sees agency as synonymous with resistance and instead viewing space to act through a broader palette of human emotions and desires. In place of the stark dichotomy of resistance or acceptance – otherwise, resistance or assimilation – we take notice instead of the space of navigation within normative structures. As such, the study of global law needs to pay attention to how jurisdictional encounters form structures or sites of exclusion and inclusion, how they are co-opted, negated, or refracted, and what that does with and to actors; in other words, how it creates or negates possibilities for agency and affects the self-understanding of actors.

This requires us to give greater consideration to emotions and, in particular, to a broad array of emotions: we must take seriously expressions of suffering, but also articulations of hope, desires, and joy.[15] Further, we should not see emotions as necessarily mapping directly onto self-interest; instead, emotional responses can deepen our understanding of stated self-interests, also by undermining such positionings. For all our cynicism about development discourse, our interviewees were keen development subjects and were forthright in articulating a hyper-individualised, entrepreneurial vision of development. Yet, when asked what brings them joy, they presented a desire for a good life that is based in community, a life in which neighbours share food and banana beer and in which they dance together. This is a different vision of development and of a desired future than that of the 'model Rwandan citizen'. To characterise the Twa as resisting development subjectivity or as being forced to perform the correct mind-set does not therefore capture their full range of daily emotions. Where a life lived in community accepting of

[15] In her work on the emotional geographies of access to water, Farhana Sultana highlights that 'a range of emotional sentiments come to constitute water–society relations'; beyond the pain and suffering, she notes, there is also pleasure, relief, joy, and contentment (2011: 168).

them brings them joy, their hope is expressed through the desire for material progress, while the daily reality is frequently one of suffering and desperation. We need to incorporate the full array of emotions into our studies in order to better understand the experience of daily life within patterns of global ordering. By paying attention to emotions within the study of law, we are more easily able to see beyond law's fixed categories, identities, and roles. In his book *Territories of Difference*, Escobar asks the question of how one can engage with the incompleteness of capitalist development without seeing resistance everywhere (2008: 83). I am suggesting that, following Klouzal (2003), part of the answer to this question lays in paying more attention to emotional expressions of well-being within development practices, including how they view all the resources at their disposal: subjective, linguistic, material, cultural.

This focus on the hopes and desires of the individuals and communities subjected to global jurisdictional claims also makes clear that the irregularity of the topography of the global is not merely a result of the different positioning of a state within a global or post-colonial landscape, or by the different form of mediated administration, but also by the desires and actions of local actors. How they respond to global subjectivities and the extent to which these claims match or facilitate their desires also plays a part in determining the extent to which these claims have resonance and reach. The Twa have transformed participation within development into national belonging. Where global narratives locate Twa in a struggle for indigenous rights, within conservationism as either indigenous or as poachers, or as potential or partially realised development subjects, they have chosen to locate themselves within the framing of development subjects as members of a national community, demanding not difference but equal concern. What the Twa are doing is a form of jurisdictional politics, repositioning themselves from one legal narrative – that of difference and of indigeneity – to another, that of national development. In doing so, they are re-subjectivising themselves – through their performance of subjectivity by playing up to the notion of mind-set – as simultaneously development's subjects and as Rwandan.

6.3 A Demand for Membership and Care

Meera Nanda has famously detailed how '"emancipation" from the West as well as all institutions of modern nation-states, even democratically elected, developmentalist states, has become the cherished end of every post-colonial social project', where the chosen vehicle of this emancipation is indigeneity (2001: 163). Good post-colonial subjects are meant to have seen through Western conceptions of reason and modernity and refuse to buy into their promises by selling out their traditional beliefs. Development has therefore come to be seen as dangerous for the marginalised and vulnerable and to be associated with destruction – of the environment, community, alternative epistemologies, and ways of life. While this is a vital critiquc of development, it obviously does not explain how development discourse has managed to capture and hold collective imaginations in order to determine reality (Escobar 1995).

In his later reflections on the idea of post-development, Escobar teases out three modalities for post-development engagement with modernity. The first of these is 'alternative development', which focuses on food security and the satisfaction of basic well-being for all; the second he labels 'alternative modernities', in which contestation by local groups against development interventions leads to the contestation of global designs; the third, and most radical, project is 'alternatives to modernity', whereby local and regional worlds are redefined and reconstructed on the basis of cultural, economic, and ecological difference (2008: 162). This attempt at categorising post-development agency according to the degree of subversiveness opens up the possibility of active engagement with development without needing to divide responses into a hard binary of either resistance or co-optation. Our interviewees do not see development as a neo-colonial imposition. They instead see it as the promise of a better life: decent housing, access to sanitation, sufficient food, access to healthcare, a good education, and belonging. If we were to place the Twa in Escobar's scheme, they are seeking alternative development, one in which their basic needs are met and where they come in from the margins. This 'virtual dimension' of progress is development as desire or as transcendental (Beard 2007; de Vries 2007: 29). Twa agency within development subjecthood is in part the demand for the promised imaginary of progress to be realised. The Twa are thus not seeking an alternative to modernity, or to radically unsettle existing understandings, but rather membership in it. Their claim to inclusion is a claim to membership in the modern, globalised world, with all the benefits of material progress that capitalism promises (Ferguson 2006).

Demands for access to the fruits of capitalism have long been a central part of the decolonisation agenda. In his analysis of the interrelation between capitalism and colonialism in *The Wretched of the Earth*, Fanon captured this succinctly in his statement: 'you are rich because you are white, you are white because you are rich' (1963: 40). Demanding inclusion in material progress does not need to be seen as co-optation into a capitalist development model but can equally be understood as a claim to equal humanity – or, in Ferguson's terms, inclusion in the first rank (2006: 187). Ownership of their own home or of livestock was offered up to our interviewers as proof not only of being a good development subject but also that they matter. The Twa are thus engaged in struggles over symbolic meanings, as well as over access to material resources; that is, their demand for inclusion is a struggle against ideas that define them as less worthy of care and respect. This is not a call for equal rights – even less is it a claim for recognition of difference – but is a demand for equal care. When, for example, Twa appeal to norms of non-discrimination to assert their inclusion, it is vernacularised through the framework of care and community, such as sharing a beer. This can be read as an attempt to reformulate their development subjecthood from a hyper-individualism into membership in the community: as Twa are demanding care, they are also expressing community with and seeking it from fellow citizens. The good life – as our interviewees repeatedly told us – requires food to eat, but also food to share. The call for membership based on a notion of care is thus a demand for a form of community-based politics beyond the transactional relationship between state and citizen imagined by liberal theories of rights, whereby the space of agency is created here by engaging with the state as plural; that is, by dividing the local authorities from the state and by engaging with the latter via criticism of the local. Seeking membership is thus a creative engagement with the idea of Rwandanness that can involve an attempt to rewrite what membership means, both nationally and within global discourse.

For Twa, the politics of care finds expression in equal access to material goods as well as in (the enforcement of) full inclusion in Rwandan society. This demand for equal care is an assertion by Twa of their dignity, both in relations with fellow Rwandans and with the authorities. It is thus at its core a claim to inter-connectedness – a searching in daily life for recognition of their Rwandanness and not of their alterity. Yet despite this, and despite formal legal erasure, the Twa continue to exist as a community, both directly and indirectly: even as Rwandan development subjects, the Twa continue to exist at the local level as Twa in the minds of their neighbours, the local authorities, and, more importantly, their own minds. Membership does not therefore entail disappearance (cf. Escobar 2008) – at least not in the short term. This raises the question of whether allowing the recognition of cultural differentiation within a strong Rwandan identity – for example, by facilitating pride in being a Rwandan Twa – could in fact further strengthen feelings of Rwandan belonging. Barth has suggested in his work on inter-group boundaries that recognition of difference does not necessarily lead to a social boundary, and social boundaries do not inevitably lead to conflict (1969; also Broch-Due 2004). Membership does not necessarily equate to sameness, so long as acknowledgement of cultural difference does not become a justification of marginalisation.[16]

This study suggests that the combined formulation of progress and belonging here is working to legitimise the political project of creating development subjects from ethnic subjects – at least in relation to the Twa. White has noted in the context of the global narrative that development is 'determinedly colour-blind' (2002: 407), and the focus here on poverty and vulnerability has allowed the Rwandan state to de-ethnicise the concept of progress. Where we started in this project from the position that the criminalisation of ethnicity would constitute a barrier to the participation of Twa, our data suggests that the opposite is the case. The hard stance taken, reflected in the criminalisation of ethnicity, has instead provided the ontological security upon which the Twa are crafting a space for agency. However, as is also clear from this tale, de-ethnicising is not necessarily to de-politicise progress: ethnicity is not the only possible basis for political contestation. If there is little space to contest authority within Rwanda, that is arguably for other reasons.

Moreover, it is important to note that it is not yet clear that the Rwandan state will make good on the promise of progress that underpins Rwandanness. As recently reported by the UN Special Rapporteur on Extreme Poverty and Human Rights, while the state's efforts to reduce poverty are impressive, the benefits of economic growth are unevenly divided, and inequality is rising (De Schutter 2025). This is most evident in the growing gap between urban and rural areas, the latter being where the vast majority of Twa (and other Rwandans) live, and between the highly skilled and the rest of the population. In addition, as detailed in

[16] Yet it is important to stress the right of communities, where they choose to do so, to assert a difference that 'goes all the way down' and be recognised for it (see Tully 1995). My point is rather that the right to difference should not become an obligation to differentiate oneself or to articulate a separate identity.

Chapter 3, land ownership is key to the Twa sense of belonging, both in terms of the materiality of being able to grow one's own food and in terms of social status; and it is equally unclear whether or how the state will be able to transpose this desire for land into some other form of socio-economic well-being that it can actually deliver. The Twa choice for Rwandanness is premised – yes, in part, on the destruction of their traditional way of life – but, more importantly, on the believability of the promise of progress and inclusion made by the state. A failure to fulfil the promise will not only undermine the core message of unity but will likely also lead to wider political contestation at the local level.

6.4 The Curious Case of Rwanda?

This book has told a tale of the Twa and therefore also of contemporary Rwanda.[17] This tale sees Rwanda's Twa – for as far as our data is generalisable – choosing the promise of progress and belonging offered by the state. What, though, if anything, does this tell us about indigeneity in Africa or about the global development state more broadly? Put differently, is Rwanda a unique case?

Critical development scholarship of the last decades has unpacked how the Global South state is viewed as defective, whereby development and human rights interventions are needed to reconfigure the state (e.g. Picciotto 2000; Tan 2011). Simultaneously with global institutions viewing the Global South state as deficient, counter-hegemonic scholars typically see the Third World state as having colonised all political space, as well as civil society space and even the life of the mind (Rajagopal 2003: 419; Nandy 2010). From a post-colonial African perspective, Mamdani and Mbembe describe a post-colonial society in which the citizen has little to no direct relationship with the state. Instead, the family, the lineage, the kin, and even the religious community stand between them, and are responsible for ensuring individual well-being or survival (Mamdani 1996; Mbembe 2001: 45). But our interviewees do not experience the Rwandan state as deficient or distant. It is the state, mediated through the local authorities, that is the repository of our interviewees' hopes and that is the focus of their demands for care.

Rwanda has responded to the inter-group violence of the twentieth century with a totalising narrative of unity: every aspect of the state is

[17] My thanks to Ambreena Manji for suggesting that I consider the ideas detailed in this section.

geared towards achieving 'unity as Rwandanness'. Having goals is one thing, but the Rwandan state – with its small, heavily centralised state; tradition of a single 'father-type' leader standing above politics; and shared language and culture across ethnic groups (McDoom 2020) – is also able to enact its plans: for example, the strong commitment to pro-poor programming has led to significant improvements in poverty reduction, despite the many structural challenges that Rwanda faces. Similarly, the state has overcome the complex webs of alternative belongings by requiring participation in state development programmes, and through the formation of collectives and other forms of institutionalised community co-operation, such as *umuganda*. These programmes also work to tie individuals to physical place – to territorialise and localise them – in place of connections to networks of belonging that flow past state borders and risk the possibility of destabilisation from outside. It is the participation in these programmes and the related institutions, as well as the structural memory – nurtured by the state – of the violence that tore the country apart, that ties the individual to the state, giving the state its dominant presence in the daily socio-political life of all Rwandans (Thomson 2013).[18] And, if this re-education or sensitisation fails, the law – constitutional and criminal law, and administrative decrees – is used to enforce the eradication of ethnicity from the public realm. The combination of clarity of purpose and the capacity to make it real is what makes the promises of inclusion in an imagined future Rwanda believable. The Rwandan state has been able to harness the global development narrative to its reconciliation and unity agenda, creating a powerful force that is able to speak directly to the yearning of its citizens for a better life.

In addition to delivering on the promise of progress, the Rwandan state has sought to legitimise itself internally by presenting the country as charting its own course, with emphasis on its post-colonial credentials through *agaciro* and home-grown solutions. Using the rhetorical technique of before-and-after storytelling (Barthes 1977), the state claims 1994 not as the before-and-after of genocide but as the culmination of colonial rule, thereby allowing the current regime to be the start of the post-colonial era. In this story, global narratives are co-opted by the state into a national renewal project.

Yet while unity-as-Rwandanness is set as the highest moral value, it represents nonetheless a Rwanda-in-the-world. Rwanda is not precious

[18] The problems created by a top-down developmental state in Rwanda have been well documented elsewhere (Ansoms 2009, 2011; Sundberg 2016: 42–43).

about language or culture, with English becoming the dominant language of education and success. Traditional culture is packaged for tourists as a means of providing financial support to communities, but – with the exception of the Kigali Convention Center – there is little pride in these traditions within state policy. In contrast, then, to the 'lexicographers, philologists, grammarians, folklorists, publicists and composers' of nineteenth-century European nationalism (Anderson 1983: 75), Rwanda's nationalism is led by politicians who position themselves as administrators and moral leaders, and is supported by entrepreneurs, religious leaders, and park officials. Rwanda is situating itself as a global state economically – accepting almost without question the broad lines of the global narratives on development and conservationism[19] – yet presents itself at home as in full control over Rwanda's 'morality' and over how the Rwandan nation is constituted internally. This focus on home-grown solutions can be read as a way of sublating the colonial inheritance, of achieving epistemic freedom. From a different angle, however, Rwandan morality looks very similar to the civilising ethics of the coloniser. The relationship of the state to its citizens is itself part of a global tale, whereby states became forcefully embedded in relationships of power, racial ideologies, and notions of what being human is (property, God, nation), and out of which forms of global legal ordering have emerged.

The Rwandan state is able to combine the legitimacy[20] of its unity agenda with the capacity to deliver it to an impressive degree. It is thus not so much any unique position of Rwanda in global figurations that might explain the story told here but rather the Rwandan state's clear focus on and dedication to achieving its goals. However, where Reyntjens asserts that law has been used to 'reconfigure the ethnic map' (2024: 175), and while it is the case that the Twa, like all Rwandans, are forcefully citizenised through the legal articulation of Rwanda's unity narrative, the willingness of Twa to accept the offer of inclusion is also due to the particular circumstances of Rwanda's Twa, most of which were determined by previous regimes. It is clear that the Twa in Rwanda have lost what Escobar terms their 'history-making skills' (2008: 234): based on our data, their connection to their group past and to cultural practices in their everyday lives has been almost entirely severed. For what remains to be

[19] On how African agency is curtailed by international economic governance, see Okafor (2006).

[20] Legitimacy here refers to legitimacy in the eyes of our interviewees. I am not speaking to the overall legitimacy of the regime, which has been extensively covered elsewhere (see, inter alia, Sundberg 2016).

saved, Twa culture would need to be incorporated into Rwandanness by the state and promoted with pride – not in place of the promise of membership and progress, but within it. Moreover, we should not underestimate the depth of poverty that Twa endure and the misery and despair that it engenders. Yet, the law is never so simple as to be one thing: while what we see in Rwanda may be rule by law rather than rule of law, the legal rules here also express care. Inclusion by law is providing security to Twa and empowering a marginalised community to demand their inclusion. However, it is important to reiterate again that what is true for Twa may not be true for other groups within Rwandan society, whether other ethnic groups or other sections of society, such as women or those with disabilities. While I suggested in Chapter 1, following Taylor (2011), that Twa are an important bellwether for Rwanda society, the tiny size of the community and its marginalisation within society allow Twa flexibility within the strictures of the unity narrative. Contestation can more easily come from the margins, and the Twa, as evidenced here, are using that freedom to carve out space to negotiate their inclusion. They are acted upon, yes, but are also acting on; that is, exercising agency.

Our findings do not of course entail that Rwanda's Twa will not, at a different moment, choose to articulate their desires and hopes through the language of difference or, specifically, indigeneity rather than through the framework of Rwandanness. At such a moment, if it comes, they may, for example, claim restitution or compensation for the loss of a way of life. This can happen whether or not the state is able to deliver on the progress they so desire. As the response of Twa disappointed by redistribution efforts made clear, if the promise of progress is not fulfilled – if access to land cannot be provided – then it seems almost certain that accusations of ethnic-based discrimination will grow. What this story does not suggest, however, is that minorities or indigenous peoples are only choosing to assert their unique difference at the political level because they have not been offered anything 'better'. Simply because indigenous rights allow for political positioning (Hodgson 2011), it does not follow that the feelings and beliefs motivating such claims are not genuine or deserving of recognition and respect.[21] Moreover, a living culture rooted in a different cosmovision is unlikely to choose for estrangement from that culture because of improvements in public services and inclusion in the wider community. The choice of

[21] There is nothing in Hodgson's influential work to suggest that she is arguing otherwise.

Rwanda's Twa is their own and not a blueprint for other communities or authorities to implement.

Attempting to capture the necessary contingency of subjectivity in the post-colony – one which exists, as Werbner has noted, under conditions of marginalisation, dispossession, and exploitation (2012: 3) – Whyte uses the subjunctive: a tense or tone that is conditional, tentative; and which is responsive to uncertain futures (2012). What our interviews revealed was a community mobilising their resources – political, social, linguistic – to negotiate their material and ontological security. Yet, as Da Fina reminds us, 'the construction and presentation of identity is a process in constant development and ... one of its crucial sites of negotiation is interaction' (Da Fina 2006: 355). Twa as Rwandan is not the end stage of Rwandan Twa identity. Identities are dynamic and their fragments can be recombined to create new imaginaries of belonging in response to external events, such as unfulfilled promises and daily interactions within global jurisdictional encounters. The story told here is just one tale and, like all stories, it is open to contestation, to modification, and to being entirely rewritten.

BIBLIOGRAPHY

Adamczyk, Christiane, '"Today I Am No Mutwa Anymore": Facets of National Unity Discourse in Present-Day Rwanda' (2011) 19 *Social Anthropology/ Anthropologie Sociale* 175–188.

Adekola, Oluwafemi, Pauliina Krigsholm and Kirsikka Riekkinen, 'Towards a Holistic Land Law Evaluation in Sub-Saharan Africa: A Novel Framework with an Application to Rwanda's Organic Land Law 2005' (2021) 103 *Land Use Policy* 105291.

Adekunle, Julius, *Culture and Customs of Rwanda* (Westport: Greenwood Press, 2007).

Adelman, Sam and Abdul Paliwala, 'Beyond Law and Development?', in Sam Adelman and Abdul Paliwala (eds.), *The Limits of Law and Development: Neoliberalism, Governance and Social Justice* (London: Routledge, 2021), 15–37.

Affolder, Natasha, 'Looking for Law in Unusual Places: Cross-Border Diffusion of Environmental Norms' (2018) 7(3) *Transnational Environmental Law* 425–449.

African Commission on Human and Peoples' Rights (ACHPR) and International Working Group for Indigenous Affairs (IWGIA), 'Report of the African Commission's Working Group of Experts on Indigenous Peoples/ Communities, Submitted in Accordance with the Resolution on the Rights of Indigenous Populations/Communities in Africa', adopted by the African Commission on Human and Peoples' Rights at its 28th ordinary session (Banjul: ACHPR, 2005).

Agrawal, Arun, *Environmentality: Technologies of Government and the Making of Subjects* (Durham: Duke University Press, 2005).

Akpome, Aghogho, 'The Narrative Construction of Identity in Contemporary Rwanda: A Study of *An Ordinary Man* by Paul Rusesabagina (with Tom Zoellner)' (2014) 73(2) *African Studies* 192–210.

Ali, Daniel Ayalew, Klaus Deininger and Markus Goldstein, 'Environmental and Gender Impacts of Land Tenure Regularization in Africa: Pilot Evidence from Rwanda' (2014) 110 *Journal of Development Economics* 262–275.

Allen, Stephen, 'The UN Declaration on the Rights of Indigenous Peoples: Towards a Global Legal Order on Indigenous Rights?', in Andrew Halpin and

Volker Roeben (eds.), *Theorising the Global Legal Order* (Oxford: Hart Publishing, 2009), 187–207.

Alston, Philip and Mary Robinson (eds.), *Human Rights and Development: Towards Mutual Reinforcement* (Oxford: Oxford University Press, 2005).

Ampumuza, Christine, Martijn Duineveld and René van der Duim, 'The Most Marginalized People in Uganda? Alternative Realities of Batwa at Bwindi Impenetrable National Park' (2020) 20 *World Development Perspectives* 1–9.

Anaya, James, 'Indigenous Law and Its Contribution to Global Pluralism' (2007) 6 *Indigenous Law Journal* 3–12.

Anders, Gerhard, 'The New Global Legal Order as Local Phenomenon: The Special Court for Sierra Leone', in Franz von Benda-Beckmann, Keebet von Benda-Beckmann, and Anne Griffiths (eds.), *Spatializing Law: An Anthropological Geography of Law in Society* (Aldershot: Ashgate, 2009), 137–156.

Anderson, Benedict, *Imagined Communities: Reflections on the Origin and Spread of Nationalism* (London: Verso Books, 1983 (revised ed. 1991)).

Anderson, David G. and Eeva Berglund (eds.), *Ethnographies of Conservation: Environmentalism and the Distribution of Privilege* (Oxford: Berghahn Books, 2003).

Andersson Djurfeldt, Agnes, 'Gendered Land Rights, Legal Reform and Social Norms in the Context of Land Fragmentation: A Review of the Literature for Kenya, Rwanda and Uganda' (2020) 90 *Land Use Policy* 104305.

Anghie, Antony, *Imperialism, Sovereignty and the Making of International Law* (Cambridge: Cambridge University Press, 2005).

Ansoms, An, 'Re-engineering Rural Society: The Visions and Ambitions of the Rwandan Elite' (2009) 108 *African Affairs* 289–309.

Ansoms, An, 'Rwanda's Post-genocide Economic Reconstruction: The Mismatch between Elite Ambitions and Rural Realities', in Scott Strauss and Leo Waldorf (eds.), *Remaking Rwanda: State Building and Human Rights after Mass Violence* (Madison: University of Wisconsin Press, 2011), 240–251.

Ansoms, An, 'The End of the New Green Revolution in Rwanda?', ROAPE blog, 11 February 2020: https://roape.net/2020/02/11/the-end-of-the-new-green-revolution-in-rwanda.

Ansoms, An and Giuseppe D. Cioffo, 'The Exemplary Citizen on the Exemplary Hill: The Production of Political Subjects in Contemporary Rural Rwanda' (2016) 47(6) *Development and Change* 1247–1268.

Ansoms, An, Giuseppe D. Cioffo, Chris Huggins and Jude Murison, 'The Reorganization of Rural Space in Rwanda: Habitat Concentration, Land Consolidation and Collective Marshland Cultivation', in An Ansom and Thea Hilhorst (eds.), *Losing Your Land: Dispossession in the Great Lakes* (Woodbridge: James Currey, 2014), 163–185.

Archer, Margaret S., *Being Human: The Problem of Agency* (Cambridge: Cambridge University Press, 2000).

Austin, J. L., *How to Do Things with Words*. Ed. James O. Urmson (Oxford: Clarendon Press, 1962).

Bahuchet, Serge, *Languages of African Rainforest 'Pygmy' Hunter-Gatherers: Language Shifts without Cultural Admixture*. Historical Linguistics and Hunter-Gatherer Populations in Global Perspective (Leipzig: Max-Planck Institute, 2006).

Bahuchet, Serge, 'Changing Language, Remaining Pygmy' (2012) 84(1) *Human Biology* 11–43.

Baldwin, Gretchen, 'Constructing Identity through Commemoration: Kwibuka and the Rise of Survivor Nationalism in Post-conflict Rwanda' (2019) 57(3) *Journal of Modern African Studies* 355–375.

Balkin, Jack M., 'Understanding Legal Understanding: The Legal Subject and the Problem of Legal Coherence' (1993) 103 *Yale Law Journal* 105–176.

Ballakrishnen, Swethaa S., 'At Odds with Everything around Me: Vulnerability Politics and Its (Out of) Place in the Socio-legal Academy', in Lynette J. Chua and Mark Fathi Massoud (eds.), *Out of Place: Fieldwork and Positionality in Law and Society* (Cambridge: Cambridge University Press, 2024), 139–159.

Bamporiki, Edouard, *My Son, It Is a Long Story: Reflections of Genocide Perpetrators* (Kigali: Bamporiki Edouard, 2017).

Banerjee, Abhijit V. and Esther Duflo, *Poor Economics: A Radical Rethinking of the Way to Fight Global Poverty* (London: Penguin, 2012).

Barker, Chris and Dariusz Galasiński, *Cultural Studies and Discourse Analysis: A Dialogue on Language and Identity* (London: Sage Publications, 2001).

Barth, Fredrik, 'Introduction', in Fredrik Barth (ed.), *Ethnic Groups and Boundaries: The Social Organization of Cultural Difference* (Oslo: Universitetsforlaget, 1969), 9–38.

Barthes, Roland, 'Introduction to the Structural Analysis of Narrative', in Roland Barthes (ed.), *Image-Music-Text*, trans. Stephen Heath (London: Fontana, 1977), 79–124.

Bauman, Richard, 'Language, Identity, Performance' (2000) 10(1) *Pragmatics* 1–5.

Bayart, Jean-François, *Global Subjects: A Political Critique of Globalization* (Cambridge: Polity Press, 2007).

Bayart, Jean-François, *The State in Africa: The Politics of the Belly*, 2nd ed. (Cambridge: Polity Press, 2009).

Baynham, Mike, 'Performing Self, Family and Community in Moroccan Narratives of Migration and Settlement', in Anna de Fina, Deborah Schiffrin, and Michael Bamberg (eds.), *Discourse and Identity* (Cambridge: Cambridge University Press, 2006), 376–397.

Beard, Jennifer L., *The Political Economy of Desire: International Law, Development and the Nation State* (London: Routledge-Cavendish, 2007).

Begley, Larissa, 'The RPF Control Everything! Fear and Rumour under Rwanda's Genocide Ideology Legislation', in Susan Thomson, An Ansoms, and

Jude Murison (eds.), *Emotional and Ethical Challenges for Field Research in Africa* (London: Palgrave Macmillan, 2013), 70–83.
Beloff, Jonathan R., 'The Differences in Rwanda's Generational Engagement in *Ndi Umunyarwanda*' (2025) *African Identities* 1–22. http://doi.org/10.1080/14725843.2025.2465463.
Benda, Richard M., 'Time to Hear the Other Side: Transitional Temporalities and Transgenerational Narratives in Post-genocide Rwanda', in Natascha Mueller-Hirth and Sandra Rios Oyola (eds.), *Time and Temporality in Transitional and Post-conflict Societies* (Abingdon: Routledge, 2018), 122–191.
Benda, Richard M., 'Promising Generations: From Intergenerational Guilt to *Ndi Umunyarwanda*', in Hannah Greyson and Nicki Hitchcott (eds.), *Rwanda since 1994: Stories of Change* (Liverpool: Liverpool University Press, 2019), 189–210.
Benitez Ponce, Pablo Cesar, James Nelson Blignaut, John Kalisa et al., *A Post-Pandemic, Nature-Based Tourism and Conservation: Recovery Plan for Rwanda* (Washington, DC: World Bank Group, 2021).
Benton, Lauren, *Law and Colonial Cultures: Legal Regimes in World History, 1400–1900* (Cambridge: Cambridge University Press, 2002).
Benton, Lauren and Adam Cluclow, 'Interpolity Law and Jurisdictional Politics' (2023) 42(2) *Law and History Review* 1–13.
Bentzon, Agnete Weis, Anne Hellum and Julie E. Stewart (eds.), *Pursuing Grounded Theory in Law: South–North Experiences in Developing Women's Law* (Otta: Mond Books, 1998).
Berman, Paul Schiff, *Global Legal Pluralism: A Jurisprudence of Law beyond Borders* (Cambridge: Cambridge University Press, 2012).
Berry, John W., 'Social and Cultural Change', in Harry C. Triandis and Richard W. Brislin (eds.), *Handbook of Cross-Cultural Psychology, Social Psychology, Volume 5* (Boston: Allyn and Bacon, 1980), 211–280.
Berry, John W., 'Acculturation: Living Successfully in Two Cultures' (2005) 29(6) *International Journal of Intercultural Relations* 697–712.
Bettez Gravel, Pierre, 'The Transfer of Cows in Gisaka (Rwanda): A Mechanism for Recording Social Relationships' (1967) 69 *American Anthropologist* 322–331.
Bhabha, Homi K., *The Location of Culture* (London: Routledge, 1994).
Bhabha, Homi K., 'Introduction', in Homi K. Bhabha (ed.), *Nation and Narration* (London: Routledge, 1990), 1–7.
Bhambra, Gurminder S., 'The State: Postcolonial Histories of the Concept', in Olivia Rutazibwa and Robbie Shilliam (eds.), *Routledge Handbook of Postcolonial Politics* (London: Routledge, 2018), 200–209.
Birrell, Kathleen, *Indigeneity: Before and beyond the Law* (London: Glasshouse/Routledge, 2016).
Blackie, Laura E. R. and Nicki Hitchcott, '"I Am Rwandan": Unity and Reconciliation in Post-genocide Rwanda' (2018) 12 *Genocide Studies and Prevention* 24–37.

Blaser, Mario, 'Life Projects: Indigenous Peoples' Agency and Development', in Mario Blaser, Harvey Feit, and Glenn McRae (eds.), *In the Way: Indigenous Peoples, Life Projects, and Development* (London: Zed Books, 2004), 26–44.

Blaser, Mario, *Storytelling Globalization from the Chaco and Beyond* (Durham: Duke University Press, 2010).

Blundo, Giorgio and Pierre-Yves Le Meur, 'Introduction: An Anthropology of Everyday Governance: Collective Service Delivery and Subject-Making', in Giorgio Blundo and Pierre-Yves Le Meur (eds.), *The Governance of Daily Life in Africa: Ethnographic Explorations of Public and Collective Services* (Leiden: Brill, 2009), 1–37.

Bornstein, Erica, *The Spirit of Development: Protestant NGOs, Morality and Economics in Zimbabwe* (Stanford: Stanford University Press, 2005).

Bouka, Yolanda, '*Nacibazo*, "No Problem": Moving beyond the Official Discourse of Post-Genocide Justice in Rwanda', in Susan Thomson, An Ansoms, and Jude Murison (eds.), *Emotional and Ethical Challenges for Field Research in Africa* (London: Palgrave Macmillan, 2013), 107–122.

Bourdieu, Pierre, *The Logic of Practice*, tr. Richard Nice (Stanford: Stanford University Press, 1990).

Boyd White, James, 'Law as Rhetoric, Rhetoric as Law: The Arts of Cultural and Communal Life' (1985) 52 *The University of Chicago Law Review* 684–702.

Boyd White, James, *Acts of Hope: Creating Authority in Literature, Law, and Politics* (Chicago: University of Chicago Press, 1994).

Boyd White, James, *When Language Meets the Mind: Three Questions* (Oisterwijk: Wolf Legal Publishers, 2007).

Broche-Due, Vigdis (ed.), *Violence and Belonging: The Quest for Identity in Post-colonial Africa* (London: Routledge, 2004).

Brockington, Dan, *Celebrity and the Environment: Fame, Wealth and Power in Conservation* (London: Zed Books, 2008).

Brockington, Dan and Katherine Scholfield, 'The Conservationist Mode of Production and Conservation NGOs in Sub-Saharan Africa' (2010) 42(3) *Antipode* 551–575.

Brockington, Daniel and James Igoe, 'Eviction for Conservation: A Global Overview' (2006) 4(3) *Conservation & Society* 424–470.

Brown, David, *Contemporary Nationalism: Civic, Ethnocultural and Multicultural Politics* (London: Routledge, 2000).

Brown, Wendy, 'Doing Justice to Someone: Sex Reassignment and Allegories of Transexuality' (2001) 7(4) *GLQ: A Journal of Lesbian and Gay Studies* 621–636.

Brubaker, Roger and Frederick Cooper, 'Beyond "Identity"' (2000) 29(1) *Theory and Society* 1–47.

Buckley-Zistel, Susanne, 'Dividing and Uniting: The Use of Citizenship Discourses in Conflict and Reconciliation in Rwanda' (2006a) 20 *Global Society* 101–113.

Buckley-Zistel, Susanne, 'Remembering to Forget: Chosen Amnesia as a Strategy for Local Coexistence in Post-genocide Rwanda' (2006b) 76(2) *Africa: Journal of the International African Institute* 131–150.

Buckley-Zistel, Susanne, 'Nation, Narration, Unification? The Politics of History Teaching after the Rwandan Genocide' (2009) 11 *Journal of Genocide Research* 31–53.

Butler, Judith, *Bodies That Matter: On the Discursive Limits of 'Sex'* (New York: Routledge, 1993).

Butler, Judith, 'Further Reflections on Conversations of Our Time' (1997) 27(1) *Diacritics* 13–15.

Canessa, Andrew, *Intimate Indigeneities: Race, Sex and History in the Small Spaces of Andean Life* (Durham: Duke University Press, 2012).

Canfield, Matthew C., Julia Dehm and Marisa Fassi, 'Translocal Legalities: Encounters with Transnational Law' (2021) 12 *Transnational Legal Theory* 335–359.

Cantrell, Phillip A., *Revival and Reconciliation: The Anglican Church and the Politics of Rwanda* (Madison: University of Wisconsin Press, 2022).

Castree, Noel, 'Neoliberalizing Nature: The Logics of De- and Re-regulation' (2007) 4 *Environment and Planning A* 131–152.

Chakrabarty, Dipesh, *Provincializing Europe: Postcolonial Thought and Historical Difference* (Princeton: Princeton University Press, 2000).

Chandler, David and Julian Reid, *Becoming Indigenous: Governing Imaginaries in the Anthropocene* (London: Rowman and Littlefield, 2019).

Chemouni, Benjamin, 'Taking Stock of Rwanda's Decentralisation: Changing Local Governance in a Post-conflict Environment' (2016) 1(6) *Third World Thematics: A TWQ Journal* 763–778.

Chemouni, Benjamin and Assumpta Mugiraneza, 'Ideology and Interests in the Rwandan Patriotic Front: Singing the Struggle in Pre-genocide Rwanda' (2019) 119 *African Affairs* 115–140.

Chrétien, Jean-Pierre, *The Great Lakes of Africa: Two Thousand Years of History* (Cambridge, MA: MIT Press, 2003).

Chua, Lynette J., 'Feeling at Home Outside: Embracing Out-of-Placeness in the Study of Law and Resistance', in Lynette J. Chua and Mark Fathi Massoud (eds.), *Out of Place: Fieldwork and Positionality in Law and Society* (Cambridge: Cambridge University Press, 2024), 103–118.

Clark, Janine Natalya, 'National Unity and Reconciliation in Rwanda: A Flawed Approach?' (2010) 28(2) *Journal of Contemporary African Studies* 137–154.

Clark, Phil, *The Gacaca Courts, Post-genocide Justice and Reconciliation in Rwanda: Justice without Lawyers* (Cambridge: Cambridge University Press, 2010).

Clark, Phil, 'After Genocide: Democracy in Rwanda, 20 Years On' (2014a) 20(4) *Juncture* 308–311.

Clark, Phil, 'Negotiating Reconciliation in Rwanda: Popular Challenges to the Official Discourse of Post-genocide National Unity' (2014b) 8(4) *Journal of Intervention and Statebuilding* 303–320.

Cohen, Paul A., *History in Three Keys: The Boxers as Event, Experience, and Myth* (New York: Columbia University Press, 1997).

Collins, Bennett, Meghan C. Laws and Richard Ntakirutimana, 'Becoming "Historically Marginalized Peoples": Examining Twa Perceptions of Boundary Shifting and Recategorization in Post-genocide Rwanda' (2021) 44(4) *Ethnic and Racial Studies* 576–594.

COPORWA, *Five Year Strategic Plan 2010–2014* (Kigali, 2014): https://coporwa.files.wordpress.com/2011/08/coporwa-five-years-strategic-plan-2010-c3a0-20141.pdf.

Cowell, Fred, 'Participatory Rights in Rwanda: Genocide Ideology Laws and the Future of Political Space', in Maddalena Campioni and Patrick Noack (eds.), *Rwanda Fast Forward: Social, Economic, Military and Reconciliation Prospects* (London: Palgrave Macmillan, 2012).

Crisafulli, Patricia and Andrea Redmond, *Rwanda Inc.: How a Devastated Nation Became an Economic Model for the Developing World* (New York: Palgrave Macmillan, 2012).

Cronon, William, 'The Trouble with Wilderness; or Getting Back to the Wrong Nature', in William Cronon (ed.), *Uncommon Ground: Rethinking the Human Place in Nature* (New York: W. W. Norton & Co., 1995), 69–90.

Cutler, A. Claire, 'Historical Materialism, Globalization, and Law: Competing Conceptions of Property', in Mark Rupert and Hazel Smith (eds.), *Historical Materialism and Globalization* (London: Routledge, 2002), 230–256.

Daes, Erica-Irene, 'Protection of the Heritage of Indigenous Peoples', UN Study Series n. 10/1997.

Darian-Smith, Eve and Phillip C. McCarty, *The Global Turn: Theories, Research Designs, and Methods for Global Studies* (Oakland: University of California Press, 2017).

Dawson, Neil M., 'Leaving No-One Behind? Social Inequalities and Contrasting Development Impacts in Rural Rwanda' (2018) 5 *Development Studies Research* 1–14.

Decker, Corrie and Elisabeth McMahon, *The Idea of Development in Africa: A History* (Cambridge: Cambridge University Press, 2021).

De Fina, Anna, 'Group Identity, Narrative and Self-Representations', in Anna de Fina, Deborah Schiffrin, and Michael Bamberg (eds.), *Discourse and Identity* (Cambridge: Cambridge University Press, 2006), 351–375.

Dekker, Marleen and Nicky Pouw, 'Introduction to the Special Issue: Policies for Inclusive Development in Africa' (2022) *The European Journal of Development Research*.

De Lame, Danielle, *Une Colline Entre Mille ou Le Calms Avant la Tempete: Transformations et Blocages du Rwanda Rural* (Tervueren: Musee Royal de l'Afrique Centrale, 1996).

De Schutter, Olivier, 'End of Mission Statement: Special Rapporteur on Extreme Poverty and Human Rights, Visit to Rwanda 19 May–30 May 2025' (Kigali, 30 May 2025).

De Soto, Hernando, *The Mystery of Capital: Why Capitalism Triumphs in the West and Fails Everywhere Else* (New York: Random House, 2000).

De Sousa Santos, Boaventura, 'Law: A Map of Misreading – Toward a Postmodern Conception of Law' (1987) 14 *Journal of Law and Society* 279–302.

De Sousa Santos, Boaventura, 'Human Rights as an Emancipatory Script? Cultural and Political Conditions', in Boaventura de Sousa Santos (ed.), *Another Knowledge Is Possible: Beyond Northern Epistemologies* (London: Verso, 2007), 3–35.

De Sousa Santos, Boaventura, *Epistemologies of the South: Justice against Epistemicide* (London: Routledge, 2014).

De Sousa Santos, Boaventura and César A. Rodríguez-Garavito (eds.), *Law and Globalization from Below: Towards a Cosmopolitan Legality* (Cambridge: Cambridge University Press, 2005).

De Vries, Peter, 'Don't Compromise Your Desire for Development! A Lacanian/Deleuzian Rethinking of the Anti-politics Machine' (2007) 28(1) *Third World Quarterly* 25–43.

Des Forges, Alison, *Leave None to Tell the Story: Genocide in Rwanda* (New York: Human Rights Watch, 1999).

Des Forges, Alison, 'Land in Rwanda: Winnowing Out the Chaff', African Great Lakes Democracy Watch blog, 28 May 2006.

Doughty, Kristen Conner, *Remediation in Rwanda: Grassroots Legal Forums* (Philadelphia: University of Pennsylvania Press, 2016).

Dowie, Mark, *Conservation Refugees: The 100-Year Conflict between Global Conservation and Native People* (Cambridge, MA: MIT Press, 2009).

Eltringham, Nigel, *Accounting for Horror: Post-genocide Debates in Rwanda* (London: Pluto Press, 2004).

Eltringham, Nigel, 'The Past Is Elsewhere: The Paradoxes of Proscribing Ethnicity in Post-Genocide Rwanda', in Scott Strauss and Leo Waldorf (eds.), *Remaking Rwanda: State Building and Human Rights after Mass Violence* (Madison: University of Wisconsin Press, 2011).

Engle, Karen, *The Elusive Promise of Development: Rights, Culture, Strategy* (Durham: Duke University Press, 2010).

Eramian, Laura, 'Ethnic Boundaries in Contemporary Rwanda: Fixity, Flexibility and Their Limits' (2015) 57(1) *Anthropologica* 93–104.

Eramian, Laura, *Peaceful Selves: Personhood, Nationhood, and the Post-conflict Movement in Rwanda* (Oxford: Berghahn Books, 2017).

Escobar, Arturo, *Encountering Development: The Making and Unmaking of the Third World* (Princeton: Princeton University Press, 1995, 2nd ed. 2012).

Escobar, Arturo, 'Construction Nature: Elements for a Post-structuralist Political Ecology', (1996) 28(4) *Futures* 325–344.

Escobar, Arturo, 'Culture Sits in Places: Reflections on Globalism and Subaltern Strategies of Localization' (2001) 20 *Political Geography* 139–174.

Escobar, Arturo, *Territories of Difference: Place, Movements, Life, Redes* (Durham: Duke University Press, 2008).

Eslava, Luis, *Local Space, Global Life: The Everyday Operation of International Law and Development* (Cambridge: Cambridge University Press, 2015).

Ewick, Patricia and Susan Silbey, 'Subversive Stories and Hegemonic Tales: Toward a Sociology of Narrative' (1995) 29(2) *Law and Society Review* 197–226.

Ezeanya, Chika, 'Indigenous Knowledge, Economic Empowerment and Entrepreneurship in Rwanda: The Girinka Approach' (2014) 6 *Journal of Pan African Studies* 241–263.

Fairhead, James and Melissa Leach, *Misreading the African Landscape: Society and Ecology in a Forest-Savanna Mosaic* (Cambridge: Cambridge University Press, 1996).

Fanon, Franz, *The Wretched of the Earth*, tr. Constance Farrington (London: Penguin Books, 1963).

Ferguson, James, *The Anti-politics Machine: 'Development', Depoliticization, and Bureaucratic Power in Lesotho* (Cambridge: Cambridge University Press, 1990).

Ferguson, James, *Expectations of Modernity: Myths and Meanings of Urban Life on the Zambian Copperbelt* (Oakland: University of Californian Press, 1999).

Ferguson, James, *Global Shadows: Africa in the Neoliberal World Order* (Durham: Duke University Press, 2006).

Ferguson, James and Akhil Gupta, 'Spatializing States: Toward an Ethnography of Neoliberal Govermentality' (2002) 29(4) *American Ethnologist* 981–1002.

Fordham, Paul, *The Geography of African Affairs* (London: Pelican, 1968).

Foucault, Michel, *The Archaeology of Knowledge: And the Discourse on Language*, tr. Alan M. Sheridan Smith (New York: Pantheon, 1972).

Foucault, Michel, *The History of Sexuality: An Introduction*, tr. Robert Hurley (New York: Pantheon Books, 1978).

Foucault, Michel, *Power/Knowledge: Selected Interviews and Other Writings, 1972–1977*. Ed. Colin Gordon ; tr. Colin Gordon, Leo Marshall, John Mepham, and Kate Soper (New York: Pantheon, 1980).

Foucault, Michel, 'The Subject and Power' (1982) 8 *Critical Inquiry* 777–795.

Freedman Eric, 'When Indigenous Rights and Wilderness Collide: Prosecution of Native Americans for Using Motors in Minnesota's Boundary Waters Canoe Wilderness Area' (2002) 26(4) *American Indian Quarterly* 378–392.

Gaertner, Samuel L. and John F. Dovidio, 'The Common Ingroup Identity Model', in Paul A. M. Van Lange, Arie W. Kruglanski, and E. Tory Higgins (eds.),

Handbook of Theories of Social Psychology (London: Sage Publications, 2012), 439–457.

Gallimore, Rangira Béa, 'Vicarious Shame, Narrative, Social Reconnection and Public Recognition in Bamporiki's Sin to Them, Shame on Me' (2015) 85(1) *Présence Francophone: Revue internationale de langue et de literature*, Article 8.

Garland, Elizabeth, 'The Elephant in the Room: Confronting the Colonial Character of Wildlife Conservation in Africa' (2008) 51(3) *African Studies Review* 51–74.

Gaynor, Niamh, '"A Nation in a Hurry": The Costs of Local Governance Reforms in Rwanda' (2014) 41(143) *Review of African Political Economy* S49–S63.

Gilbert, Jérémie, 'Litigating Indigenous Peoples' Rights in Africa: Potentials, Challenges and Limitations' (2017) 66 *International and Comparative Law Quarterly* 657–686.

Goldman, Michael, *Imperial Nature: The World Bank and Struggles for Social Justice in the Age of Globalization* (New Haven: Yale University Press, 2005).

González-Hidalgo, Marien and Christos Zografos, 'Emotions, Power, and Environmental Conflict: Expanding the "Emotional Turn" in Political Ecology' (2020) 44 *Progress in Human Geography* 235–255.

Goodwin, Morag, 'What I Talk about When I Talk about Global Law' (2012) 17(2) *Tilburg Law Review* 269–275.

Goodwin, Morag, 'The Poverty of Numbers: Reflecting on the Legitimacy of Global Development Indicators' (2017) 13(4) *International Journal of Law in Context* 485–497.

Goodwin, Morag, 'Becoming Rwandan? The Impact of Two Decades of Unity Policies on the Batwa' (2021a) 63(2) *KAOW Bulletin des Séances/Mededelingen der Zittingen* 187–208.

Goodwin, Morag, 'Good Governance', in Koen De Feyter, Gamze Erdem Türkelli, and Stéphanie de Moerloose (eds.), *Encyclopedia of Law and Development* (Cheltenham: Edward Elgar, 2021b), 104–107.

Goodwin, Morag, 'Evaluating the Success of Decentralisation in Facilitating the Inclusion of Rwanda's Marginalised' (2022) 34 *The European Journal of Development Research* 2251–2271.

Goodwin, Morag, 'Equality in Development: A Reflection on Meaning', in Ingunn Ikdahl, Kristen Sandberg, Julie Stewart, Vibeke Blaker Strand, and Tone Linn Wærstad (eds.), *Hellums metode: festskrift til Anne Hellum 70 år* (Oslo: Gyldendal Academic, 2023), 95–103.

Gough, Ian and J. Allister McGregor, *Wellbeing in Developing Countries: From Theory to Research* (Cambridge: Cambridge University Press, 2007).

Grad, Hector and Lusia M. Rojo, 'Identities in Discourse: An Integrative View', in Rosana Dolón and Júlia Todolí (eds.), *Analysing Identities in Discourse* (Amsterdam: John Benjamins Publishing Company, 2008), 3–28.

Grayson, Hannah, 'A Place for Individuals: Positive Growth in Rwanda' (2017) 3 (2–4) *Eastern African Literary and Cultural Studies* 107–130.

Gready, Paul, '"You're Either with Us or against Us": Civil Society and Policy-Making in Post-genocide Rwanda' (2010) 109 *African Affairs* 637–657.

Gupta, Joyeeta, Nicky R. W. Pouw and Mirjam A. F. Ros-Tonen, 'Towards an Elaborated Theory of Inclusive Development' (2015) 27(4) *Journal of Development Research* 541–559.

Haenn, Nora, *Fields of Power, Forests of Discontent: Culture, Conservation and the State in Mexico* (Tucson: University of Arizona Press, 2005).

Hall, Stuart, 'Introduction: Who Needs Identity?', in Stuart Hall and Paul du Gay (eds.), *Questions of Cultural Identity* (London: Sage Publications, 1996), 1–17.

Hannum, Hurst, 'The Concept and Definition of Minorities', in Marc Weller (ed.), *Universal Minority Rights: A Commentary on the Jurisprudence of International Courts and Treaty Bodies* (Oxford: Oxford University Press, 2007), 49–74.

Haraway, Donna, 'Situated Knowledges: The Science Question in Feminism and the Privilege of Partial Perspective' (1988) 14 *Feminist Studies* 575–599.

Harrington, John, 'Between Nation and Empire: How the State Matters in Global Health' (2023) 43 *Legal Studies* 461–479.

Harrison, Graham, 'Rwanda: An Agrarian Development State?' (2016) 37(2) *Third World Quarterly* 354–370.

Hatzfeld, Jean, *The Strategy of Antelopes: Living in Rwanda after the Genocide*, tr. Linda Coverdale (New York: Farrar, Straus and Giroux, 2007).

Havugimana, Alexis, 'The Challenges and Examination of New Programme Ubudehe 2020 in Rwanda' (2023) 13 *American Journal of Industrial and Business Management* 287–311.

Heller-Roazen, Daniel, *The Enemy of All: Piracy and the Law of Nations* (New York: Zone Books, 2009).

Hintjens, Helen, 'Conflict and Resources in Post-genocide Rwanda and the Great Lakes Region' (2006) 63(5) *International Journal of Environmental Studies* 599–615.

Hintjens, Helen, 'Post-genocide Identity Politics in Rwanda' (2008) 8(1) *Ethnicities* 5–41.

Hodgson, Dorothy, *Being Maasai, Becoming Indigenous: Postcolonial Politics in a Neoliberal World* (Bloomington: Indiana University Press, 2011).

Hornsby, Jennifer, 'Agent', in Ted Honderich (ed.), *The Oxford Companion to Philosophy* (Oxford: Oxford University Press, 2nd ed., 2005).

Hoyweghen van, Saskia, 'The Urgency of Land and Agrarian Reform in Rwanda' (1999) 98 *African Affairs* 353–372.

Huggins, Chris, 'Historical and Contemporary Land Laws and Their Impact on Indigenous Peoples' Land Rights in Rwanda', in Forest Peoples Programme, *Land Rights and the Forest Peoples of Africa: Historical, Legal and Anthropological Perspectives* (Moreton-in-Marsh: FPP, 2009).

Huggins, Chris, 'Land in Return, Reintegration and Recovery Processes: Some Lessons from the Great Lakes Region of Africa in Uncharted Territory', in Sara Pantuliano (ed.), *Uncharted Territory: Land, Conflict and Humanitarian Action* (Rugby: Practical Action Publishing, 2009), 67–93.

Huggins, Chris, 'Land Grabbing and Land Tenure Security in Post-genocide Rwanda', in An Ansom and Thea Hilhorst (eds.), *Losing Your Land: Dispossession in the Great Lakes* (Woodbridge: James Currey, 2014), 141–162.

Ignatiev, Noel, *How the Irish Became White* (London: Routledge, 2009).

Igoe, James, 'The Spectacle of Nature in the Global Economy of Appearances: Anthropological Engagements with the Spectacular Mediations of Transnational Conservation' (2010) 30(4) *Critique of Anthropology* 375–397.

Igoe, Jim, Katja Neves and Dan Brockington, 'A Spectacular Eco-tour around the Historic Bloc: Theorising the Convergence of Biodiversity Conservation and Capitalist Expansion' (2010) 42(3) *Antipode* 486–512.

Ingelaere, Bert, '"Does the Truth Pass across the Fire without Burning?": Locating the Short Circuit in Rwanda's Gacaca Courts' (2009) 47(4) *Journal of Modern African Studies* 507–528.

Ingelaere, Bert, 'Do We Understand Life after Genocide? Center and Periphery in the Construction of Knowledge in Postgenocide Rwanda' (2010a) 53(1) *African Studies Review* 41–59.

Ingelaere, Bert, 'Peasants, Power and Ethnicity: A Bottom-Up Perspective on Rwanda's Political Transition' (2010b) 109 *African Affairs* 273–292.

Ingelaere, Bert, 'The Ruler's Drum and the People's Shout: Accountability and Representation on Rwanda's Hills', in Scott Strauss and Leo Waldorf (eds.), *Remaking Rwanda: State Building and Human Rights after Mass Violence* (Madison: University of Wisconsin Press, 2011), 67–78.

Ingelaere, Bert and Marijke Verpoorten, 'Trust in the Aftermath of Genocide: Insights from Rwandan Life Histories' (2020) 57(4) *Journal of Peace Research* 521–535.

International Work Group for Indigenous Affairs (IWGIA), *The Indigenous World 2001/2002* (Copenhagen: IWGIA, 2002).

IOB, *Transition and Inclusive Development in Sub-Saharan Africa: An Analysis of Poverty and Inequality in the Context of Transition*, IOB Study no. 422, April 2018.

Kalimba, Zephyrin, 'Case Study 1: Rwanda – The Situation of the Batwa Forest Dwellers and Conservation of the Volcanoes National Park and Nyungwe Natural Forest', in John Nelson and Lindsay Hossack (eds.), *Indigenous Peoples and Protected Areas in Africa: From Principles to Practice* (Moreton-in-Marsh: FPP, 2003), 47–86.

Kalua, Fetson, 'Homi Bhabha's Third Space and African Identity' (2009) 21(1) *Journal of African Cultural Studies* 23–32.

Kamer, van Volksvertegenwoordigers, *Bijzondere commissie belast met het onderzoek over Congo Vrijstaat (1885–1908) en het Belgisch koloniaal verleden in Congo (1908–1960), Rwanda en Burundi (1919–1962), de impact hiervan en de gevolgen die hieraan dienen gegeven te worden*, Doc. 55, 1462/003, Brussels, 17 July 2021.

Karanja, Wambui, 'Development, Research, and the Commodification of Poverty in Africa: Rethinking Research Narratives', in George J. Sefa Dei and Cristina Jaimungal (eds.), *Indigeneity and Decolonial Resistance: Alternatives to Colonial Thinking and Practice* (Gorham: Myers Education Press, 2018), 153–182.

Kimonyo, Jean Paul, *Transforming Rwanda: Challenges on the Road to Reconstruction* (London: Lynne Rienner Publishers, 2019).

Klouzal, Linda, 'The Subjective Side of Development: Sources of Well-Being, Resources for Struggle', in Kum-Kum Bhavnani, John Foran, and Priya Kurian (eds.), *Feminist Futures: Re-imagining Women, Culture and Development* (London: Zed Books, 2003), 256–262.

Kneas, David, 'Chest Hair and Climate Change: Harrison Ford and the Making of "Lost There, Felt Here"' (2017) 22 *Environmental History* 516–526.

Kokunda, Sylvia, Haven Nahabwe, Jeremiah Nahamya, Samari Niwamanya, Ronald Mazirwe, Samrawit Gougsa, Elizabeth Kemigisha and Nicole Redvers, 'Batwa Indigenous Peoples Forced Eviction for "Conservation": A Qualitative Examination on Community Impacts' (2023) 3(8) *PLOS Global Public Health* e0002129.

Kothari, Ashish, Ariel Salleh, Arturo Escobar, Federico Demaria and Alberto Acosta (eds.), *Pluriverse: A Post-development Dictionary* (Southborough: Tulika Books, 2019).

Kothari, Uma, 'Power, Knowledge and Social Control in Participatory Development', in Bill Cooke and Uma Kothari (eds.), *Participation: The New Tyranny?* (London: Zed Books, 2001), 139–152.

Kothari, Uma, '*A Radical History of Development Studies: Individuals, Institutions and Ideologies*', in Uma Kothari (ed.), (London: Bloomsbury Publishing, 2019a).

Kothari, Uma, 'From Colonial Administration to Development Studies: A Post-colonial Critique of the History of Development Studies', in Uma Kothari (ed.), *A Radical History of Development Studies: Individuals, Institutions and Ideologies* (London: Bloomsbury Publishing, 2019b).

Kotsakis, Andreas, 'Community Participation in Biodiversity Conservation: Emerging Localities of Tension', in Amanda Perry-Kessaris (ed.), *Law in the Pursuit of Development* (London: GlassHouse, 2010), 131–145.

Krisch, Nico (ed.), *Entangled Legalities beyond the State* (Cambridge: Cambridge University Press, 2021).

Kubai, Anne, '"Confession" and "Forgiveness" as a Strategy for Development in Post-genocide Rwanda' (2016) 72(4) *HTS Teologiese Studies/Theological Studies* a3562.

Kwibuka, Eugene, 'What Does "Ndi Umunyarwanda" Mean to You?', *The New Times*, 3 December 2013.

Lambek, Michael, 'Nuriaty, the Saint, and the Sultan: Virtuous Subject and Subjective Virtuoso of the Postmodern Colony', in Richard Werbner (ed.), *Postcolonial Subjectivities in Africa* (London: Zed Books, 2002).

Lander, Jennifer, *Transnational Law and State Transformation: The Case of Extractive Development in Mongolia* (London: Routledge, 2021).

Latour, Bruno, 'Agency at the Time of the Anthropocene' (2014) 45(1) *New Literary History* 1–18.

Lawry, Steven, Rebecca McLain, Margaret Rugadya, Gina Alvarado and Tasha Heidenrich (eds.), *Land Tenure Reform in Sub-Saharan Africa: Interventions in Benin, Ethiopia, Rwanda and Zimbabwe* (London: Routledge, 2023).

Leach, Michael C., 'A Kaleidoscope of Meaning Fragments: Understanding the Rule of Law's Paradoxes in International Development', doctoral thesis, Tilburg University, 2021.

Lehman, Karen, 'Protecting the Space Within', in Majid Rahnema and Victoria Bawtree (eds.), *The Post-development Reader* (London: Zed Books, 1998), 353–358.

Lemarchand, René, *Rwanda and Burundi* (Westport: Praeger Publishers, 1970).

Lemarchand, René, 'Burundi in Comparative Perspective: Dimensions of Ethnic Strife', in John McGarry and Brendan O'Leary (eds.), *The Politics of Ethnic Conflict Regulation: Case Studies of Protracted Ethnic Conflicts* (London: Routledge, 1993), 83–105.

Lemarchand, René, *The Dynamics of Violence in Central Africa* (Philadelphia: University of Pennsylvania Press, 2009).

Lemarchand, René and Maurice Niwese, 'Mass Murder, the Politics of Memory and Post-genocide Reconstruction: The Cases of Rwanda and Burundi', in Béatrice Pouligny, Simon Chesterman, and Albrecht Schnabel (eds.), *After Mass Crime: Rebuilding States and Communities* (Tokyo: United Nations University Press, 2006), 165–189.

Lewis, Jerome, *The Batwa Pygmies of the Great Lakes Region* (London: Minority Rights Group, 2000).

Lewis, Jerome, 'BaYaka Pygmy Multi-modal and Mimetic Communication Traditions', in Daniel Dor, Chris Knight, and Jerome Lewis, *The Social Origins of Language* (Oxford: Oxford University Press, 2014), 77–91.

Lewis, Jerome and Judy Knight, *The Twa of Rwanda: Assessment of the Situation of the Twa and Promotion of Twa Rights in Post-war Rwanda* (Chadlington: World

Rainforest Movement and International Work Group for Indigenous Affairs, 1995).

Li, Tania Murray, 'Articulating Indigenous Identity in Indonesia: Resource Politics and the Tribal Slot' (2000) 42(1) *Comparative Studies in Society and History* 149–179.

Li, Tania Murray, *The Will to Improve: Governmentality, Development, and the Practice of Politics* (Durham: Duke University Press, 2007).

Lindahl, Hans, *Fault Lines of Globalization: Legal Order and the Politics of A-Legality* (Oxford: Oxford University Press, 2013).

Lindahl, Hans, *Authority and the Globalisation of Inclusion and Exclusion* (Cambridge: Cambridge University Press, 2018).

Lindijer, Koert, *Een Wolkenkrabber op de Savanne: Veertig jaar correspondentschap in Afrika* (Amersfoort: Atlas Contact, 2023).

Lingsma, Tjitske, 'Rwanda opereert zoals Oost-Duitsland met de Stasi', *De Groene Amsterdammer*, 6 April 2022.

Local Administrative Entities Development Agency (LODA), *VUP Programme Document* (Kigali: Republic of Rwanda, October 2022).

Longman, Timothy, *Christianity and Genocide in Rwanda* (Cambridge: Cambridge University Press, 2010).

Longman, Timothy, *Memory and Justice in Post-genocide Rwanda* (Cambridge: Cambridge University Press, 2017).

Luoma, Colin, *Fortress Conservation and International Accountability for Human Rights Violations against Batwa in Kahuzi-Biega National Park* (London: Minority Rights Group, 2022).

Mahmood, Saba, 'Feminist Theory, Agency and the Liberatory Subject' (2006) 42(1) *Temenos* 31–71.

Mahmood, Saba, *Politics of Piety: The Islamic Revival and the Feminist Subject* (Princeton: Princeton University Press, 2011).

Makhunga, Lindiwe D., 'Post-genocide Rwanda and Discursive Construction of Legitimacy: Contesting Seemingly Dichotomous Political Narratives' (2019) 45(3) *Social Dynamics* 382–394.

Mamdani, Mahmood, *Citizen and Subject: Contemporary Africa and the Legacy of Late Colonialism* (Princeton: Princeton University Press, 1996).

Mamdani, Mahmood, *When Victims Become Killers: Colonialism, Nativism, and the Genocide in Rwanda* (Princeton: Princeton University Press, 2001).

Manchanda, Nivi, 'The Imperial Sociology of the "Tribe"', in Olivia Rutazibwa and Robbie Shilliam (eds.), *Routledge Handbook of Postcolonial Politics* (London: Routledge, 2018), 134–143.

Manji, Ambreena, *The Politics of Land Reform in Africa: From Communal Tenure to Free Markets* (London: Zed Books, 2006).

Maquet, Jacques Jérôme, *The Premise of Inequality in Ruanda* (London: Oxford University Press, 1961).

Martin, Adrian, Nicole Gross-Camp, Bereket Kebede, Shawn McGuire and Joseph Munyarukaza, 'Whose Environmental Justice? Exploring Local and Global Perspectives in a Payments for Ecosystem Services Scheme in Rwanda' (2014) 54 *Geoforum* 167–177.

Mayersen, Deborah, '"Fraternity in Diversity" or "Feudal Fanatics"? Representations of Ethnicity in Rwandan Presidential Rhetoric' (2015) 49 *Patterns of Prejudice* 249–270.

Mazrui, Ali A., 'Racial Self-Reliance and Cultural Dependency: Nyerere and Amin in Comparative Perspective' (1973) 27(1) *Journal of International Affairs* 105–121.

Mbembe, Achille, *Afriques indociles: christianisme, pouvoir et Etat en société post-coloniale* (Paris: Karthala, 1988).

Mbembe, Achille, 'Provisional Notes on the Postcolony' (1992) 62(1) *Africa: Journal of the International African Institute* 3–37.

Mbembe, Achille, *On the Postcolony* (Berkeley: University of California Press, 2001).

McAuslan, Patrick, *Land Law Reform in Eastern Africa: Tradition or Transformative? A Critical Review of 50 Years of Land Law Reform in Eastern Africa 1961–2011* (London: Routledge, 2013).

McClintock, Anne, *Imperial Leather. Race, Gender, and Sexuality in the Colonial Context* (New York: Routledge, 1995).

McDoom, Omar Shahabudin, *The Path to Genocide in Rwanda: Security, Opportunity, and Authority in an Ethnocratic State* (Cambridge: Cambridge University Press, 2021).

McDoom, Omar Shahabudin, 'Securocratic State-Building: The Rationales, Rebuttals, and Risks behind the Extraordinary Rise of Rwanda after the Genocide' (2022) 121 *African Affairs* 535–567.

McGarry, John and Brendan O'Leary, 'Introduction: The Macro-political Regulation of Ethnic Conflict', in John McGarry and Brendan O'Leary (eds.), *The Politics of Ethnic Conflict Regulation: Case Studies of Protracted Ethnic Conflicts* (London: Routledge, 1993), 1–40.

McKay, Andy and Verpoorten, Marijke, 'Growth, Poverty Reduction, and Inequality in Rwanda', in Channing Arndt, Andy McKay, and Finn Tarp (eds.), *Growth and Poverty in Sub-Saharan Africa* (Oxford: Oxford University Press, 2016), 1–10.

McLean Hilker, Lyndsay, 'Everyday Ethnicities: Identity and Reconciliation among Rwandan Youth' (2009) 11 *Journal of Genocide Research* 81–100.

McNamee, Terence, 'Such a Long Journey: Peacebuilding after Genocide in Rwanda', in Terence McNamee and Monde Muyangwa (eds.), *The State of Peacebuilding in Africa: Lessons Learned for Policymakers and Practitioners* (Heidelberg: Springer, 2021), 379–395.

Medina, Laurie Kroshus, 'Governing through the Market: Neoliberal Environmental Government in Belize' (2015) 117(2) *American Anthropologist* 272–284.

Menzel, Anne, 'The Perils of Recognising Local Agency: A Situational Concept of Agency and the Case of Victims of Sexual Violence and the Sierra Leone Truth and Reconciliation Commission (TRC)' (2020) 23 *Journal of International Relations and Development* 584–606.

Mertens, Charlotte, Stéphanie Perazzoneb and David Mwambari, 'Fatal Misconceptions: Colonial Durabilities, Violence and Epistemicide in Africa's Great Lakes Region' (2022) 14(1) *Critical African Studies* 2–18.

Meyerstein, Ariel, 'Between Law and Culture: Rwanda's *Gacaca* and Postcolonial Legacy' (2007) 32(2) *Law & Social Inquiry* 467–508.

Mgbako, Chi, 'Ingando Solidarity Camps: Reconciliation and Political Indoctrinations in Post-genocide Rwanda' (2005) 18 *Harvard Human Rights Journal* 201–224.

Milz, Manuel, 'The Authoritarian Face of the "Green Revolution": Rwanda Capitulates to Agribusiness', Grain blog, 8 August 2011.

Ministry of Environment, 'National Biodiversity Strategy and Action Plan' (Kigali: Republic of Rwanda, December 2019).

Ministry of Environment, 'National Land Policy 2019' (Kigali: Republic of Rwanda, 2019).

Ministry of Finance and Economic Planning (MINECOFIN), *Poverty Reduction Strategy Paper* (Kigali: Republic of Rwanda, 2002).

Ministry of Finance and Economic Planning (MINECOFIN), *Vision 2020* (Kigali: Republic of Rwanda, revised 2012).

Ministry of Finance and Economic Planning (MINECOFIN), *Economic Development and Poverty Reduction Strategy II, 2013–2018* (Kigali: Republic of Rwanda, 2013).

Ministry of Finance and Economic Planning (MINECOFIN), *Vision 2050* (Kigali: Republic of Rwanda, 2015).

Ministry of Lands and Forestry, 'National Forestry Plan 2018' (Kigali: Republic of Rwanda, 2018).

Ministry of Lands, Environment, Forests, Water and Mines, 'National Land Policy 2004' (Kigali: Republic of Rwanda, 2004).

Ministry of Local Government (MINALOC), *National Social Protection Strategy* (Kigali: Republic of Rwanda, 2011).

Ministry of Local Government (MINALOC), *Assessment of the Impact of Decentralisation Policy Implementation in Rwanda (2001–2017)* (Kigali: Republic of Rwanda, 2018a).

Ministry of Local Government (MINALOC), *Governance and Decentralization Sector Strategic Plan (2018/19–2023/24)* (Kigali: Republic of Rwanda, 2018b).

Moss, Sigrun Marie, 'Beyond Conflict and Spoilt Identities: How Rwandan Leaders Justify a Single Recategorization Model for Post-conflict Reconciliation' (2014) 2(1) *Journal of Social and Political Psychology* 435–449.

Moss, Sigrun Marie and Johanna Ray Vollhardt, '"You Can't Give a Syringe with Unity": Rwandan Responses to the Government's Single Recategorization Policies' (2016) 16 *Analyses of Social Issues and Public Policy* 325–359.

Mudimbe, V. Y., *The Invention of Africa: Gnosis, Philosophy, and the Order of Knowledge* (Bloomington: University of Indiana Press, 1988).

Mudimbe, V. Y., *The Idea of Africa: African Systems of Thought* (Bloomington: Indiana University Press, 1994).

Mukashema, Immaculée and Etienne Mullet, 'Reconciliation Sentiment among Victims of Genocide in Rwanda: Conceptualizations, and Relationships with Mental Health' (2010) 99(1) *Social Indicators Research* 25–39.

Mukasonga, Scholastique, 'Cattle Praise Song', *The New Yorker*, 5 November 2018.

Mukasonga, Scholastique, *The Barefoot Woman* (Paris: Editions Gallimard, 2018).

Muleefu, Alphonse, 'Double Legitimacy: A Danger to African Governance', *The New Times*, 3 June 2024.

Munir, Laine, 'Women and Changing Sociolegal Landscapes in Rwandan Mining Formalization' (2023) 97 *Journal of Rural Studies* 167–176.

Musahara, Herman and Chris Huggins, 'Land Reform, Land Scarcity, and Post-conflict Reconstruction: A Case Study of Rwanda', in Chris Huggins and Jenny Clover (eds.), *From Ground Up: Land Rights, Conflict and Peace in Sub-Saharan Africa* (Pretoria: Institute of Security Studies, 2005), 269–346.

Mutandwa, Edward and Richard Kanyarukiga, 'Understanding the Role of Forests in Rural Household Economies: Experiences from the Northern and Western Provinces of Rwanda' (2016) 78(2) *Southern Forests: A Journal of Forest Science* 115–122.

Mwambari, David, '*Agaciro*, Vernacular Memory, and the Politics of Memory in Post-Genocide Rwanda' (2021) 120 *African Affairs* 611–628.

Nanda, Meera, 'We Are All Hybrids Now: The Dangerous Epistemology of Post-colonial Populism' (2001) 28 *The Journal of Peasant Studies* 162.

Nandy, Ashis, *The Intimate Enemy: Loss and Recovery of Self under Colonialism* (Oxford: Oxford University Press, 1983).

Nandy, Ashis, 'State', in Wolfgang Sachs (ed.), *The Development Dictionary: A Guide to Knowledge as Power* (London: Zed Books, 2010), 295–307.

Natarajan, Usha, 'Who Do We Think We Are? Human Rights in a Time of Ecological Change', in Usha Natarajan and Julia Dehm (eds.), *Locating Nature: Making and Unmaking International Law* (Cambridge: Cambridge University Press, 2022), 200–228.

National Unity and Reconciliation Commission, *The Road towards Unity and Reconciliation: Ten Years after (1994–2004)* (Kigali: Republic of Rwanda, 2004).

National Unity and Reconciliation Commission, *The National Policy on Unity and Reconciliation* (Kigali: Republic of Rwanda, 2007).

National Unity and Reconciliation Commission, *2009 Strategic Plan 2009–2012* (Kigali, Republic of Rwanda, 2009a).

National Unity and Reconciliation Commission, *Review Magazine* (Kigali: Republic of Rwanda, 2009b).

National Unity and Reconciliation Commission, *I Am Rwandan: The Right Path to Regaining the Dignity Lost by Rwandans* (Kigali: Republic of Rwanda, 2013).

National Unity and Reconciliation Commission, *Rwanda Reconciliation Barometer 2010* (Kigali: Republic of Rwanda, 2015).

National Unity and Reconciliation Commission, *Unity and Reconciliation Process in Rwanda* (Kigali: Republic of Rwanda, 2016).

National Unity and Reconciliation Commission, *Rwanda Reconciliation Barometer 2015* (Kigali: Republic of Rwanda, 2020).

National Unity and Reconciliation Commission, *Rwanda Reconciliation Barometer 2020* (Kigali: Republic of Rwanda, 2025).

Ndahinda, Felix Mukwiza, *Indigenousness in Africa: A Contested Legal Framework for Empowerment of 'Marginalized' Communities* (The Hague: T. M. C. Asser Press, 2011).

Ndahinda, Felix Mukwiza and Alphonse Muleefu, 'Revisiting the Legal and Socio-Political Foundations and (Western) Criticisms of Gacaca Courts', in Tom Bennett, Eva Brems, Giselle Corradi, Lia Nijzink, and Martien Schotsmans (eds.), *African Perspectives on Tradition and Justice* (Cambridge: Intersentia, 2012).

Ndikubwimana, Jean-Baptiste, Kathleen Ayako Anangwe, Jack Busalile Mwimali, Kabwete Mulinda Charles and Oriare Nyarwath, 'A Re-conceptualisation of the Batwa's Right to Recognition as a Minority and Indigenous People in Rwanda: A Human Rights-Based Approach' (2024) 10(10) *Heliyon* e30848.

Ndulo, Muna, 'One Nation, Multiple Identities: Ethnicity, Inclusivity, and Constitution-Making', in Muna Ndulo and Cosmas Emeziem (eds.), *The Routledge Handbook of African Law* (London: Routledge, 2022), 153–178.

Neumann, Roderick P., *Imposing Wilderness. Struggles over Livelihood and Nature Preservation in Africa* (Oakland: University of California Press, 1998).

Newbury, Catherine M., 'Ethnicity in Rwanda: The Case of Kinyaga' (1978) 48 *Africa: Journal of the International African Institute* 17–29.

Newbury, Catherine M., *The Cohesion of Oppression: Clientship and Ethnicity in Rwanda, 1860–1960* (New York: Columbia University Press, 1988a).

Newbury, Catherine M., 'Ethnicity and the Politics of Rwanda' (1988b) 45(1) *Africa Today* 7–24.

Newbury, Catherine M., 'High Modernism at the Ground Level. The *Imidugudu* Policy in Rwanda', in Scott Strauss and Leo Waldorf (eds.), *Remaking Rwanda: State Building and Human Rights after Mass Violence* (Madison: University of Wisconsin Press, 2011), 223–239.

Newbury, Catherine M. and David Newbury, 'A Catholic Mass in Kigali: Contested Views of the Genocide and Ethnicity in Rwanda' (1999) 33 *Canadian Journal of African Studies* 292–328.

Newbury, David, 'The Clans of Rwanda: An Historical Hypothesis' (1980) 50 *Africa: Journal of the International African Institute* 389–403.

Newbury, David, 'Understanding Genocide' (1998) 41 *African Studies Review* 73–97.

Newbury, David, *The Land beyond the Mists: Essays on Identity and Authority in Precolonial Congo and Rwanda* (Athens: Ohio University Press, 2009).

Ngounou, Boris, 'Rwanda: Volcanoes Park to Be Expanded by 23% with $255 Million Investment', Paris: Afrik21.africa, 14 April 2022.

Nilsson, Pia, Mikaela Backman, Lina Bjerke and Aristide Maniriho, 'One Cow Per Poor Family: Effects on the Growth of Consumption and Crop Production' (2019) 114 *World Development* 1–12.

Ntakirutimana, Richard and Bennet Collins, '"Am I Twa or HMP?": Examining the "Historically Marginalized People" Label and the Acculturation of the Twa in Rwanda', Aegis Working Paper PB 005, September 2017.

Nussbaum, Martha C., *Women and Human Development: The Capabilities Approach* (Cambridge: Cambridge University Press, 2000).

Nussbaum, Martha C., *Creating Capabilities: The Human Development Approach* (Cambridge, MA: Belknap Press, 2011).

Nyamnjoh, Francis B., '"A Child Is One Person's Only in the Womb": Domestication, Agency and Subjectivity', in Richard Werbner (ed.), *Post-colonial Subjectivities in Africa* (London: Zed Books, 2002).

Nyenyezi Bisoka, Aymar and An Ansoms, 'State and Local Authorities in Land Grabbing in Rwanda: Governmentality and Capitalist Accumulation' (2020) 41(2) *Canadian Journal of Development Studies/Revue canadienne d'études du développement* 243–259.

Nyenyezi Bisoka, Aymar, Cécile Giraud and An Ansoms, 'Competing Claims over Access to Land in Rwanda: Legal Pluralism, Power and Subjectivities' (2020) 109 *Geoforum* 115–124.

Okafor, Obiora Chinedu, 'Poverty, Agency and Resistance in the Future of International Law: An African Perspective' (2006) 27(5) *Third World Quarterly* 799–814.

Olivier de Sardan, Jean-Pierre, *Anthropology and Development: Understanding Contemporary Social Change* (London: Zed Books, 2005).

Organisation for Economic Co-operation and Development, 'A Comprehensive Overview of Global Biodiversity Finance, OECD Environment Policy Papers', 6 April 2020.

Page, Tiffany, 'Sustaining Life: Rethinking Modes of Agency in Vulnerability' (2018) 33 *Australian Feminist Studies* 281–298.

Pahuja, Sundhya, *Decolonizing International Law: Development, Economic Growth and the Politics of Universality* (Cambridge: Cambridge University Press, 2011).

Pahuja, Sundhya, 'Laws of Encounter: A Jurisdictional Account of International Law' (2013) 1(1) *London Review of International Law* 63–98.

Palmer, Nicola, 'Re-examining Resistance in Post-genocide Rwanda' (2014) 8(2) *Journal of Eastern African Studies* 231–245.

Paradis, Rozlyn M., 'The Intersectional Experience of *Ndi Umunyarwanda*: An Interdisciplinary Analysis of Identity and Removing Ubwoko in Rwanda' (2020) 3(2) *Undergraduate Journal of Global Citizenship* 1–27.

Parfitt, Trevor, 'Towards a Post-structuralist Development Ethics? Alterity or the same?' (2010) 31(5) *Third World Quarterly* 675–692.

Parmar, Sejal, 'Reckoning with the Past? Rwanda's Revised Genocide Ideology Law and International Human Rights Law on Freedom of Expression', in Paul Behrens, Olaf Jensen, and Nicholas Terry (eds.), *Holocaust and Genocide Denial: A Contextual Perspective* (London: Routledge, 2017), 94–117.

Peluso, Nancy Lee, 'What's Nature Got to Do with It? A Situated Historical Perspective on Socio-natural Commodities' (2012) 43(1) *Development and Change* 79–104.

Perry-Kessaris, Amanda, 'Law and Development', in Peer C. Zumbansen (ed.), *The Oxford Handbook of Transnational Law* (Oxford: Oxford University Press, 2021), 377–390.

Petersmann, Marie and Dimitri Van Den Meerssche, 'On Phantom Publics, Clusters, and Collectives: Be(com)ing Subject in Algorithmic Times' (2024) 39(1) *AI & Society* 107–124.

Pfeffer, Max J., John W. Schelhas and L. A. Day, 'Forest Conservation, Value Conflict and Interest Formation in a Honduran National Park' (2001) 66(3) *Rural Sociology* 382–402.

Phillips DeZalia, Rebekah A., 'Being Rwandan: The Use of Language, History, and Identity in Post-genocide Rwanda', in Scott L. Moeschberger and Rebekah A. Phillips DeZalia (eds.), *Symbols That Bind, Symbols That Divide* (Heidelberg: Springer, 2014), 157–180.

Picciotto, Sol, 'Liberalization and Democratization: The Forum and the Hearth in the Era of Cosmopolitan Post-industrial Capitalism' (2000) 63(4) *Law and Contemporary Problems* 157–178.

Polanyi, Karl, *The Great Transformation: The Political and Economic Origins of Our Time* (Boston: Beacon Press, 1944, 2nd ed. 2001).

Potel, Jossam, Gloria Owona and Wilson Tumsherure, 'The Paradox of Poverty amidst Potentially Plentiful Natural Resources of Land in Rwanda', in Walter Timo de Vries, John Tiah Bugri, and Fatima Mandhu (eds.), *Responsible and Smart Land Management Interventions* (Boca Raton: CRC Press, 2020), 37–48.

Pottier, Johan, *Re-imagining Rwanda: Conflict, Survival and Disinformation in the Late Twentieth Century* (Cambridge: Cambridge University Press, 2002).

Pottier, Johan, 'Land Reform for Peace? Rwanda's 2005 Land Law in Context' (2006) 6(4) *Journal of Agrarian Change* 509–537.

Povinelli, Elizabeth A., *The Cunning of Recognition: Indigenous Alterities and the Making of Australian Multiculturalism* (Durham: Duke University Press, 2002).

Prunier, Gérard, *From Genocide to Continental War: The 'Congolese' Conflict and the Crisis of Contemporary Africa* (London: Hurst, 2009).

Purdeková, Andrea, 'Civic Education and Social Transformation in Post-genocide Rwanda: Forging the Perfect Development Subjects', in Maddalena Campioni and Patrick Noack (eds.), *Rwanda Fast Forward: Social, Economic, Military and Reconciliation Prospects* (London: Palgrave Macmillan, 2012), 192–209.

Purdeková, Andrea, *Making Ubumwe: Power, State and Camps in Rwanda's Unity Building Project* (Oxford: Berghahn Books, 2015).

Purdeková, Andreá and David Mwambari, 'Post-genocide Identity Politics and Colonial Durabilities in Rwanda' (2021) 14(1) *Critical African Studies* 19–37.

Radcliffe, Sarah A., 'Imagining the State as a Space: Territoriality and the Formation of the State in Ecuador', in Thomas Blom Hansen and Finn Stepputat (eds.), *States of Imagination: Ethnographic Explorations of the Postcolonial State* (Durham: Duke University Press, 2001), 123–146.

Radcliffe, Sarah A., *Dilemmas of Difference: Indigenous Women and the Limits of Postcolonial Development Policy* (Durham: Duke University Press, 2015).

Radkau, Joachim, *Nature and Power: A Global History of the Environment* (Cambridge: Cambridge University Press, 2008).

Rajagopal, Balakrishnan, *International Law from Below: Development, Social Movements and Third World Resistance* (Cambridge: Cambridge University Press, 2003).

Rajah, Jothie, 'Review of Darian-Smith, Laws and Societies in Global Contexts' (2014) 48(2) *Law & Society Review* 479.

Republic of Rwanda, 'Rwanda 6th National Report to the Convention on Biological Diversity' (Kigali, 2020).

Reyntjens, Filip, 'Rwanda, Ten Years On: From Genocide to Dictatorship', in Stefaan Marysse and Filip Reyntjens (eds.), *The Political Economy of the Great Lakes Region in Africa: The Pitfalls of Enforced Democracy and Globalization* (London: Palgrave Macmillan, 2005), 15–47.

Reyntjens, Filip, 'Constructing the Truth, Dealing with Dissent, Domesticating the World: Governance in Post-genocide Rwanda' (2011) 110 *African Affairs* 1–34.

Reyntjens, Filip, 'From Ethnic Amnesia to Ethnocracy: 80% of Rwanda's Top Officials Are Tutsi', *African Arguments*, 24 November 2021.

Reyntjens, Filip, *Modern Rwanda: A Political History* (Cambridge: Cambridge University Press, 2024).

Rist, Gilbert, *The History of Development: From Western Origins to Global Faith* (London: Zed Books, 4th ed., 2021).

Rodríguez-Garavito, César and Luis Carlos Arenas, 'Indigenous Rights, Transnational Activism, and Legal Mobilization: The Struggle of the U'wa People in Columbia', in Boaventura de Sousa Santos and César Rodríguez-Garavito (eds.), *Law and Globalization from Below: Towards a Cosmopolitan Legality* (Cambridge: Cambridge University Press, 2005), 241–266.

Rodrik, Dani, *One Economics, Many Recipes: Globalization, Institutions, and Economic Growth* (Princeton: Princeton University Press, 2007).

Rojas, Christine and Shannon Kindornay, 'The Politics of Governing Development', in Heloise Weber (ed.), *The Politics of Development: A Survey* (London: Routledge, 2014), 10–30.

Rostow, W. W., *The Stages of Economic Growth: A Non-communist Manifesto* (Cambridge: Cambridge University Press, 1960).

Roth, Robin, 'Spatial Organization of Environmental Knowledge: Conservation Conflicts in the Inhabited Forest of Northern Thailand' (2004) 9(3) *Ecology and Society* 5.

Ruhara, Charles Mulindabigwi and R. Charles Kayitana, 'Mind-Set and Entrepreneurial Activities in Rwanda: A Firm Level Investigation', in Almas Heshmati (ed.), *Rwanda Handbook of Economic and Social Policy, Volume I* (Jönköping: Jönköping International Business School and University of Rwanda, 2017), 1–16.

Russell, Garnett S., 'Global Discourses and Local Practices: Teaching Citizenship and Human Rights in Postgenocide Rwanda' (2018) 62(3) *Comparative Education Review* 385–408.

Rutazibwa, Olivia U., 'Studying *Agaciro*: Moving beyond Wilsonian Interventionist Knowledge Production on Rwanda' (2014) 8(4) *Journal of Intervention and Statebuilding* 291–302.

Rutazibwa, Olivia U., 'On Babies and Bathwater: Decolonizing International Development Studies', in Sara de Jong, Rosalba Icaza, and Olivia U. Rutazibwa, *Decolonization and Feminisms in Global Teaching and Learning* (London: Routledge, 2019), 158–180.

Rutazibwa, Olivia U., 'Decolonising Westernised Solidarity through Epistemic Blackness', Johannesburg Institute for Advanced Studies (JIAS) seminar, 18 March 2020.

Sachs, Wolfgang, 'Introduction', in Wolfgang Sachs (ed.), *The Development Dictionary: A Guide to Knowledge as Power* (London: Zed Books, 2019).

Sanders, Edith, 'The Hamitic Hypothesis: Its Origin and Functions in Time Perspective' (1969) 10(4) *The Journal of Africa History* 521–532.

Santos, Florence, Diana Fletschner and Giuseppe Daconto, 'Enhancing Inclusiveness of Rwanda's Land Tenure Regularization Program: Insights from Early Stages of Its Implementation' (2014) 62 *World Development* 30–41.

Sassen, Saskia, 'Visible Formalizations and Formally Invisible Facticities' (2013) 20 *Indiana Journal of Global Legal Studies* 3–27.

Schiff, Brian and Chaim Noy, 'Making It Personal: Shared Meanings in the Narratives of Holocaust Survivors', in Anna de Fina, Deborah Schiffrin, and Michael Bamberg (eds.), *Discourse and Identity* (Cambridge: Cambridge University Press, 2006), 398–425.

Schlosser, Markus, 'Agency', in Edward N. Zalta (ed.), *The Stanford Encyclopedia of Philosophy* (Winter 2019 Edition), https://plato.stanford.edu/entries/agency.

Scott, James C., *Weapons of the Weak: Everyday Forms of Peasant Resistance* (New Haven: University of Yale Press, 1985).

Scott, James C., *Domination and the Arts of Resistance: Hidden Transcripts* (New Haven: University of Yale Press, 1990).

Scott, James C., *Seeing Like a State: How Certain Schemes to Improve the Human Condition Have Failed* (New Haven: Yale University Press, 1998).

Sebahutu, Evariste Erwin, 'Rwandan Ethnoscape More Than 400 Years Later: The Failure of De-ethnicization Policy?' (2022) 3 *International Journal of Global Community* 251–272.

Sen, Amartya, *Commodities and Capabilities* (Amsterdam: North-Holland, 1985).

Sen, Amartya, *Development as Freedom* (Oxford: Oxford University Press, 1999).

Sentama, Ezechiel, 'National Reconciliation in Rwanda: Experiences and Lessons Learnt', EUI Research Project Report: Issue 2022/05.

Shayne, Julia D., 'Culture and Resistance: A Feminist Analysis of Revolution and "Development"', in Kum-Kum Bhavnani, John Foran, and Priya Kurian (eds.), *Feminist Futures: Re-imagining Women, Culture and Development* (London: Zed Books, 2003), 285–300.

Sieder, Rachel and Anna Barrera, 'Women and Legal Pluralism: Lessons from Indigenous Governance Systems in the Andes' (2017) 49 *Journal of Latin American Studies* 633–658.

Silva, Denise Ferreira da, *Toward a Global Idea of Race* (Minneapolis: University of Minnesota Press, 2007).

Skouteris, Thomas, *The Notion of Progress in International Law Discourse* (The Hague: T. M. C. Asser Press, 2010).

Smith, Anthony D., *National Identity* (Reno: University of Nevada Press, 1991).

Smith, Dorothy E., 'Texts and the Ontology of Organizations and Institutions' (2001) 7(2) *Studies in Cultures, Organizations and Societies* 159–198.

Sommers, Marc, *Stuck: Rwandan Youth and the Struggle for Adulthood* (Athens: University of Georgia Press, 2012).

Soyinka, Wole, *Of Africa* (New Haven: Yale University Press, 2012).

Ssuuna, Ignatius, 'Genocide: Debate Rages on over Call for Apology', *The East African*, 20 July 2013.

Stavenhagen, Rodolfo, 'Ethnodevelopment: A Neglected Dimension in Development Thinking', in Raymond Apthorpe and András Krähl (eds.), *Development Studies: Critique and Renewal* (Leiden: E. J. Brill, 1986), 71–94.

Stegeborn, Wiveca, 'Sri Lanka's Forests: Conservation of Nature versus People' (1996) 20(1) *Cultural Survival Quarterly.*

Strauss, Scott and Leo Waldorf (eds.), *Remaking Rwanda: State Building and Human Rights after Mass Violence* (Madison: University of Wisconsin Press, 2011a).

Strauss, Scott and Leo Waldorf, 'Seeing Like a Post-conflict State', in Scott Strauss and Leo Waldorf (eds.), *Remaking Rwanda: State Building and Human Rights after Mass Violence* (Madison: University of Wisconsin Press, 2011b).

Sullo, Pietro, 'Writing History through Criminal Law: State-Sponsored Memory in Rwanda', in Berber Bevernage and Nico Wouters (eds.), *The Palgrave Handbook of State-Sponsored History after 1945* (London: Palgrave Macmillan, 2018), 69–85.

Sultana, Farhana, 'Suffering for Water, Suffering from Water: Emotional Geographies of Resource Access, Control and Conflict' (2011) 42 *Geoforum* 163.

Sundberg, Molly, *Training for Model Citizenship: An Ethnography of Civic Education and State-Making in Rwanda* (London: Palgrave Macmillan, 2016).

Suryanarayana, M. H., *Inclusive Growth: A Sustainable Perspective* (Mumbai: UNDP Report, 2013).

Sylvain, Renée, 'Disorderly Development: Globalization and the Idea of "Culture" in the Kalahari' (2005) 32(3) *American Ethnologist* 354–370.

Takacs, David, *The Idea of Biodiversity: Philosophies of Paradise* (Baltimore: The Johns Hopkins University Press, 1996).

Takeuchi, Shinichi and Jean Marara, 'Land Law Reform and Complex State-Building Processes in Rwanda', in Shinichi Takeuchi (ed.), *African Land Reform under Economic Liberalisation* (Heidelberg: Springer, 2022), 137–152.

Tan, Celine, *Governance through Development: Poverty Reduction Strategies, International Law and the Disciplining of Third World States* (London: Routledge, 2011).

Taylor, Charles, 'Foucault on Freedom and Truth', in David C. Hoy (ed.), *Foucault: A Critical Reader* (Oxford: Basil Blackwell, 1986), 69–102.

Taylor, Charles, *Sources of the Self: The Making of Modern Identity* (Cambridge, MA: Harvard University Press, 1989).

Taylor, Charles, 'The Dialogical Self', in David Hiley, James Bohman, and Richard Shusterman (eds.), *The Interpretive Turn* (Ithaca: Cornell University Press, 1991), 304–314.

Taylor, Christopher C., *Milk, Honey, and Money: Changing Concepts in Rwandan Healing* (Washington, DC: Smithsonian Institution Press, 1992).

Taylor, Christopher C., 'Dual Systems in Rwanda: Have They Ever Really Existed?' (2004) 4(3) *Anthropological Theory* 353–371.

Taylor, Christoper C., 'Moulders of Mud: Ethnogenesis and Rwanda's Twa' (2011) 76 *Ethnos* 183–208.

The Rwandan, 'Opinion: Ndi Umunyarwanda (I Am Rwandan) and Other Similar Campaign Initiatives: Reconciliation or Social Division?', 14 December 2013, www.therwandan.com/ndi-umunyarwanda-i-am-rwandan-and-other-similar-campaign-initiatives-reconciliation-or-social-division.

Thomson, Susan, 'Ethnic Twa and Rwandan National Unity and Reconciliation Policy' (2009) 21 *Peace Review* 313–320.

Thomson, Susan, 'Getting Close to Rwandans since the Genocide: Studying Everyday Life in Highly Politicized Settings' (2010) 53 *African Studies Review* 19–34.

Thomson, Susan, 'Whispering Truth to Power: Everyday Resistance to Reconciliation in Postgenocide Rwanda' (2011) 110 *African Affairs* 439–456.

Thomson, Susan, *Whispering Truth to Power: Everyday Resistance to Reconciliation in Postgenocide Rwanda* (Madison: University of Wisconsin Press, 2013).

Thomson, Susan, *Rwanda: From Genocide to Precarious Peace* (New Haven: Yale University Press, 2018).

Trouillot, Michel-Rolph, *Silencing the Past: Power and the Production of History* (Boston: Beacon Press, 1995).

Trubek, David M. and Marc Galanter, 'Scholars in Self-Estrangement: Some Reflections on the Crisis in Law and Development Studies in the United States' (1974) *Wisconsin Law Review* 1062–1102.

Tshipa, Sharon, 'Environmental Protection Is Deeply-Held Practice in African Spirituality: What Happens When It Is Re-shaped by Christianity and Capitalism?', *Africa Is a Country*, 15 November 2023.

Tsing, Anna Lowenhaupt, 'Natural Resources and Capitalist Frontiers' (2003) 38(48) *Economic and Political Weekly* 5100–5106.

Tsing, Anna Lowenhaupt, *Friction: An Ethnography of Global Connection* (Princeton: Princeton University Press, 2005).

Tsing, Anna Lowenhaupt, *The Mushroom at the End of the World* (Princeton: Princeton University Press, 2015).

Tully, James, *Strange Multiplicity: Constitutionalism in an Age of Diversity* (Cambridge: Cambridge University Press, 1995).

Turner, Simon, 'Making Good Citizens from Bad Life in Post-genocide Rwanda' (2014) 45(3) *Development and Change* 415–433.

Twagilimana, Aimable, *The Debris of Ham: Ethnicity, Regionalism, and the 1994 Genocide* (Lanham: University Press of America, 2003).

Twining, William, *General Jurisprudence: Understanding Law from a Global Perspective* (Cambridge: Cambridge University Press, 2012).

Twizeyimana, Albert-Baudoin, 'Rwanda: La propreté à marché forcée', *InfoSud Belgique*, 29 June 2006.

Unger, Corinna R., 'Development', in Mlada Bukovansky, Edward Keene, Christian Reus-Smit, and Maja Spanu (eds.), *The Oxford Handbook of History and International Relations* (Oxford: Oxford University Press, 2023), 348–362.

United National Development Programme, *Human Development Report 1990: Concept and Measurement of Human Development* (New York: UNDP, 1990).

United National Development Programme Rwanda, 'National Human Development Report: Rwanda 2014' (Kigali: UNDP, 2015).

United National Development Programme Rwanda, *Rwanda National Human Development Report 2018: Policy Innovations and Human Development – Rwanda's Home-Grown Solutions* (Kigali: UNDP, November 2020).

United National Development Programme Rwanda, *Annual Report 2021: Financing Innovation and Innovating Finance* (Kigali: UNDP, 6 June 2022).

United Nations, 'Report of the Independent Expert on Minority Issues, Gay McDougall – Mission to Rwanda', UN Doc A/HRC/19/56/Add.1, 28 November 2011.

United Nations Environment Programme, 'The State of Finances for Nature in the G20: Leading by Examples to Close the Investment Gap' (Nairobi, 2022).

United Nations Environment Programme – World Conservation Monitoring Centre, 'Protected Area Profile for Rwanda from the World Database on Protected Areas', February 2023.

Unrepresented Nations and Peoples Organisation, 'A Report of the UNPO Mission with APB: Investigating the Situation of the Batwa People of Rwanda', 28 September to 15 December 1994.

Unrepresented Nations and Peoples Organisation, 'Indigenous Peoples: Invisible Peoples – Earth, Exploitation and Survival' (2015): unpo.org/article/18575.

Unrepresented Nations and Peoples Organisation, 'Submission to the UN Office of the High Commissioner for Human Rights for the Consideration of the Expert Mechanism on the Rights of Indigenous Peoples, Concerning "The Right to Health and Indigenous Peoples", with a Particular Focus on Children and Youth' (Brussels: UNPO, 2016).

Unrepresented Nations and Peoples Organisation, 'Batwa: Recent Attacks Wake Memories of Ethnic Conflict', 16 July 2018.

Urueña, René, *No Citizens Here: Global Subjects and Participation in International Law* (Leiden: Martinus Nijhoff, 2012).

Uvin, Peter, *Aiding Violence: The Development Enterprise in Rwanda* (West Hartford: Kumarian Press, 1988).

van Beemen, Olivier, *Ondernemers in het Wild* (Amsterdam: Uitgeverij Promethus, 2024a).

van Beemen, Olivier, 'Hè, zij waren toch de good guys?', *De Groene Amsterdammer*, 18 April 2024b.

Van Hoyweghen, Saskia, 'The Disintegration of the Catholic Church of Rwanda: A Study of the Fragmentation of Political and Religious Authority' (1996) 95 *African Affairs* 379–401.

Vandeginste, Stef, 'Political Representation of Minorities as Collateral Damage or Gain: The Batwa in Burundi and Rwanda' (2014a) 49(1) *Africa Spectrum* 3–25.

Vandeginste, Stef, 'Governing Ethnicity after Genocide. Ethnic Amnesia in Rwanda versus Ethnic Power-Sharing in Burundi' (2014b) 8(2) *Journal of Eastern African Studies* 263–277.

Vansina, Jan, 'Western Bantu Expansion' (1984) 25 *Journal of African History* 129–145.

Vansina, Jan, *Paths in the Rainforests: Towards a History of Political Tradition in Equatorial Africa* (Madison: University of Wisconsin Press, 1990).

Vansina, Jan, 'Historical Tales (Ibiteekerezo) and the History of Rwanda' (2000) 27 *History in Africa* 375–414.

Vansina, Jan, *Antecedents to Modern Rwanda: The Nyiginya Kingdom* (Madison: University of Wisconsin Press, 2004).

Verbraeken, Anneke, *Rijke Mensen Sterven Niet: Confronterende ontmoetingen in Congo en Rwanda* (Amersfoort: Atlas Contact, 2017).

von Benda-Beckmann, Frans and Keebet von Benda-Beckmann, 'Transnationalisation of Law, Globalisation and Legal Pluralism: A Legal Anthropological Perspective', in Christoph Antons and Volkmar Gessner (eds.), *Globalisation and Resistance: Law Reform in Asia since the Crisis* (Oxford: Hart Publishing, 2007), 53–80.

Wachira, George Mukundi and Tuuli Karjal, 'Advocacy for Indigenous Peoples' Rights in Africa, in Ridwan Leher and Korir Sing'Oei (eds.), *Indigenous People in Africa: Contestations, Empowerment and Group Rights* (Pretoria: African Institute of South Africa, 2014), 104–123.

Wade, Peter, *Race and Sex in Latin America* (London: Pluto Press, 2009).

Wainaina, Binyavanga, *How to Write about Africa* (London: Hamish Hamiliton, 2022).

Walker, Neil, 'Late Sovereignty in the European Union', in Neil Walker (ed.), *Sovereignty in Transition* (Oxford: Hart Publishing, 2003), 3–32.

Walker, Neil, *Intimations of Global Law* (Cambridge: Cambridge University Press, 2015).

Wama Marobe, Marobe, 'We-versus-They: Building a Paradigm Community in Rwanda' (2015) 28 *Politikon* 121.

Wearing, Michael, *Social Identity* (Hauppauge: Nova Science Publications, 2011).

Weismantel, Mary J., *Cholas and Pishtacos: Stories of Race and Sex in the Andes* (Chicago: University of Chicago Press, 2001).

Werbner, Richard (ed.), *Postcolonial Subjectivities in Africa* (London: Zed Books, 2002).

West, Paige, James Igoe and Dan Brockington, 'Parks and People: The Social Impact of Protected Areas' (2006) 35 *Annual Review of Anthropology* 251–277.

White, Sarah C., 'Thinking Race, Thinking Development' (2002) 23 *Third World Quarterly* 407–419.

Whyte, Susan Reynolds, 'Subjectivity and Subjunctivity: Hoping for Health in Eastern Uganda', in Richard Werbner (ed.), *Postcolonial Subjectivities in Africa* (London: Zed Books, 2002), 171–190.

Williamson Sinalo, Caroline, *Rwanda after Genocide: Gender, Identity and Post-traumatic Growth* (Cambridge: Cambridge University Press, 2018).

Willis, Owen, 'Forgotten People in a Remembered Land: The Batwa and the Genocide' (2005) *International Insights: Special Issue* 126–148.

Wing, Adrien Katherine and Mark Richard Johnson, 'The Promise of a Post-genocide Constitution: Healing Rwandan Spirit Injuries' (2002) 7 *Michigan Journal of Race and Law* 247–315.

Wittgenstein, Ludwig, *Philosophical Investigations*, ed. G. E. M. Anscombe and R. Rhees, tr. G. E. M. Anscombe (Oxford: Blackwell, 1963).

Wolf, Dianne L. (ed.), *Feminist Dilemmas in Fieldwork* (Boulder: Westview Press, 1996).

Wolff, Jonathan and Avner de-Shalit, *Disadvantage* (Oxford: Oxford University Press, 2007).

World Bank, *WAVES Country Report* (Washington, DC: World Bank Group, 2015).

World Bank, *Rwanda: Poverty Reduction Strategy Paper (PRSP) and Joint Assessment* (Washington, DC: World Bank Group, 2022).

Wrong, Michela, *Do Not Disturb: The Story of a Political Murder and an African Regime Gone Bad* (London: Harper Collins, 2021).

Young, Crawford, 'Ethnicity and the Colonial and Post-colonial State in Africa', in Paul Brass (ed.), *Ethnic Groups and the State* (Totowa: Croom Helm, 1985), 57–93.

Ziegler, Margaret, 'Breaking the Silence on the Rwandan Genocide: An Interview with Edouard Bamporiki', *Peace Magazine*, 16, July–September 2013.

Zorbas, Eugenia, 'What Does Reconciliation after Genocide Mean? Public Transcripts and Hidden Transcripts in Post-genocide Rwanda' (2009) 11 *Journal of Genocide Research* 127–147.

Zumbansen, Peer C., 'Manifestations and Arguments: The Everyday Operation of Transnational Legal Pluralism', in Paul Schiff Berman (ed.), *Oxford Handbook of Global Legal Pluralism* (Oxford: Oxford University Press, 2020), 230–262.

Zumbansen, Peer C., 'Transnational Law: Theories and Applications', in Peer C. Zumbansen (ed.), *The Oxford Handbook of Transnational Law* (Oxford: Oxford University Press, 2021), 3–30.

Rwandan Legislation

Law N° 22/1999 of 01/08/2016 regarding Matrimonial Regimes, Liberalities and Successions.

Law N° 47/2001 of 18/12/2001 on Prevention, Suppression and Punishment of the Crime of Discrimination and Sectarianism.

Law N° 04/2005 of 08/04/2005 Organic Law determining the modalities of protection, conservation and promotion of environment in Rwanda.

Law N° 10/2007 of 01/03/2007 modifying and complementing Organic Law n°16/2004 of 19/6/2004 establishing the organisation, competence and functioning of Gacaca Courts charged with prosecuting and trying the perpetrators of the crime of genocide and other crimes against humanity, committed between October 1, 1990 and December 31, 1994 as modified and complemented to date.

Law N° 17/2008 of 20/06/2008 Establishing the National Forest Authority (NAFA) and determining its Organisation, Functioning and Responsibilities.

Law N° 18/2008 of 23/07/ 2008 related to the punishment of the crime of genocide ideology.

Law N° 43/ 2013 of 16/06/2013 Governing Land in Rwanda.

Law N° 47bis/2013 of 28/06/2013 Determining the Management and Utilisation of Forests in Rwanda.

Law N° 63/2013 of 27/08/2013 determining the mission, organization and functioning of Rwanda Environment Management Authority (REMA).

Law N° 84/2013 of 11/09/2013 on the Crime of Genocide Ideology and Other Related Crimes.

Law N° 48/2018 of 13/08/2018 on the Environment.

Law N° 72/2019 establishing the Rwanda Forest Authority.

Law N° 27/2021 of 10/06/2021 Governing Land.

Law N° 01/2023 of 13/01/2023 Governing National Parks and Nature Reserves.

INDEX

For EU product safety concerns, contact us at Calle de José Abascal, 56–1°, 28003 Madrid, Spain or eugpsr@cambridge.org.

www.ingramcontent.com/pod-product-compliance
Ingram Content Group UK Ltd.
Pitfield, Milton Keynes, MK11 3LW, UK
UKHW020200290926
15471UKWH00005B/975
* 9 7 8 1 0 0 9 7 6 8 5 3 5 *